Mind-Head Soul-Head

Mind-Head Soul-Head
The Condition of Post-Sufficiency

BRIAN L. NYGAARD

RESOURCE *Publications* • Eugene, Oregon

MIND-HEAD SOUL-HEAD
The Condition of Post-Sufficiency
Copyright © 2010 Brian L. Nygaard. All rights reserved. Except for brief quotations in critical publications or reviews, no part of this book may be reproduced in any manner without prior written permission from the publisher. Write: Permissions, Wipf and Stock Publishers, 199 W. 8th Ave., Suite 3, Eugene, OR 97401.

Resource Publications
An Imprint of Wipf and Stock Publishers
199 W. 8th Ave., Suite 3
Eugene, OR 97401
www.wipfandstock.com

ISBN 13: 978-1-60899-765-7

Manufactured in the U.S.A.

*This book is dedicated to my parents,
Roger and Marilyn Nygaard,
for the creation of a secure and loving home in my youth,
and for their enduring influence on my personal
values, worldviews, and outlooks.*

Contents

Foreword • ix

Acknowledgments • xi

Introduction: The Two-Percent Solution • 1

1. Machines and Souls • 13
2. Mutually Assured Destruction • 44
3. "We Really Are Better!" • 76
4. Controlling the Uncontrollable • 95
5. "It Just Runs" • 131
6. Back to the Basics • 153
7. "Here's the Deal" • 159
8. The Values Delusion • 166
9. Organizational Teleology • 192
10. Growth Defines Life • 203
11. Free-Agency and Trust • 213

Conclusion • 229

Definitions to Commonly Used Words • 231

Foreword *by Brandon Lee Nygaard*

I HAVE HAD A difficult relationship with math going back to my days in elementary school. Of all the violence the subject has done to me, its greatest injustice was the so-called story problem. My charges against this cruel invention of modern education are two-fold. First, they are horrible stories. Forget poignant drama, colorful descriptions, and engaging characters. The most for which one may hope is that the train leaving point A will actually crash into the train leaving point B (which never happens, by the way). Telling a fifth grader this constitutes a story ought to be outlawed. Second, I feel that there are deeper problems than simple math. "Susie has 4 cats. She gives away 2. The mommy cat has 4 kittens. How many cats does Susie have?" If Susie can't keep track of how many cats she has, I wonder if she is responsible enough to have pets (let alone kittens). I furthermore fail to see what application these trains and cats really have to a fifth grader. The point is this: stories are never that simple, and problems are never that straightforward.

Many people view the world as a story problem. If they can just extract the basic arithmetic from the setting and characters, they can solve anything. During his career, my dad realized that the world is not this simple. Story problem solutions are of little help; in fact they may even do more harm than good. You cannot ignore the people and focus on the numbers. This was the genesis of my Dad's book: you have to engage both the numbers and the people; Mind-Head and Soul-Head. The problem is that many organizations, baptized into the story problem mentality, engorge the Mind-Head at the expense of a starving Soul-Head. The result is the death of interaction and imagination that eventually kills the organization. My dad is working to change this. He is attempting to put the characters back into the story problem equation. This is a complicated task because people are not the "placeholders" they are in fifth grade math problems. People have values and desires, a need for acceptance within their communities. Through the course of this book, my dad will show how leaders can refocus on community, unleash creativity, and put their organizations on a path to durability.

The path to this book was not an easy one. Dad, as a favor to his un-employed son, brought me in to help with the book. He and I think a lot alike, so I was able to provide (hopefully) helpful critiques. Dad began with a collection of ideas and observations, which would have read more like a journal than a book. We agreed there needed to be more cohesion. Through a lot of labor, I think he was able to do this. Dad also aimed to "humanize" what he deems as a overly process-driven world. In doing this, he references a good deal of philosophy.

My fear was that he might come across as a Greek philosopher "wanna-be." He worked to clarify a lot of the language. What I hope you will see is an appeal to first principles, and not a display of intellectualism. This book was also an emotional struggle. Throughout his career, my dad has seen the disastrous effects of Mind-head management. His first response was to take up the role of a rebel, launching assaults on the formula-loving corporate world. I encouraged him to view himself as a liberator, not just pointing out all that is wrong with organizations, but suggesting a path back to a healthy Soul-Head. I hope that you will resonate with his frustration, but also see his suggested path of opportunity going forward.

It is easy to get frustrated with the story problem approach that many organizations take. I believe you will find in this book a remedy. People are not throwaways in the pursuit to finding some magic formula. They are not cogs in a big corporate machine. People are literally the soul of the organization. This book shows how that soul can be nurtured and grown to the benefit of organization, while reversing the process-focused approaches that are so disastrous. I might be a bit biased, but I believe dad's solution work. Even better, it doesn't involve counting cats.

Acknowledgments

I WOULD LIKE TO extend my sincere thanks to my son, Brandon L. Nygaard, whose overall editorial assistance and ongoing encouragement was absolutely critical in the shaping of this work. Additionally, I would especially like to thank Quintin Steiff, Pastor of Valley Church in West Des Moines, IA; Ken Nordhoff, City Manager of San Rafael, CA; and Anthony E. Greene, Partner at Atticus Advisers, LLC in Atlanta, GA; for their editorial work on the manuscript.

Introduction

The Two-Percent Solution

> Large and successful organizations believe they continue to do all the right things, yet they lose sight of what they are becoming. The change in "who they are" moves them in the direction of long-term under performance and limited durability.

MAYBE I SHOULD HAVE learned the answer to one of the most intriguing questions in the realm of organizational metaphysics when I was in business school. I must have been sick that day. The question to which I am referring initially came to mind when I was entering the securities industry while I was in my early twenties. I was studying for the investment industry regulatory exams when I came across a couple of data points that would forever change the way I think about the world, and more broadly, the world of groups of people working together towards a common end.

The data that I absorbed that day suggested that over time, small businesses had created returns for their owners of around ten percent, while big businesses had created returns of about eight percent. Small organizations, it appeared, represented better investments than larger ones, ostensibly as a result of better organizational performance. That seemed completely backwards to me. I reacted quite strongly to this information and the reason for the emotional response was that my existing presuppositions had brought me to just the opposite conclusion. I had grown up thinking that big businesses (actually big anything) ruled the world. I had always assumed a more naturally-derived pecking order. In my perceived "order," it was understood that the goal of the less-than-big-and-powerful was to struggle with all their might, over extended periods of time, to become as profitable and indomitable as the already-mighty. I actually remember thinking that I had somehow read the data incorrectly. So I read it again. But I had not, in-fact, read it wrong. And the question that was formulated on that day almost three decades ago continues to be as profound for me today as it was in the early 1980s.

The question, simply stated, was this: If big businesses—and large and successful organizations in general—have access to nearly all the finest graduates from the most prestigious universities, all the required investment capital they could possibly deploy, a legacy of years and years of accumulated brand building, and all the protections provided by scaled and highly-efficient operations, why (or how) could small organizations possibly perform better in a direct comparison of their financial results? Moreover, why did these Lilliputians even *exist* if the potentially higher returns were somehow "available" in the marketplace? While it may be argued, as with all data points, that the truth is sometimes not exactly as displayed in a simple set of numbers (ten percent versus eight percent), if this data was even directionally correct, the question for me was the same. Something was wrong here, and I had a very strong desire, what might even be described as a compulsion, to figure out what the *something* was.

The first and obvious conclusion to which I immediately came was this: large and successful organizations must be "*doing* something wrong." That was obviously brilliant. I went on to conjecture that they must have had some type of operating handicap of which I was unaware. All I had seen to that point in my life were the relative advantages. There was obviously something wrong with my understanding of the world (believing the large and successful to be completely dominate), and the perceived magnitude of my personal "wisdom gap" seemed to be very wide. I felt very vulnerable to this *thing* that I did not at all understand.

I was, at the time, working in one of those large and successful institutions, and it appeared important to my future career growth (read compensation) to understand how my newly minted observation should impact how I thought and acted. I had a wife and a couple of little kids at home that were counting on my paycheck to avoid homelessness as a lifestyle.

I began asking myself whether there was something inherent or somehow inculcated into large collections of human beings working together (referred to as "human institutions") that created, almost by definition, their relative under-performance. And if that inherency was the case, I wondered what the *nature* of the thing really was. Was it a communications-related issue? Was it a strategy and execution issue? Or, was it a function of pure randomness? Was it just a function of the lazy response to the passage of inexorable time? Was it something in the water? And more troublingly to me was whether this thing, whatever it might be, was the same ingredient that leads many human institutions to their ultimate failure, and in their honored placement in the Great Dustbin of History? Rightly or wrongly, it just seemed to me that this was a question of tremendous significance.

As one looks back over the last several decades, the percentage of "Nifty-Fifty" large capitalization stocks of the sixties and seventies that still exist today in any meaningful way is troubling. Remember that failed and troubled companies get taken out of the major stock indexes. How could these "rocks" have been chipped apart? More broadly, as you look back at the history of the world's preeminent civilizations during five thousand years, an equally troubling picture emerges. The noted historian Arnold Toynbee tells us that only a small remnant of the world's once-great civilizations remain extant.

It would seem there exists a large or maybe even infinite number of potential opportunities for the failure of human institutions. And that conclusion would point to an equally dizzying array of associated causes. Closer to home, for each of us personally, what has been the history of the associations, broadly defined, in which each of us has participated? Seemingly, wherever one looks, against the wishes of the members of the particular institution, we see the rise and fall of the once-thriving. It seems equally interesting that while nearly everyone *knows* that "perpetual human institutions" have a tendency to experience something akin to a biological life cycle that so many institutions just "fade away." This often observed negative consequence comes in spite of the best thinking and best efforts of all of those concerned. They vanish from existence and no one even seems to notice. And yet a tremendous price is paid by the institution's members, and in many instances, by society as a whole, when our once-proud institutions fail.

My intuition would lead me to hope that a very bright, self-interested, and committed group of leadership people within any successful organization would design and implement better survival strategies.

While nearly all institutions are focused on the notions of innovation and growth, many are on a path of decay if the truth of the current situation could be known. That is what history tells us. And most institutions will likely see their incipient failure over a span of a relatively small number of years; in some cases, less than a generation. Failure and decline is, looking back in time, much easier than continuous growth and ongoing success.

So why don't they, the institution's leadership and members, figure it out? As a young and aspiring business-type, that question came to really bother me. "Why don't they just put their heads together and come up with a solution?" I asked myself, "Don't they recognize the havoc and personal dislocation that is felt when a human institution fails and people lose their jobs? Don't they see what is being forfeited? Don't they understand the consequences to themselves personally? Have they not considered the seriousness of the future implications on their constituencies? Should all the historic efforts of their institutions simply come to naught?" The problem surely seemed apparent enough.

In the following years, I subsequently started asking myself a related question. In my quest for answers, I wondered if there might be some type of "organizational orthodoxy" that if followed religiously, would lead to the durability and sustainability of human institutions as we know them. The notion of "organizational durability" became an important part of my thinking. Rather than focusing on the simple notion of the *under-performance* of the large and successful, I broadened my search to encompass a more straightforward and systematic approach to organizational success. My search was for a *formula* I could apply that would allow me to demonstrate my exceptional value to my superiors (read compensation). And I was looking for that same formula to practically guide my actions and drive the "right answers," as those are the things that formulas are designed to do. I was at a point in my career where the world seemed to be moving so fast that I almost had to find a systematic way to concurrently keep my sanity and direct my actions.

As it turns out, twenty five years later I had worked for four large organizations, all within the financial services industry. And during that time I looked at my large and successful institutions and tried to determine what might be happening that could lead to their under-performance . . . or even worse outcomes. And I was looking for that mystical formula that would both magically solve for the durability and underperformance problem, and at the same time serve to keep my managerial head above water.

The problem I constantly experienced was that this was a very negative and ofttimes cynical quest for answers. It came to feel like a form of black art or a branch of forensic science. Turning over rocks to look for unsightly little creatures is not most people's idea of a good time. At various points along the way, I had to stop the process, as the search for the truly ugly is never fun. The search could only be ultimately personally fulfilling based on the contingent development of a theory that actually intellectually "held together" and that would help me to manage my life. It was always so much easier to look for comity within one's organizations and in life in general. But I was looking for an important answer to what I considered an even more important question. So I pressed on.

In those early days, while I was yet in my twenties, the simple and classical answer to the under-performance question (which I accepted rather naively), went something like this: "The smaller institutions take more risks, they are more entrepreneurial, and they seize on opportunities more quickly than larger institutions." It seemed that this answer, at least for the most part, was true. The rather banal theory sufficed for several years as I went about thinking about how to build revenues and profits in my large institutional affiliations.

Some years later the blindingly obvious question occurred to me, and I began thinking about *why* the little guys actually did these kinds of things and the big guys just did not. Why wouldn't the "intelligent capital" in big businesses take the same type and magnitude of risks if they naturally lead to significantly higher returns over the long-term? It would seem that the largest organizations would actually have a better view of risk assumption, and a broader base of resources on which to draw in assessing those risks. It also seemed rather obvious that if "big businesses" were short on entrepreneurship, they should just go out and hire more entrepreneurial people. And why wouldn't they just *decide* or *will* to be more imaginative and innovative, and then direct their significant resources towards moving those valuable ideas into the market with expediency? But it became very clear, upon further review, that the answers to those questions were far more complex than I might have initially expected.

As the years went by there were many other "would-be-and-apparent" answers that occurred to me relative to the under-performance of large and successful institutions which ultimately proved to be both completely dank and unworkable. There were also fairly long periods of time where I just threw up my hands and concluded that an answer might not exist (or at least be discernable by me) in spite of all my best efforts to identify one. I had also, by that time, developed a new methodology and "formula" to deal with the speed of the world (without answering the core questions), and my life was working just fine. It was during my thirties that I also came to recognize that the big underperformance question—that I had *discovered*—was not even new. I had previously convinced myself that I was onto something both new and novel. At the same time, of the "answers" that continually crossed my path (mostly in the form of books that I had read and consultancy approaches that came my way), which might somehow explain my conundrum, none seemed to substantively obviate the high failure rates. Nor did they fundamentally address the ability of organizations to stem their own ultimate and stumbling decline. What I generally saw with respect to those who were addressing the organizational performance question was simple profiteering from the issue in the form of approaches that all basically said the same thing: "The problem you have is definitely X. So if you do exactly Y, you will solve for all your problems." Apparently this distressing level of simplicity is attractive to its intended audiences.

All of the approaches were emotionally attractive, but simply represented disingenuous and single-dimensioned solutions which promised infinitely more than they could possibly ever hope to deliver. I sat down one day and put together a list of fifty of these quick-fixes. The list included everything from empowerment to diversity, and from market segmentation schemes to value-added accounting techniques. There was inherently nothing wrong with any of the prescriptions. They were just not of a medicinal quality to cure for what ailed the patient. I could straightforwardly conclude the lack of efficacy of these single-track approaches from casual observations within my institutional surroundings.

More importantly, none of the answers seemed to appropriately link the real root causes of the problem and the related effects as I viewed them in my organizational life. This collection of answers seemed to only address the readily observable *symptoms* and *effects*, and seemed to venture no where close to the real root causes. As a result, the question that I had asked earlier in my career was again reformulated many years later as: "What are the real, foundational and root-level causes of the relative underperformance and limited durability of the large and successful?"

This new phase of the experiment took the form of identifying and observing whether there were any demonstrable attitudes, mindsets, behavioral insights or value systems that might naturally and unavoidably separate the performance and durability of the big from the small. I had heretofore looked at the things that organizations *did*, like strategic planning processes, communications protocols and the management and allocation of scarce resources in an attempt to find the answers to my question. I had found essentially nothing of value in any of those hiding places. I found a whole collection of processes and "concepts" with little correlation to the question at hand. The major breakthrough in my thinking came when I completely changed the nature of the search. The once-again re-formatted question went roughly like this: "Do these large and successful organizations *do* something different that causes them to regularly trip and fall, or do they in-fact *become* something entirely different?"

James Sire commented in *Naming the Elephant* that "ontology precedes epistemology." That comment seemed to hold a great deal of truth in but three words. What he was saying was that you cannot have a theory of knowledge, without first having an adequate sense of the objects opposite which the knowledge is to be applied. I had been looking for differences in the ways organizations acted, and saw what appeared as randomly occurring effects. When I began to actually look into the ontology of these institutions, and more deeply at the nature of their *being*, the picture became much less opaque. And the conclusion reached was that the outcomes of organizations are not a simple function of what they *do*. The outcomes are rather a direct result of who they *are*.

I have now been experimenting, using my re-formatted and broadened question, for another ten years. As mentioned, I have worked for four large financial services companies, each of which has been considered historically successful in their competitive fields. All of these organizations were S&P 500 companies. And all have experienced both huge "ups" and huge "downs" during the period of my working life. One of them has now completely failed. Another is essentially treading water as I write these words. And two now appear to be headed backwards. My observations are clearly and obviously shaped by my experiences within these institutions, which I believe represent a cross section of life within the large and successful organization space.

Operating under the presupposition that rarely are things as they appear at first glance, I have attempted to seek out a level of truth that I would have missed had I not at least attempted to see deeper into the muddled organizational maze. To simply believe that things are rarely as they appear, however, is of limited value. To determine what the reality actually *is* would be to create something of much greater value. My hope is that I have discovered some of the ontological realities faced by large organizations. The conclusions from my years of observation, along with a prescription for the improvement of outcomes of these human institutions, form the basis of this book.

Art and Science

At the same time, and to take a step back, my other set of interests (as opposed to my vocational interests) has always been in the areas of philosophy, history, economics, and theology. Throughout most of my adult life, my vocational interests and my personal interests have operated on separate and disparate tracks. My vocational interests could be described as "utilitarian," as I had my family and a set of ego needs that needed sating. My personal interests, essentially interests of the heart, were an escape from the pressures of corporate performance demands and a "place for my brain to go" that was not forced to coincide with the next quarter's "earnings release." What I am going to attempt to define in some detail in this book is the amplified realization that my mechanistic, formulaic, utilitarian and "processy" notions of how the world of human institutions actually works were fundamentally misdirected. My quest for an "orthodoxy formula" was equally misguided and actually quite dangerous. I was in need of a new way to think about the issues.

The answers to the organizational performance and durability question that I have subsequently come to view as "the truth" were actually to be found in *meaning*, and not in *doing*. More directly, I have now come to see that meaning is the basic driver of doing. And as a result, it is not that organizations are doing the wrong things that cause them problems. They are likely doing the same things they have always done, but with withering results. Were it not for my essential and deeply felt heart interests, I would likely never have come to these conclusions. It is difficult to underestimate the impact of these interests, my human-nature interests, on how I have come to think about human institutions.

My quest has shown that the answers to the question of the underperformance of human institutions are only successfully addressed with the tools of the social "sciences." They are found in looking into the nature of our humanity, and not into the nature of our processes. They are found in the answers to the *why* questions, and not the questions that address the what's, how's, where's and when's. They are found in looking at *faith* systems and not physical or psychological systems. They are found in the establishment of solid *human foundations* that fundamentally support these institutions, and not on a series of "substitute" foundations. They are found in a whole series of paradoxical notions of human behavior that obfuscate and confuse our organizational existences. And they are found in understanding what could be described as a set of nefarious forces that play on the frailty of all humanity.

After years and years of looking, it turns out that I found the answers to my question in a place that I did not even intend to look. I found the answers in the soft-sciences, the "social-arts," and not in the rigor of the applied organizational sciences, broadly described. As a "business guy", to have been associated as a member of the "social sciences crowd" during my college days would have been an insult. These were the people that we used to laugh at for their lack of personal direction and self-discipline. This was the people group whose job training, it was quipped, consisted of mastering the phrase, "Would you like fries with your order?" Worse yet, they might have been political liberals. But my experimentation and observations have confirmed these social science insights: the essential "human" learnings. And the gleanings have really nothing to do with business and capitalism, other than that the world of business is a world made up of people working together.

The conclusions reached herein essentially retain a guarded spirit of optimism. I have come to believe that human institutions contain within themselves the opportunity for continued high-performance and essential durability. At the same time, my belief is that the gate through which organizational durability is navigated is quite narrow, and the challenges both numerous and widely dispersed. From where I stand today, to be resigned to complete "institutional fatalism" as a conclusion is not, however, more than a day's walk away. I continue to believe that the long-term trajectory for most human institutions is that of a skipping stone. Were it not for the goodness and persistence of the human spirit, most human institutions would fail almost immediately as a function of their organizational engineering, leadership structures, and development processes. I have been the most startled in my quest to find how easily we forget and contort the historic underpinnings of our success, as well as how easily our once virtuous behavior can be turned (by ourselves) against us.

Throughout the book I will do my best to show both sides of coin, the positive as well as the negative, as well as to adumbrate alternative approaches that facilitate appreciably better outcomes. I will also attempt to develop and describe a set of universal imperatives that I believe apply to all human institutions. And while this prescription may not represent a successful "organizational orthodoxy", it does represent, in my experience, a foundation on which durable success can be built. It also represents an approach that seeks to connect the essential elements of humanity that are expressed with the more mechanical and altogether necessary—but completely insufficient—processes that are already successfully employed in most large human institutions.

There are times within this book where my expressions might best be described as a jeremiad, a lament. I had thought about lessoning the emotion that I will at times express, but decided against it as there are so many things that I have experienced that have created exceptional levels of personal frustration. You can be the judge as to whether I have over-reacted. At the same time, it is not my goal to enflame, but rather to coach . . . mostly to coach myself. It is easier for some of us to be rebels than liberators. It is often more rewarding to be a cynic than a saint. Negativity is a well-positioned defense mechanism that often serves as protection from life's uncertainties. But in the end, all of us want to be a part of the solution. And that is my goal as well.

This book is about avoiding organizational heartache. This book is about pain-avoidance at the institutional and personal level. This book is about membership in fragile human institutions and the seemingly unseen forces that drive organizations onto the pages of history. This book is mostly about humanity and organizational philosophy. And my thesis comes from simple observation. Yogi Berra once said something like "A lot of important observations can be made by watching what's going on." That was my method, and Mr. Berra stated it more succinctly than I ever could.

The poet Emerson once commented that "The end of the human race will be that it will eventually die of civilization." In civilizations, all the piece-parts work together in a highly-functional manner until something rudely interrupts the existing peace and serenity. It might not seem that the difference between investment returns of eight percent and ten percent are of much significance. It is only two percent, after all. But that two percent is actually a very, very large number. This difference is not a picture of peace and serenity. And the two percent difference belies the real magnitude of the issues that underlie the real problems. The differences in the *conditions* that drive those disparate return levels of return could not be more polar. And that is where we will begin Chapter One.

1

Machines and Souls

Large and successful organizations are born with two heads; a Mind-Head and a Soul-Head. The ongoing failure to address the questions of "who they are," leads to the malnourishment of the Soul-Head, and the gorging of the Mind-Head.

"What you must do, do quickly." These are the words that flow in an environment of betrayal. The first time I ran across the phrase had something to do with a guy by the name of Judas, and was linked to the alleged payment of thirty pieces of silver. The last time I ran across them came in an executive meeting where the CEO effectively said the very same thing. The latter setting was prompted by a completely nonsensical RIF (reduction-in-force, or forced layoffs of staff) that we were being told to execute. RIFs are a nice way of sanitizing the fact that people are losing their jobs, their incomes, and potentially much more. While I could understand the rationale for the RIF within the very political context in which were operating, that was not what essentially struck me. The thing that came screaming out was how emotionally callow and cold the comment was in its pretentiousness. I was hoping to hear something about the human tragedy of job loss and how we should exercise as much sensitivity as possible toward those that were about to become unemployed. This was especially true given we were enduring the worst economic downturn we had experienced in many decades. But all we heard was, "What you must do, do quickly." I had expected, or maybe just hoped for, a little more heart, or a little more *soul* to have been expressed. But the "*mind* of the machine" had spoken.

The understanding of humanity in terms of the separate and distinct notions of the mind and the soul go back to the first written accounts of human thought. Some of us have concluded that we are but mind and body, flesh and bone. And some of us discuss the possibility of a soul, either in an eternal or temporal light. The notion of the supremacy of the *mind* was well-established by many of the ancient philosophers. Others from the same era took a much more soulish approach to their philosophy. The inventor Thomas Edison considered his body just something to carry his brain around. Gnostics separate the body and soul and consider them distinct elements of a two-dimensioned entity called a person. While disagreement will always exist, the thing on which most of us can agree is that a soul is a difficult concept to define, and even more challenging to fundamentally agree upon, than the mind. The mysticism attached to any description of a soul provides a very rich field for diverse opinions and even heated controversy.

Regardless of its roots, an appreciation that people are different than machines and that our minds are more than just "computers made of meat" is widely held. It is also generally agreed that minds and souls are essentially of a different nature. For purposes of making progress in our discussion, all we have to conclude is that there is something special and very different between people and either hydroelectric power plants or begonias. Our minds actually do have some similarities with power plants. But, it is our souls that make us different from the inorganic and from our inventions. And the needs of a soul are different than anything else with which we come into contact.

It is always interesting to me, that as we interact with each other, it seems as if we are interacting on two levels. On one level our minds are interacting with one another. On another level our souls appear to be in direct contact. Interactions of the mind are useful and instructive. Interactions of the soulish type take on a different dynamic. More is at risk in these soulish conversations as more of "who we really are" is being exposed. More is at risk in soulish contact because no given soul has any type of unique power over another in this type of discourse. More is at risk as it is much easier to be "disagreed with" than "not accepted."

Soulish contact is that which deepens our respect, and creates an interest in developing greater levels of trust for "the other." Souls interact at the level of values and shared experience. And in shared values and commonality of experience is found trust. We earnestly desire to trust each other in the most sincere way, as it creates both relational and physical security. And it is in an environment of security-based trust that we can advance the human condition. It is in this environment that we are free to act, and free to use our imaginations to create a better future. I have come to see this interaction, our relating to one another at the level of both mind and soul, as if we humans were a type of two-headed creature. One head effectively houses our mind, the other, our soul. Allow me some latitude to explain.

When I talk with someone, I envisage myself talking with this "two-headed person." And I assume that I look the same to them. The question is then "What head is interacting with what head?" To be fully human, interactive and imaginative, this has to be a four-way conversation. But so many times, human dialogue ends up being just a two-way conversation, with the Mind-Heads doing all the talking. And it is easy to see why. Mind-Heads are always in a big hurry and are in need of getting "something very important" done. Soul-Heads want to talk about their vacations, some line from an old movie, their love life or SEC football. Mind-Heads are disciplined and orderly and thoughtful. Soul-Heads are forgetful and unruly. Soul-Heads are also passionate and sentimental.

Mind-Heads look like Mitt Romney's head (businessman and politician): cool, professional, and logical, with very nice hair. Mind-Heads are easy to talk with as you can generally project what is going to come out of their mouths. Mankind will someday create a computer program to replicate the capabilities of the Mind-Head. Soul-heads look like Jerry Garcia's head, Jerry of the Grateful Dead: artist, iconoclastic, unconventional, and with the hair of a werewolf. You have no idea as to what is "going on" in a Soul-Head, and that is as it should be. There is no code. There are no rules. All you can know when you connect with a Soul-Head is that it is very likely you are going to experience something new. Mind-Heads express themselves in the observable and the knowable. Soul-Heads express themselves in the vernacular of hopes and fears. Mind-Heads calculate and de-construct. Soul-Heads seek to assemble, and they long for a place called home.

That we exist with two unique heads is a very important part of who we are and how we act. When it is said that two heads are better than one, I am just going to assume this is what was meant. If we neglect the existence of either our Mind-Head or our Soul-Head, that head will just shrivel up and become completely useless. Some of us will actually cut-off one of our heads as we come to think of it as either non-productive or not very interesting. But we were all meant to have these two separate heads. It is what makes us human. With only one head, we cannot see the world as it really is. With but one head we can only view the world in a single-dimensioned way that is distortive of reality. At the same time, Soul-Heads, especially in our institutional lives, are much more nettlesome than Mind-Heads, and so it is apparent why having a shrunken Soul-Head might appear a positive thing. But lo, it is not.

I was talking with a business associate about a common acquaintance whose actions and attitudes would be considered, at least by most, highly undesirable. My colleague commented, in analyzing the situation, "Eddie has no soul." That seemed a little stark to me. But the comment was essentially a statement that captured what we were seeing in his actions. Eddie was driven not by any source of empathy or internal notion of the good, but rather by what he could personally extract from the world in any and all situations. "Eddie would charge into a burning building to rescue a nickel, but not his mother" was what I heard next. And while I laughed, the reality of the situation was that this was in-fact the sad truth.

We all recognize and appreciate the characteristics that emanate from somewhere deep within us human-types that create a willingness and ability to see beyond our own self-serving interests and to seek after a common good. Mother Theresa is a certifiable goddess in our memories as a result of her exhibition of unbounded soulishness. Our heroes are all, by definition, selfless and soulish. Without the presence of souls, all human interaction would be subject to the forces of valuesless entropy, and chaos would immediately ensue. In Eddie's case, he had clearly severed his own Soul-Head. And in his case, it was likely removed with an old rusty fork. And so we find that having but one head is the truly monstrous picture of a man.

ORGANIZATIONAL SOULS

We have all had experience in dealing with those whose "hearts have been broken." We have all had opportunities to see the impact of abusive relationships and simple neglect. The presence of "lives of quiet desperation" are virtually everywhere. The joyful times we enjoy in our existences sit immediately adjacent to the significantly painful ones. As much as we would like to live in a world of completely positive experiences, it just doesn't happen. Our human experience is also universally and humanly common. But it is in our soulishness that we see a future filled with an increasing amount of "the good" that provides the hope that propels each of us forward. We live as individuals in the hope of a better and increasingly joyful future. Our souls are the eyes through which we view that future.

On a personal basis, if we stay away from theories as to the eternal, this rough definition of a soul is acceptable to most of us. Souls serve the purpose of guiding us outside ourselves and towards a sense of creative optimism as to what is to come next in our lives. Souls are our internal honest agents and are incapable of intentional distortions of the truth. Our minds will rationalize anything; our souls cannot. In this view, souls are fundamental to happiness, decency, progress and to all that is worthy of being held in high-regard. But if we just stop there, we lose an insight into the nature of human institutions. We truncate our understanding of the work of the soul.

Simply put, I have come to conclude that it is not correct to see the world as a large collection of individuals all possessing souls, operating in the context of a set of diverse human institutions that are themselves essentially non-soulish. Human institutions have souls as well. Contrary to Marxist thought that capitalistic organizations are ineluctably "soulless" and amoral, the truth is that all human institutions have souls. This conclusion comes in the face of my traditional Anglo-Protestant notion of the accountability of individuals and a related and very strong native cynicism towards the efficacy of feckless and despotic human institutions . . . of any kind.

I had, up to a point in time, seen all human institutions as "necessary evils" at best. It is natural for people like me to exalt the personal responsibility of individuals and condemn all human institutions as defective and corrupt by nature. A brief study of the history of institutions would validate much of the prophylactic cynicism. However, I came to see institutions as a collection of soulish individuals. The aggregation of individual souls creates not just a "group," but rather a *"synthesis of souls."* And in that view the institutions *themselves* become soulish. My attitude towards human institutions, given this conclusion, was then forever changed. And so did my level of hope and respect for those institutions.

A more proper rendering, as I have concluded, is to see the world as a collection of both individuals and their institutions as by nature "soulish." I have come to see institutions as two-headed entities with an infinite ability for good, parked immediately adjacent to an infinite supply of "bad." In that light I began to see the answer to the question of the performance of large institutions in terms of the relative nourishment, and the associated level of health, of their institutional souls. Not to be confused with morality and ethics, or "right and wrong," this type of soulishness is that which honestly and fundamentally points us towards a beneficent and more prosperous future.

My conclusion is that large and successful institutions incrementally lose their Soul-Heads, usually as the simple result of atrophy from lack of use, and that this loss leads directly and unmistakably down a path to their ultimate decline. The atrophy of the Soul-Head occurs as an indefatigable *process* and not as a noteworthy *event*. The loss can occur over many years or even centuries, or it can happen over a period of just a few months. Whether the Soul-Head of the institution is intentionally or unintentionally shed, or just shrinks from malnourishment, is irrelevant. All human institutions need two healthy heads.

SOULISHNESS DEFINED

Individual souls are like human faces, all unique. But all share some characteristics that are highly differentiating from the world of the abjectly non-soulish. A few of these characteristics would include the fundamental notion that souls are relational, as opposed to material. Minds seek after comfort and aesthetics and the achievement of the complete personal control over the future enjoyment of the same. Comfort and aesthetics are the currency of the material. Souls seek after other souls. Souls share a very serious bent towards being admired and accepted by other souls, and pay little heed to accomplishment in the material realm. Souls are more concerned about values and virtuous behavior than they are about winning or prevailing over an opponent. "Mindishness" creates plans and strategies, while the soul creates desired end-states. Souls tend toward humility, while minds tend towards arrogance. The soul is mobilized by passions; the mind is motivated to relieve anxiety and improve predictability. Souls are not controlled by rationality; they are controlled by something which looks more like feelings. And it is in the connection with "feeling" that comes much contempt for the soul, as it is impossible to control how someone else feels, as opposed to how someone thinks or acts. Policies can be created and enforced, but values cannot be "implemented." Souls are subjective and the voice of opinion, while minds are objective and systematic. Souls are the consummate free-agents, for better or for worse. Minds watch the clock, while souls enjoy the time.

In theory, if each of us were completely "rational" in our thinking, we would all agree on everything. I see bumpers stickers in my San Francisco suburb that say, "One Planet, One People." Interesting concept, but wholly utopian and naïve as it relates to the work of the soul. Our souls take each of us in very different directions as to our view of how the world works and how we each fit in the overall scheme. Given a common set of facts, we all come to different conclusions as to their interpretation, and needless to say, their impact on our future actions.

Souls are the source of very divergent opinions. From our souls come a set of values that number with the stars. These values, when processed through our intellect and placed in our own unique contextual frameworks form our "worldviews." And our worldviews shape our systems of criticism and evaluation. And herein is the connection between the sub-optimal performance of large and successful organizations and the loss of the institutional soul. As the worldviews of individuals within an institution (and the values that are implicit in those worldviews) diverge, the fabric of the community is stretched and in many cases ripped. A community cannot retain relational and emotional cohesion in the face of conflicting values and worldviews. And it is the failure of many large organizations to retain a consistent set of worldviews that cripple their institutional souls and their ability to effectively and profitably coexist within their environment. More significantly, communities-in-conflict are not able to generate any real level of imagination, nor are they able to see and agree upon the nature of their challenges. And even beyond that, the ability of large and successful organizations to speak in a language of "soulishness and community" is lost along the path to success and predictable prosperity.

Accordingly, if a human institution's situation is such that both internal cohesion and progress are possible without people effectively working together, then the idea of an institutional soul is irrelevant. At the same time, a group of completely "dis-integrated" or disconnected people that just happen to be working together does not represent a human institution, and certainly not a community. Ultimately, tribal alliances form and conflict is created and the "organization" is rendered detritus. On the other hand, my experience has been that the relationships and resulting cooperation between individuals is *the* critical element in ongoing adaptation, progress and the survival of our institutions. Whether the issues are those of original imagination or the execution of agreed-upon tactics, the complexities of the world seem to dictate the effective cooperation of both minds *and* souls.

The differences in the outcomes of souls that are both dedicated and healthy versus those that are tangential and wounded cannot be overstated, especially in the intermediate to long-term. It is possible to cajole or coerce a wounded soul, of either the personal or institutional variety, into some form of action in the short-term. But a soul-sick institution is in need of more than threats or spurious incentives. It needs to be made *well* before it can contribute. For me to look at a soulishly sick institution creates the same type of emotional response as to look at a mistreated animal. The wagging tail belies the seriousness of the threat posed by the situation.

The foundation of the soul is its sense of origin. The answer to the age-old question of why each of us is here is critical to our understanding of the world and how we interact with it. This origin shapes how the "soul-bearer" perceives the world, and it provides the set of tools for understanding events and evaluating responses due to the conception of its origin. The soul's distinct origin gives rise, in turn, to a unique nature. If the origin shapes the worldview, the nature of the soul is the worldview fully formed. A soul's worldview answers the question "How does the world work?" The answer to this question forms the basis for how the soul interacts with the world around it. The answer to this question also defines the nature of the soul, illustrating how different values, facts, presuppositions, and inclinations interweave to make a united and (as best as the soul-bearer can) cohesive understanding of reality. This overarching understanding leads to different ways of interacting with the world. The soul has a relational element that governs our interactions with people in terms of their value systems, their goal orientations and their perceived ability to be trusted. This "system" of the soul is always on duty and is infinitely careful. Breaches to the system are never a good thing and this element of the soul is a meticulous evaluator of the farcical; as a means of personal protection.

The soul also has a very critical faith component. This part of the soul addresses the non-quantifiable, the mystic, the transcendent and our unknowable futures. This system flips on and off as needed. But it represents our source of hope, and is therefore indispensable. When the relational system of the soul malfunctions, people get hurt. When the faith systems fail, people "die." Without hope, the future is not our ally.

If we can get past the answer to the question of how we got here, the natural next question, and a domain of the soul, is to determine what we are actually here *for*. Call this purpose or meaning or destiny or whatever you will, but the important question that the soul is looking for answers to is simply "So what?" Given the soul's complex network of values and beliefs, its purposes go beyond perforce goal setting. The soul's purpose could more adequately be defined in terms of duty. "Because I am like this and the world is the way it is, I must do or become this." Expressions of the soul's purpose can be seen every day, from philosophy to pop-culture. "You can do anything you set your mind to" is the oft-voiced sentiment of the popular and successful. And while this is obviously not true (I couldn't run a four minute mile with all the best training in the world, and never could), the spirit of the comment is probably reasonably well-intended and directed at establishing a meaningful purpose.

Many people end up degrading their sense of purpose by defining it in purely materialistic terms, immortalized by the now old eighties slogan "whoever dies with the most toys wins." From experience, however, I would say that most people do not start with this philosophy. More likely than not, we live our adult lives with the higher realities of family, community, passing on a legacy of character and wisdom, and contributing to the greater good. Suffice to say that those of us who struggle with determining any purpose for our lives, a purpose that fails to satisfy the desires of our souls, are truly unfortunate. Moreover, the "lost-ness" that accompanies a lack of purpose eliminates the possibility of any meaningful contribution. Only in the course of determining a mutuality of interest with those around us is our faith in the system of life maintained.

As individuals, we all relate very quickly with the notions of where we "grew up" and the impact of one's upbringing on each us as individual adults. For some of us it is a joyful reckoning and for others it is not. We can all acutely feel and identify our senses of "what is important to me" and "this is where I would like my life to go." We all have goals and we all have fears. But the important thing is that when we are talking about the soul, we remember how *deep* the soul goes within each of us. It is essentially "who we are" at a very fundamental level. There is no human interaction that doesn't touch our souls.

Within each of our Soul-Heads is an essential set of "truths" that are driven by a combination of our experiences and our personal systems of faith. In this case, faith is anything in which we place our trust that is not "verifiable" scientifically, but in which we nonetheless believe. Each of us is a massive collection of both experiences and faith-based beliefs. The expression of our Soul-Heads is that of a set of values reflective of the truths which exists within us. They are a unique set of values in that our personal experiences are all different and our beliefs systems are equally personal. As our Soul-Heads come into contact with other Soul-Heads, it is the communication of value-systems that is important. Consistent value sets are the basis for trust which is the core ingredient for all human progress, relationally or physically. It is trust which allows us to operate in a state of freedom and liberty that allows *imagination* to thrive, and it is imagination which is uniquely human. Imagination is essentially the soulish phenomenon.

INSTITUTIONAL SOULS AND HOMES

Human institutions exhibit the same soulish characteristics as do individuals. It was in that observation that the world began to look very different from the one that I had grown up to imagine. One cannot have a worldview and values-set which necessitates X, without having an appropriate and consistent purpose Y, leading to a hopeful outcome Z. Within an individual, there will always be cohesion of these factors or we would call the condition a form of mental illness. The same is a true and observable condition within our institutions. Values always lead to ideas, and ideas are turned into actions, and actions lead to outcomes. To the extent that this chain of cause and effect is perceived by each of us as beneficial and cohesive, we participate with passion. The opposite is also true.

Organizations with healthy souls are comprised of individuals who see in their institution a place where the values are aligned, the cause worthy, and the outcomes attractive. An emotional unity is formed that provides the bulwark for progress and effective community. Community is not simply a collection of people, as in "I live in such and such a community." Community is too rarely seen in its purest form anymore, as true community is experienced only in the presence of healthy and aligned souls. A community is the place where we *live*. And the ultimate purpose and ultimate longing of the soul is to find our "home."

It is only natural then that we might consider this definition of communal and soulish unity home. Our own personal homes have similar attributes. Within our homes, we all have the same origins, whether that is defined as a physical address, a last name, or our legal and biological ties. We frequently have similar worldviews and values as they are taught and exhibited in the environment of a home. And to the extent those worldviews are attenuated, the more challenging becomes the environment. Members of successful homes understand and agree with their roles and work together towards the accomplishment of a common, but individually applicable purpose. The destination is always simply defined as "being home." Our community forms the core of our existence. And though we as individuals are always changing, accomplishing varied purposes and moving in different directions, we will never transcend our need and identification with home. The only difference between communities and families is the size of the membership. All other factors impacting the group's soulish health are identical.

The 1980s television show "Cheers" created the scene of a neighborhood bar with a small group of patrons, each with their own critically distinctive personalities and quirkiness. Although the individual players were all uniquely troubled in some way as human beings (and each of us could personally identify with their faults and frailties), they were just as critically successful as a human institution. As a group they had an identity as a community and they shared a collective soul. Their dialogue was between their Soul-Heads, as their Mind-Heads were told to keep their mouth shut. They didn't need to have their roles explained and they certainly didn't see themselves as a "large and successful" human institution. Almost as critical to our enjoyment of the show as the plots and acting was the theme song. The song said that we all long to go "Where everybody knows your name... where everybody's glad you came." And this form of organization is bound to perennially succeed. The fragility of the people gave the semblance of disorder and chaos. But the reality was complete interpersonal cohesion and real community. The fabric was resilient and the strands were individually strong. The Cheers bar was a home for its inhabitants.

All human institutions share this collective soul. The only question within any assemblage of humanity is its relative soulish *health*. And all institutions share the common attributes of a home, however functional or dysfunctional it may be. It is uniformly easy to understand why we all fancy the idea of being at home. First, homes are a place where we are unconditionally accepted. Second, homes are a place where the outcomes are, to the extent possible, secure, predictable, and comfortable. Homes are also a place were everyone has a desire to contribute; not in a sense like chores, but rather like "A+" test scores on the refrigerator. The report card is positioned immediately adjacent to the family picture from the last vacation to Yellowstone. They are the "markers" that all the members of the household can rejoice in and take pride in. And lastly, homes are a place where the fruits-of-abundance are felt more relationally, than either materially or physically.

I am not at all certain that Steven Spielberg would have believed that the little line "ET phone home" might be considered, at least by some, one of the most profound lines in all of movie history. Those few well-defined words haunt you, don't they? As we watched the movie, we all found ourselves clinging to the hope that our new little friend would find his way home. As completely alien as the creature was, our hearts reached out to him because we all related to a solitary and universally apparent notion: the notion of longing to be in a place we consider home. Although we all knew or believed he would eventually make it, within each us was a longing to get him there quickly, and to see how the whole story would be revealed. It made you wish, as you watched the story unfold, that you could somehow help, even if in but some small way. I was never sure whether his little expression "ET phone home" was a question or a declarative, but the sentiment is clearly the same. You felt a tremendous connectedness with the funny looking little specimen who had but one simple request: "Please take me home. I really want to be home." That's it... just home.

We truly thrive as individuals only in instances when we experience the benefits of home. Some of our human institutions are very good at creating a home. Others are not. It really wouldn't make any difference that this was the case in most organizations if it weren't for the fact that people work in them. If people didn't need to be comfortable in their surroundings to maximize their performance, it would also be irrelevant. If people didn't need to be both accepted and trusted to be effective it would be a mute point. It wouldn't be at all significant if people didn't need to understand their environment, nor have a say in what was going on. If people had no interest in where they were going in life, home would be of no import. It also wouldn't have any real impact if trust weren't the cornerstone of all progress. It wouldn't create any demonstrable benefit if people were their own unique imagination agents. It wouldn't have an impact in a world where people weren't natively tribal and bellicose. And it would be insignificant in a world where logic was the sole driving force in the realization of progress. But none of these are consistent with our observed realities and humanity.

THE ALTERNATIVE REALITY

Imagine for a moment a different kind of home. The morning begins early. Every family member receives an email announcing that showers have been replaced by two packets of moist towelettes. This in an effort to cut down on the "spend" on the water bill. Breakfast is at Seven AM and the menu consists of Cheerios. It is the same every day, because someone decided that the family "doesn't like change." Over his bowl of cereal, middle-schooler Johnny asks his mom for advice on dating. Mom proceeds to give Johnny statistics on dating and STDs. Johnny is confused and frustrated. He had asked for something resembling practical ideas about how to ask Jenny to the dance on Friday, and all he got back in return was data. As mom pulls out the spreadsheets tracking the family budget, Susie, the precocious sister, packs her bags silently. Susie was an exceptional university student with a promising future in a highly-lucrative field. Unfortunately, the family's new risk-adjusted investment return formula determined that the risk she might become an Art History major was too great, and the algorithm suggested she be terminated from the family. The risk formula also determined that a better investment proposition would be to retain the older twin boys: George who works at Wal-Mart, and Fred who creates expense-minimizing formulas for a large financial services firm. Dad breaks the melancholy of Susie's termination from the family by announcing that the family had "performed better" in the last calendar quarter than expected. Between the slim but steady Wal-mart checks, the cost-cutting formulas, and the moist towelette strategy, expenses were down and some cash flow had been freed-up. Dad quickly adds that the family vacation has been cancelled, but reassures them that maintenance of the "family brand name" was what is truly important. Commitment to the family is all that really matters. He pontificates for a few moments about the family's core values: integrity, caring, and "doing the right thing." Breakfast resumes. Mom goes back to her spreadsheets. Fred heads off to see what other expenses can be minimized. Johnny's mind drifts to a possible future in Art History and a fear that the deodorant budget might be cut next.

This is not the kind of home anyone would want to be a part of. In fact, it barely constitutes a home at all. This is because people are not machines, nor do they become machine-like or mechanical when you put them together to accomplish some set of tasks. It is a very unnatural human state. And while we would likely all agree and acknowledge this truth, large institutions often take on this same look and feel. The sheer complexity associated with many large and successful organizations, their huge number of "moving parts," and the physical dispersion of the participants all contribute to the mechanization process. They begin to look like machines given the emotional and relational distance between the people within the organization. They begin to look like machines as a result of the language we use to describe the workings of the organism. Think about words like "headcount" or FTEs. They begin to look like machines because we begin thinking about them in scientific and materialistic terms. We think about how to gain *leverage* in the business model and how to utilize our *output algorithms* to best improve operating margins. We come to believe that if *it* can be systematized into a process, that the continual reengineering of that process will provide for infinite mechanistic progress. And they begin to look like machines as the people within them begin to feel like parts in a machine, as opposed to members of a real community. The understanding that our institutions act like machines is not in any way a novel observation. The oddity is that the negativity attached to the observation is not matched with any real actions to offset the negative and known implications of the mechanization process. Mind-Heads would rather manage a machine than a group of unpredictable and sometimes irrational humans.

As a result, our institutions become less like home and largely devoid of soul. They are soulish by nature, and soul-less as a consequence of malnourishment. We begin to see the mechanization of our lives in ways that are humanly disturbing to each of us. We cannot offset the loss of the community's soul with the improvement in our material lives. It may work for a season, but it is clearly not maintainable because of the importance of the institutional soul. Over time, organizations proceed to abandon the souls that they at one time possessed, and pursue the more "intellectually logical" strategies, that while clearly not canards, are organizationally non-foundational.

If asked, most organizational leaders would say that their organizations are not "mechanized," but rather retentive of their original humanity, freedom, and imagination. They would also agree that the mechanization and bureaucratization of organizations is truly a bad outcome and a precursor to a downdraft in the life of their institution. But most are mislead for two reasons. The first is that the mechanization process occurs in most organizations in such an "awareness dulling" fashion that few notice it happening. Consistent with watching the biological growth of almost anything, the sequential changes are far too gradual for direct observation. Time-lapse photography of an organization's soul would be revealing and educational. Only in stepping away, and then in stepping back, can the changes be seen.

The second reason that leaders are mislead is that leadership people are often not caught up in the machine. They sit on top of the machine and don't see its pernicious ways. What they see is what comes out of the machine, and it is both partial in its disclosure and sanitized in its outputs. The problem with partial truths is that they contain a grain of reality, resulting in a misleading level of reliance. As organizations change leaders, they often transition from a leader who comfortably lived within the machine, and was conscious of its realities, to one who chooses to sit on top. Moreover, any leader without a well-functioning Soul-Head is unable to see the mechanization process and the concurrent loss of community.

We all love being members of growing and healthy human institutions. The growth we see in our organizations is a positive reinforcement of our personal contributions to the cause. Growth is the most obvious evidence of "life" in a thriving and healthy community. The attractiveness of any "growth cult" is highly contagious and a mighty force in any human institution. At the same time, we as individuals are the essential problem to the continued success of the institution. Our human natures are that which causes both the growth and the ultimate stagnation. The ingredient is a constant: us. The results are not.

DIVERGENT PATHS

At some point in the life of any successful institution a crossroad is reached. Or maybe it would be better to position the situation as a fork in the road. The path to the left is one littered with the intellectualism of The Enlightenment. The path to the right is impacted by the history of moral, human and religious philosophy. The reason that the organization is at some point in time positioned at the fork in the road is that in the progression of all large and successful institutions they are forced to make a fundamental decision as to their core disposition toward the world. One of the options is to determine that they have conquered the enemy and stand relatively unopposed in their quest. Everything is now possible. The claim is one of infinite progress. The organization claims that it has developed the requisite capabilities to guarantee a glorious future. and to manage by the powers of the mind, their own destiny. In a word, the organization has become completely "sufficient." As a matter of self-identity, it is now lacking in nothing that it cannot itself provide. It has become, in its own mind, autarkic. While this positioning is never claimed as wholly absolute, it is experienced within the institution as something very closely related.

The second option is for the organization to continue to declare that it is "needy" and continuously linked to its history of deprivation and metaphorical poverty. These institutions see themselves as perennially lacking and reliant on a whole raft of factors in order for them to continue to exist and thrive. They claim neither to know, nor stake any claim in the future, but rather seek to position themselves to adapt to the future's unfolding. The former positioning, the completely sufficient, has the advantage of feeling more secure and confident. The latter position has the advantage of being consistent with the realities of life.

Organizations that choose the path to the left are "Post-Sufficient," and their appended condition is "Post-Sufficiency." They have crossed a line in their own minds where they are no longer reliant on anything or anyone for their continued success. This condition is an organizational disease that is always fatal. Mild cases can linger in the patient for years and be disguised as other ailments. It is almost always misdiagnosed for long periods of time. The treatments that are applied are ineffective given this very unfortunate misidentification. More virulent strains can take long-standing and proud organizations down-to-their-knees in literally a few months. An organization's soul can be almost completely destroyed in an instant. The *mind* of the organization may live on with the help of life support for some extended period of time; but the heart and the soul has already died.

On the other hand, organizations that chose the path to the right are those that might be euphemistically called "Insufficient Organizations." These are organizations whose soulish health is being preserved and built. These are organizations with well-functioning Mind-Heads, along with serious representation and involvement from their Soul-Heads.

The manner of the progression of Post-Sufficiency is incredibly deceptive as it represents a set of "seeds" that always produce much fruit. It is in the nature and volume of the fruit wherein the danger lies. These seeds also have embedded within them the absolute opportunity to choke out other important sources of sustenance that suffer at the expense of the growth of Post-Sufficiency. Like so many things in life, the question is one of finding a middle point that flourishes between the fatal extremes. Post-Sufficiency, by its nature, abandons the planting of seeds that produced the fruit that was consumed in their youth; in their Insufficiency. Post-Sufficiency, more profoundly, does not see the impact of the growth of the new seeds until they have taken over the field of their souls. It is impossible to do battle with an enemy that goes undetected.

The seeds of Post-Sufficiency are a set of "isms" that have been glamorized over the last few hundred years. In and of themselves they have represented powerful forces in the advancement of mankind, and have provided for a significant reduction in the suffering of many of the world's denizens. The apparent "good" provided by this set of approaches and philosophies has become so pervasive that they represent the theology of the age. But the new progress-based theology, while beneficial to the whole, has a type of orthodoxy that is too narrow for the perpetuation of individual institutions *within* the system. The system advances at the expense of its participant institutions. And it is the failure to understand the intolerance and massive shortcomings of this faith system that is at the root of the problems faced by Post-Sufficient organizations. Internal disaffection occurs within any system when the results as ascribed to the individual system's participants appear inconsistent with the results experienced by that of the whole.

Through observation, more than from the study of the "theological elements," it is relatively easy to identify four "isms" that thread their way through organizations in a Post-Sufficient state. The first of the elements is something that might be referred to as Scientism. Scientism creates a high degree of value on data and facts, and worships the fields of math and statistics. Scientism says that there is an answer for everything that can be mechanically derived if we can just gain the knowledge to figure out the salvific formula. Scientism thinks well of all of science and is vitriolic towards the perceived frailties of humanity. Science, as Gustave Le Bon says, is "deaf to our lamentations." The word *knowledge* is indicative of the store of value that is the object of scientism.

The second of the elements is simple Materialism. Materialism is the god of consumption and co-incidentally, the god of efficient output. Materialism places a high value on "things" versus relationships. If the word *knowledge* captures the essence of scientism, the word *more* captures the essence of materialism. This second element exists in a milieu of "quantity as god." Jeremy Bentham could be the spokesman for materialism with his algorithm of Felicific Calculus. Samuel Gompers, the nineteenth century labor leader once was quoted as saying that the goal of organized labor was just "more." Productivity improvements dominate the agendas of Post-Sufficient entities.

The next element was popularized by J.S. Mill and is commonly referred to as Utilitarianism. Utilitarianism as a philosophy is largely in the grave of philosophies long since dead and buried (even by Mill), but as an organizational and political concept it lives on. It declares that there exists a common definition of the good, and that to the extent we formulaically follow the definition, the greatest amount of benefits to the largest number of people will ensue. If knowledge is the food source for the Mind-Head, Utilitarianism is the waste product. For purposes of this discussion, suffice to say that Utilitarianism is an approach where the cold logic of the situation can drive the presumptive "right" decisions. It also claims the merit of being so logical that it can provide a process by which we can all come to agree on issues of collective concern, and in so doing avoid the clutter of divergent opinions. To keep with the ongoing theme of philosophers, Rousseau's notion of the "General Will" falls under the category of utilitarian.

Lastly, is the notion of totalitarianism. This one is easy to envision as it is so pervasive in the world around us. It is a description of power emanating from the center. As a political concept, most Americans soundly reject it, or anything that even remotely looks like it. In organizational contexts however, the idea of centralized planning is alive and well. The poet Yeats objection that "Things fall apart, the center cannot hold." has gone unheeded. And this is not centralized planning with any sort of broad or democratic input base. It is just leadership from on-high, creating ubiquitous central pressure. And it is usually radically distant from any other reality than the effective use of power.

Collectively, I refer to the elements of Scientism, Materialism, Utilitarianism and Totalitarianism as seen and manifest in human institutions as *SMUT*. Accordingly, organizations that ascribe to these concepts as *wholly sufficient* to provide for their future success are *SMUTy* organizations. The key thought that comes out of these elements is that they are all focused on "what we do" as an organization. This stands in direct opposition to "who we are." They are focused on decisions and their perceived outcomes, and they utilize output and "progress" as the barometers of success. This is where the humanity is lost. And this is where Post-Sufficiency takes root.

The core of the SMUTy focus of the Post-Sufficient organization is "The Plan." The Plan represents the strategy of the organization, including the volume and type of outputs that are going to be created in the future. The core value of the SMUTy organization is "rightness," defined as making decisions connected with the best logic and data available for the decision-making process. The key challenge that is perceived to exist in SMUTy organizations is whether The Plan can be appropriately and completely orchestrated, and executed on time. The best outcome for a SMUTy organization is to distill the entirety of the enterprise into a simplified "formulaic model" that everyone in the organization can grasp, and that can serve as the guide to all future decisions.

This is the approach to organizational health that I developed early in my life. It is outstanding in its details and in its scope. On its face it looks very attractive and very thorough. It is also wholly inadequate to create durable and high-performing human institutions. It is an exact prescription for the loss of an institution's soul. I used to think of these "isms" and The Plan as the supporting infrastructure on which the rest of the entity rests. I now see them as appendages (at best) and possibly malignant growths that should be surgically exorcised. At a minimum, SMUT only addresses a part of the overall picture of any human institution. It represents the non-human part. It is the Mind-Head talking, and talking tendentiously. Mind-Heads, by the way, don't have functioning ears.

"Be advised that given the inclement weather, all yard privileges for all inmates are, for this afternoon, revoked ... the Warden." Actually, I have never seen that message. But you can conceivably imagine seeing that sign being posted on a prison door. The message that I really saw was delivered via email and said this: "Be advised that given the inclement weather, all non-essential personnel are released at 12:00 today." This was signed: "Head of Human Resources." Out of the hearts of men crawl all sorts of interesting sentiments. In this case the sentiments were not very sentimental. In-fact, they are the optimal usage of the mechanical and utilitarian mindset. And in this case they were delivered by the so-called head of all-things-human. It should also be added that we never heard from this person otherwise; so this was their "message-of-the-year."

The notice could have been worded: "We are concerned about the snow storm that is being forecast for our vicinity. So we have decided to error on the side of being safe. We are asking everyone whose jobs are providing for the immediate and direct needs of our clients to stay through their normal working hours. We are asking everyone else to consider leaving at noon to avoid getting stuck somewhere you would rather not be. Thanks to all of you who will be staying. The rest of us truly appreciate it! And by the way, there is a day's worth of comp-time for those of us who are staying."

So how did we fix this message? First, no legalese and no terms of inferred slavery would be a beneficial start. When you start a communication with "be advised", anything that follows is suspect. Secondly, when you use the word "release", it sounds like something that happens when you are "out on good behavior", and the authorities will be locking you back up when you return. And lastly, the word "non-essential" hardly needs commentary given the scope of its absurdity. I would like to believe that everyone in the community is essential. If you want to talk about creating an internal caste system: this is as good as it gets. This is just a silly little example, but where does this stuff come from? It comes from SMUTy thinking. And SMUTy thinking comes from the people with only one head.

Another message I received from a CEO communicates much the same: "In my message to you earlier about our company's 20XX priorities I discussed our shareholder expectations about taking our company to a higher level of performance. Key to this is growing our earnings faster than everyone else in our industry. To accomplish this goal, we're building on the work done over the last several years by implementing a series of "performing better than the competition" measures focused on growing the top-line and improving our profit margins. As part of improving margins, we are taking a hard look over a three year period at where we work and how we do our work:

We are a global company and we need a global operating model that provides the highest quality service to our clients and the best economics to our shareholders. So, across the company and around the world we're asking ourselves whether this type of work really needs to be done in a major metropolitan area, or whether it could it be done equally well in a growth center such as Sioux Falls or the UK's Dorchester, or Singapore or Mumbai. The question of how we do our work is about efficiency, which involves our ongoing process re-engineering and technology automation efforts, again looking across the company as a whole.

The changes we are making to our operating model will affect a number of our employees, and I want to be straight with you about that. We expect to move or eliminate 5,000 positions in 20XX. We will use attrition and business growth to reduce the impact of the changes on individuals where possible. Employment in our Global Productivity Centers and in some of our Centers of Quality will expand as positions are migrated, which will also mean increased opportunities for professional growth for employees there. Today, these locations are home to just under one quarter of all staff. By 20XX we expect these locations will represent 50% of our total population.

We will, of course, preserve significant presence in our key market centers across the globe such as New York, Hong Kong and Cleveland. In many cases they are where our clients, regulators and senior management are located. All of which must have a proper level of business and shared-service support. All of us in the services industry face an increasingly competitive environment. The initiatives I have described today are essential not just to compete, but to perform better than our competition. We're committed to meeting our shareholder's expectations of first-decile earnings growth while doing what is best of our company, clients, and employees. I am confident we can."

Herein lays so much of what Post-Sufficiency looks like.

First, the announcement is almost pure SMUT. The scientism is seen in the formulaic "Global Productivity Model" amongst other places. The materialistic is found in found in "first-decile earnings growth" and in the entire notion of performance at levels in excess of the peer group. The utilitarian is observable in multiple locations, but is marvelously displayed in the comment ". . . reduce the impact of changes on individuals *where possible*." The totalitarian can be observed in the statement that senior management will need support and it appears that none of them will be asked to move. While this may or may not be the case, the choice of words is very poor given the desired response from associates. And look no further than "process re-engineering and technology automation" to see the circling of the "we are really a machine" philosophy of mechanization. If this announcement was to be actually directed at the *people* within the community, it is difficult to see the anticipated human linkages.

As a matter of fact, this announcement would appear to be directed at securities analysts and shareholders, as opposed to the organization's members. While securities analysts and shareholders are important, they both create conflicts within the company's internal community. And lastly, the notion of "doing what is best for our company, clients and employees" is so devoid of the realities of the trade-offs that are experienced between these constituencies such as to make it either laughable, pathetic, or both.

From the standpoint of the associate member, the announcement essentially assumes that the member's interests are secondary. It is very clear the focus of the company's strategy is to serve the interests of shareholders first, and everyone else second or third. Rather than focusing on and acknowledging the impact on members' lives, the message focuses on the half-truth of "highest quality service" and his inglorious self-abnegating "I want to be straight about that." Is it to be assumed that unless he indicates that he is being candid that the group should assume otherwise? What was actually being communicated was that the organization was focusing on lowering expenses and that it might come at the cost of some of the member's jobs. The value system being addressed was very clear. And the value system is by no means wrong. But what was being said is that if expenses can be reduced at the cost of the members, and that the reduction in expenses can move the price-earnings ratio up, it is a trade-off the organization's leaders were willing to make. The informal contract with members had been reformatted to include a clause that now said the organization was predisposed to identifying cost savings and that a member's job may be the next casualty. As very little reference is made to actually making the organization any better than it is, the assumption is left that the organization is going to shrink itself into increased profitability and that the key ingredient in the formula is potentially one's job.

From the standpoint of the message, the announcement is likely even more clear in terms of the values that it mandates. The hypocrisy of the message from the standpoint of an individual employee is either forgotten or waived. Rather than *socializing* the entire group and indicating that the organization was doing "what's best for our company, clients and employees" the wording should have been "for most of our employees." Given that no one working for the organization in a major metropolitan area had any confidence now in retaining their job, this statement of support around *employees* rings very hollow. And this was true as everyone was effectively being asked to assume the worst. They had to. The use of terms like "Global Productivity Centers" and "Centers of Quality" are buzz words that mean nothing to most associates and look to most of us more like self-rationalizing obfuscation. If I did not work in a Center of Quality, what did I actually work *in*? "Yes, I must have worked in a Center of Sloppy."

From the standpoint of communicating anything of the meaning as to the organization's outputs, there are none. The announcement reinforced the notion that the company was about improving earnings and nothing more. You might add "client service" to the list, but nothing more significant than that. There is seemingly no grander good than first-decile earnings and the lofty *expectations of shareholders* to which the company was subject. This organization existed for a reason, and that was now very clear. This was to understand capitalism from a textbook. It was to understand humanity from the front porch of an antebellum plantation.

From the standpoint of measurement, the scorecard couldn't be clearer: "The key is growing our earnings faster than our competitors." Well, I guess the math is right. This is the diatribe of an automaton. In light of this, even the expressed notion of "highest quality service" is rendered completely utilitarian. The concept of any foundational growth as a company and as individuals as a means of providing a hopeful future is absent-without-leave. This is the voice of the Mind-Head behind the curtain.

This type of announcement could have actually added to the soulishness of the organization. Instead it was completely soul-destroying. It almost could not have been written in a more soul-ravaging fashion without saying, "You cogs are really just not very important in the effective running of my machine." But that was not the real problem. The real problem is that people cannot operate in ways that are inconsistent with their values. If this set of "cog" values is brought to bear on an enterprise every day, the results will be that the organization is in an exit strategy.

Without re-writing the entire announcement, the following would have been the voice of an Insufficient organization . . . one with a Soul-Head left to speak for the organization:

"As leaders, we have to make some very hard decisions that we believe will benefit the company over the long term. And we fully recognize that these decisions will negatively impact many of our individual associates. Our goal remains that of building security and opportunity for every member of the team. Our organization is engaged in a worldwide struggle within our industry. As a result, over the next several years we will be shifting the work that we are currently doing to new locations on the globe, that will allow us to do our work less expensively. This will result in about twenty-five percent of all jobs being shifted to new locations over the next five years.

The recent and well-documented changes in the world require that we make decisions that will advance our ability to provide our significant array of high-quality solutions to all corners of the globe.

We are absolutely committed to remaining competitive in our markets. Our organization has a proud heritage of improving the ways in which financial markets operate around the world. In doing this, we bring a raft of benefits to markets that are on the path to becoming more free, with greater transparency, and in so doing, spreading global prosperity. We will continue to do that, and at the same time do the best job that we possibly can at balancing the personal needs of our entire group of committed worldwide associates with the needs of the business.

We measure success within our organization in many ways. The reporting of our earnings is very important for reasons that are apparent. At the same time, we know that the skills, abilities and energies that our associates bring to work every day are what drive those earnings. The announcement we are making today is with the acknowledgement that some in the organization will be personally disappointed at the results. And we will do what we can to ease the impact of that disappointment." But SMUTy leaders do not think that way.

I was out running in Louisville, Kentucky one day as we visited our son, and I saw and responded to what I believe was an interesting microcosm of life. It was significant to me as I caught myself being hopelessly non-soulish. I share the story as it represents a sentiment that is at the core of Mindishness. As I was running by a particular house an old man of at least 85 years of age was out in his massive front yard. The yard consisted of a million blades of grass and one small two-foot tall bush positioned right out in the middle of the yard. He had a scissors in his hand and was trimming the little bush very lovingly and carefully. It appeared to me that the man considered his activity an important task, as he approached it with great interest and care.

It was eerily simple to come up with a number of fairly cynical responses to this scene, and to do it in short order. And that is exactly what I did. I asked myself, "I wonder why he has that one silly little bush right out there in the middle of his massive front yard?" Then I continued, "Doesn't he have anything better to do with his time than to trim that bush with a scissors?" As I was moving beyond the scene I concluded with this: "I wonder if the old dude has lost his mind to Alzheimer's?" What would you be thinking? I immediately put the man and his condition in a negative and inferior light. I moved myself up the totem pole and I moved the old guy down. But, what does this scene have to do with the notion of soulishness?

The point is that in the scientific, progressive, materialistic and utilitarian world in which we live, we often overlook the humanity in much of what we observe and experience. We look past the soul, and peer directly into the perceived *value* of the activities of both ourselves and of others. We do the intellectual math and find that the result of the efforts of someone else is small in relative and quantifiable terms. When we think about the value of the activity, instead of the value of the person, we come to very poor conclusions. When I review the questions that I asked as I ran by (and note that at over fifty years of age I was still fortunate enough to be able to run) I became mindfully ashamed of my response. After all, I was doing "something of value", and he was not. And yet, I had clearly missed the point. On the contrary, this was a man with a mission. It was his unique mission, and I may not have understood it, but it was his business. And I couldn't, or didn't, see it. Or more specifically, I intentionally chose not to see it. I chose to see something else. With the old man, I was acting SMUTy, and accordingly, I had no place for him in my community, or in my home.

LONG-TERM EXIT STRATEGIES

Post-Sufficiency signals the reality that the institution is fighting for its life, whether the condition is acknowledged or not. And the reality of most situations is that the diseased situation both exists and is simultaneously unacknowledged. The organization is slowly dying from soul loss, and management applies the ineffective balm of more SMUT as a solution to all that ails the patient. Meanwhile, the sense of being *home* is lost, and the adjacent loss of true community and meaningful purpose is palpable. If for no other reason, the frenetic mind-numbing nature of SMUT creates loss of community. And the foundations on which to build a prosperous future are crumbling. Ironically, some of the best and brightest individuals actually thrive in this environment, at least in a relative sense, as they are the self-initiating progenitors of all the false focus. But that should be an even brighter warning sign. People no longer share any sense of unity of purpose and destiny. Infighting begins. In many cases the only remaining question for the organization is "How long does our exit period last?"

One could argue that the demise of institutions (at a macro-level) is not a systemic problem, but is rather part of Schumpeter's *Creative*

Destruction: a theory of the basis for all capitalistic progress. The simplified notion of the theory is that as one institution overcomes another, it improves the outcomes of the overall system, as the emergent institution is "better" than the precedent. I would suggest that one can agree with Schumpeter's notion at the level of the entire economic system, and at the same time agree, that like everything else, life comes with trade-offs. Alternatively, one could argue that organizational durability is just a function of *randomness* (read luck) in the system, and the associated rightful strategy is just to cross your fingers and hope for the best. That would, however, be defeatist such as to tilt toward the prophetic. Lastly, it could be debated that ultimately the future of an organization is absolutely linked to its selection of strategies. But that would be to ignore the nature of the developmental causes of successful strategies within organizations.

Progress and durability can be created within organizations without creating both the massive loss of "the good" that is ascribed to all failed organizations and without creating the personal, material, and psychological dislocation and loss of identity that co-exists with all failings. It is just very painful for the system and for individuals within the system when institutions fail, irrespective of the positive implications to the system as a whole. The institutional failings of once very constructively contributing organisms within the system create a loss of security and trust for all the system's members. That loss is always destabilizing to the whole of the community. When faith is lost in our institutions, our collective souls are badly bruised. Our Soul-Heads mourn. Our Mind-Heads just say "Whatever."

Finding ourselves in an environment with less people who would describe themselves as lost and without a home sans their institutional failures would be a very stabilizing and mobilizing factor for all concerned. We all want our institutions to succeed. The overall systemic economics matter little to us personally. The real human cost to failed institutions is immeasurably high.

I will close this chapter with a story of my experience with an organization that I have observed fall into Post-Sufficiency: The Home Depot.

It was a nice Saturday morning in San Rafael, California, and we just wanted to get a few things for the house . . . a new trash can, some replacement screens for our windows, and some carpet cleaner. So Mary and I went to the local Home Depot, in the heart of Marin County, to pick up the stuff. This had to be one of the highest grossing stores in the Home Depot system. However, if ever there was a Post-Sufficient customer experience, representing a Post-Sufficient organization, this was it.

The first scene is the packing lot. It is a danger-zone. We arrived at about eleven in the morning, and no one from the store had bothered to retrieve all the carts from the parking lot. They were strewn all over; including those big ones that once freed from their moorings can do great damage to things like car doors. This wouldn't be so bad except that there was an employee wiping down the new grills in front of the store that already looked quite clean. My immediate, simplistic, and cynical thought was that what we had here was a classic case of snafu.

Having survived the parking lot, we set out for the trash cans. The problem was that after sifting through about a hundred various lids, we couldn't find a can lid that fit our selected bin. "Well, this must be an inventory management problem. No big deal. We will venture a little farther from the house to another local establishment that always has what we need." Then we started looking for our second object of desire, the screening material. After wandering around for about ten minutes, we tried to find someone who could point us in the right direction. I couldn't find a Home Depot employee anywhere. A hundreds shoppers littered about the store, but seemingly no one to help any of us lost do-it-yourselfers. I guess it might be, "You can do it, we can help . . . but only if you are lucky enough to find one of us." We did successfully find the carpet cleaner, and eventually the screen and some other items.

At this point the story gets more interesting. After listening to the intercom literally begging for more help to come to the front to help check people out, we found two registers open with ten people in each line and a backlog of at least a dozen people at the self-service check-outs. Remember, this is a Saturday morning. So we got in the self-service line, extended back into the adjacent isle so that no one could get through the front of the store. After about fifteen minutes we got up to one of the three self-service check-outs (the forth one had an orange cone sitting on top of it).

We proceeded to scan our items and the coupon that we had for five-dollars off on any purchase above fifty dollars. At that point we are so-far-so-good. Then I scanned my credit card. At that point the screen said that I needed to talk with the cashier. Oh oh. Upon getting his attention, the cashier proceeded to tell me that it was probably the coupon that messed us up. His comment was "The self-service kiosks do not accept coupons." At that point I reminded the individual that the machine had literally spoken to me and said, "Please scan your items and coupons." At that point the cashier basically threw up his hands. "What do you want me to do?" The transaction didn't seem to be completed, but we just walked away having been given no other real options. The charge did actually hit our credit card, so we didn't have to write a letter to the company telling them what we owed them. It seemed everything about the store was out of control. It was almost as if they were trying to discourage us from coming back. But why was it that the store just worked so poorly?

Interestingly, Home Depot also owned another store in our community called Home Depot Yardbirds. Yardbirds was an independent chain in northern California that was acquired by Home Depot some years earlier. The following weekend I went to that store to buy stain for my front porch. The short story is that by the time I had spent ten minutes in that store, not less than three people had asked me if they could help me. Apparently, Post-Sufficiency had not yet trickled down into the acquired company.

The story goes on, but the point has been made. The weed seeds had been planted, watered, nurtured and seen their maturation at Home Depot. The whole experience within every Home Depot I have been in during the last ten years reeks of Post-Sufficiency. They spend massive amounts of money on advertising for an institution that is in an exit strategy unless something dramatically changes. And I won't be back to shop there again.

Each of us could sight one example after another of this sad commentary in our personal experience. Do the members of the Board of Directors of Home Depot ever shop there? No, they just look at the Board Presentation Books (the books with all the statistics and numbers) at the quarterly meetings. At least they were smart enough to get rid of their former CEO who I have seen as the poster child for Mind-Head Post-Sufficient management. What I do believe is that the Board of Home Depot does not understand that the organization has completely lost its soul. And their stock price over the last ten years is indicative of that.

The Directors thinks it's an advertising issue . . . or a product display issue . . . or an inventory management issue . . . or a competitive issue. "Surely it is those slimy predators over at Lowes that represents the fundamental problem we have with growing this business!" The list of possible rationalizations literally goes on indefinitely. They might think it is a supply chain management issue or a store location and density issue. They might believe it a store manager training issue, or a process-orientation issue. They may even think their poor performance has to do with an inappropriate level of market focus, and that if they could just be more like Target, all would be fine.

But one or two questions need to be asked. Does anyone think that the answer to this sort of endemic and troubling organizational situation is simply one of "the need for better management or customer service training?" Or, that the fix might be found in "the better alignment of purchasing, merchandising and vendor management?" If those are the types of thoughts that come to your mind, I would ask that you think more deeply about the causes. Home Depot is today an organization in a period of troubling decline, and it will take more than training and process improvement to turn the organization in a positive direction. It seems that management's current thought is that "free-financing" on consumer purchases and significant advertising expenditures are the answer. They are sorely wrong. How many times have we seen this before? And it is too bad for Home Depot's hundreds of thousands of employees—many of which will be subject of RIFs over the next ten years—as Home Depot continues to struggle through their exit strategy.

What was the real problem with The Home Depot? The real problem was that they had lost there sense of home and community and have become Post-Sufficient. They are in-fact just lost. Home is no longer accessible at the Home Depot. Maybe they should change their name to Lost Depot.

"We have trouble right here in River City." In the case of *The Music Man*, the signs of the problems of community lost-ness were seen in the form of the local pool hall. The message of the peddler of musical instruments was that if you ignore the warnings signs, your community will be lost. Your historic home will become unrecognizable to you, and it may actually be destroyed. The town's people wondered how they could have gotten themselves into such a predicament. They clearly did not like what they had perceived they were becoming, and they were quick to "buy a cure" at any cost. In their case, trumpets and trombones were the answer. But the core question of "How could we have gotten *here*?" was a very good question. It was exactly the right question.

* * * * *

Post-Sufficiency emerges within large and successful organizations when they forget who they are, and become something completely different. Their performance issues stem not from their actions, but from who they have morphed into. They focus their energies on the "outputs" of their Mind-Head and they lose their ability to operate as a cohesive community. They lose any sense of home. Mindish leadership succumbs to a litany of forces, that while positive in and of themselves, are completely lacking in the elements needed to create organizations with long-term durability. In the short-term, the shortage of Soul-Head input into the organization seems a non-issue. But when the soul of an organization begins to die, the *best thoughts* coming from the Mind-Head are unable to reverse the inevitable decline.

"How could we have gotten *here*?" It is to that question towards which we will next turn.

2

Mutually Assured Destruction

> Large and successful organizations starve their Soul-Heads, and the effect is a condition called Post-Sufficiency. Post-Sufficiency is the natural result of organizations who fail to recognize the significance of very potent forces, ultimately crushing human institutions.

Being born in 1958, I was a kid during the height of the Cold War. One of my early memories was riding my bike past one of the government buildings in my small northern Minnesota town. The building had one of the yellow and black signs indicating that it was an official Nuclear Fallout Shelter. Clearly these troubling square metal signs were a sobering indicator of the times. I remember mulling Defense Secretary McNamara's words over in my head one at a time... mutually—assured—destruction. I thought by doing that little "word exercise" that some less ominous meaning might somehow emerge. But all three words left much to be desired in my young mind. It was hard for me to believe that people could truly harbor enough hatred towards another group of people that they might actually kill each other by the millions. Unfortunately, the *Planet of the Apes* didn't seem that far-fetched to me at the time.

    I wondered what the probabilities of a real nuclear attack might be. I remember thinking about what I considered to be the most logical geographic targets for an attack. It was my first exposure to the grave outcomes that may await my existence on the planet, and some of my first thinking about the presence of evil in the world. It was also the first time I began mulling the presence of the forces that exist as the result of the sentiment of groups of people who did not care about each other.

I can still picture the building in my mind, along with its prominently posted sign. I was personally exposed for the first time to the question "How in the world did we get *here*?" I can only assume that the fallout shelter experience forever heightened my awareness to the dangers associated with any and all warning signs.

So it comes as no surprise that I continue to be keenly aware of all manner of warning signs that direct my attention towards a broad array of threats to both my family and my institutions. I have a heightened sensitivity to the signs as a function of my early life experience. In each of our lives, new and threatening danger signs continue to pop up at an increasingly dramatic rate. And they are literally everywhere. Whether they present themselves as labels on the foods we consume, flashing lights that focus our attention on any manner of dangers, or an obnoxious relative providing un-requested investment advice, the signs are clearly ever-present. As individuals we are bombarded by many more warning signs than most of us have any real desire to receive. Frankly, I already know that if I slam my fingers in the big metal doors of the ferry boat that I take to work that it might be bad. It might even hurt. The sign posted on the doors (with the picture of throbbing fingers) is not, at least in my mind, really necessary.

On the organizational front, however, life is different. Our society has determined that human institutions must fend for themselves. It is collectively assumed that we as individuals have to be protected from them, and not the other way around. No one is out there warning organizations with imposing and well-lit speed limit signs, nor is anyone informing them of the threat to their pregnancies posed by the consumption of alcohol. Every organizational leader's daily commute takes them right by the symbolic graveyards of organizations that have passed into history. But these graveyards are not marked as such. The dangers are not set out for analysis, nor disclosed in any public way. For organizations, the dangers are just not labeled.

As a kid I was warned about the threat of mutually assured destruction. Yet, as members of our human institutions we seldom discern the signs and ask the all-important question, "How in the world did we get here?" We generally miss the signs until we reach a point of deep regret. Worse yet, we find ourselves having missed the signs for so long that all the options for continued survival have long-since passed.

The problem is that we simply ignore the signs. When things are going well, and when life is comfortable, it is very challenging to actually look for nascent problems. It is so much easier to just assume that all is well and that there are "no dark clouds on the horizon." But there are always dark clouds on the horizon. We cannot create heaven on earth. If the boom-bust cycles of the economy don't prove this, I don't know what will. If the experience of our own lives does not show us this, I am not certain that we are paying attention. Large and successful organizations, nevertheless, refuse to believe that they may succumb to the same sickness as others before them. We have become professional sign-ignorers in our institutional lives. By this action we insure that we are headed to the mutually assured destruction that is Post-Sufficiency.

I will never forget my experience in walking into the home office of H&R Block Financial Advisors for the first time as the newly appointed President of that organization in 2001. The building was dilapidated and crude, like so much of downtown Detroit. The hallways were stacked to the ceiling with boxes of papers that had yet to make their way to offsite storage. The granite steps between floors were all rounded-off and dangerous. The place smelled like a soggy wet tennis shoe. But I can tell you that the working conditions were not the problem. The problems were much more deeply personal. These people were metaphysically homeless. They literally looked like a group of refugees; unwanted rabble who had somehow become the ward of an alien nation.

How did they get there? How had they become refugees in their own city, and in their own company, and in the building they had occupied forever? How could they have so effectively communicated with their faces the deep sense of desperation that had overtaken the whole lot? Did this occur over a long period of time, or had it happened quickly? How could the situation have devolved to this point? What the group effectively told me was this: "We are lost, we are afraid, we are angry, and we want to go home right now."

I walked away from that first day with the responsibility for taming the effects of a disease for which both the diagnosis and the cure were equally uncertain. I had now been exposed to the remnants of a once proud organization that had lost its way. It had become homeless and it was a contagion amongst the members. I literally felt sick as I left the building on that dreary November day. But it was my job to turn the company into something new, and for me to break down and start crying at that point (although maybe appropriate) was likely not the best way to start off my relationship with them. We obviously needed to do something significant and fundamental. We had to go back to first principles. And it was at that point that I began to see the significance of the definition of an institutional home.

The organization that I visited that day had been purchased a couple of years earlier from Ernie Olde, who was a pioneer in the discount brokerage industry. He and Charles Schwab were maybe the most visionary leaders of their time within the retail financial services business. The entity had been purchased by H&R Block for the heady price of eight hundred and fifty million dollars in 1999. Now, two years later, it was alive, but just about flat-lining, and it was worth absolutely nothing. It was actually a big liability. And while the company was hemorrhaging cash, that was not the fundamental problem, at least as far as the organization was concerned. The real issue was that the organization had completely lost its soul. No progress was going to be made until that situation was repaired. In retrospect, I wish that I would have more clearly understood how recondite the issue was at the time I was actually experiencing it.

But the reason to share this story is not to reflect on the business failings of that organization. Rather, the reason is to focus on the human failings. The home office staff of Olde Discount Securities had completely lost their sense of unconditional acceptance. They had simultaneously lost any sense for the predictability of their futures. They felt as if they had been discarded. As a matter of fact, they had come to fear that the operation was going to shut down and moved to Kansas City, the home of H&R Block. And they were being viewed very publicly as faulty cogs in a big wheel, which left them stripped of their group dignity. In short, they had toiled for years in the hot sun, with little in the way of resources, and now they were being told that they were of no value, and besides, they had very wrinkly and old-looking skin. They wanted to go back to the old days, or in their case, the Olde days, because that was where their home was. I looked at them and sincerely asked, "It is apparent to everyone else that you can't go back in time, so why do you keep looking backwards? You cannot go back home. Your home no longer exists." Later it occurred to me that it was the only direction they *could* look, until we had created a new place that they could call home.

A year after the group had been moved to new quarters in downtown Detroit, an explosion occurred in the basement of the vacated old building. The foundation of the old building was damaged. The funny thing is that the foundations of the old human organization had been even more severely damaged just a few years before.

It took years to restore the dignity that had been taken from them. But they rose to the occasion and turned themselves into something they had once been: a proud group of people who felt the comforts and rewards of being at home. And their reaction was both predictable and exceptionally positive. Some referred to it as a miracle. I just saw it as sending them back to where they belonged. All they were saying was this: "We are not a set of used machine parts! We are not refugees. We are an important part of your organization. And we have a claim to this piece of ground." And they did. And I could not have respected them more for what they had accomplished and who they had became.

FAULTY FOUNDATIONS

When Post-Sufficiency creeps into the picture, no one talks about it, but everybody feels it. It is not yet pouring down rain outside, but the storm clouds are gathering overhead and the drizzle is beginning to come down. Everyone is getting wet and cold. The big building that was supposed to keep everyone dry and comfortable is seemingly no longer fit for the task. Our natural response is to go outside and look at the roof to see if we can figure our where the leaks are starting. But we look in vain. We are looking in the wrong direction.

Organizational homelessness is never the result of a bad roof. It is not what is above us that create the problems. Rather, we are being exposed to the harshness of the elements as a direct result of "what is below": a faulty foundation. And when the foundations crack and falter, the entire infrastructure of the organization, roof included, is compromised. Building more superstructure on top of an already bad foundation will only makes matters worse. The attempt to accurately identify the frail foundations of the organization is an important exercise. Providing the right materials to fundamentally reinforce or rebuild those foundations is even more important. And this is the work of the Soul-Head.

If you ask a group of organizational leaders "What is the foundation on which your organization is built?" what would you expect as the collection of answers? This would seem, at least to me, an important question. I have a notion, however, that many organizations do not think of themselves as being built on identifiable and observable foundations. This seems contrary to how it would appear the universe (more broadly) actually works. Everything we observe seems to have a *sine qua non*. All things structural have physically identifiable foundations, or they just collapse under their own weight. All things intellectual have foundations in logic and analytical thinking. And all things spiritual have their foundations in God. Yet for some reason we don't often think of human institutions in terms of the foundations on which they are built. We would rather occupy ourselves with that which is "above ground," aesthetically pleasing, and "warm and dry."

Perhaps we avoid discussions of organizational foundations as they are tricky things to define. They are even thornier to discuss in an intelligent and coherent fashion. It could be that the reason we ignore foundations is that they are neither natively attractive nor compelling. They are not the thing itself . . . they just *support* the thing. Foundations are controversial as well, as their failures are broadly felt, and their causes are usually actively disputed. And yet they are, unfortunately, much too important to ignore.

As organizations grow, they become much "heavier" and inherently more complicated, and it becomes increasingly difficult to discern how each part relates and connects to the next. The contingencies and observable dependencies multiply and mutate at an exponential rate. Actions and their consequences become logically detached. Both observers and participants of the system share this same challenge. The seemingly labyrinth-like quality of growing institutions often overwhelms, or at least disorients, many of their leaders and nearly all of the group's members. In that miasma, it is very easy to lose sight of an organization's true and historic foundations. The understanding and belief in the underlying foundation that initially both supported the organization's growth, and that propelled it towards the previously experienced heights of success, has now been erased or altogether forgotten.

In the previous chapter, the attempt was to show how all institutions have a foundation in community and that the community is a soulish creation with a distinct set of very human needs. When leaders lose sight of this, the first warning signs of Post-Sufficiency go up. Organizations that lose sight of their original foundation in community are generally marking a subtle shift towards one of three faulty foundations. These shifting bases include an over-reliance on the organization's strategy, an excessive focus on a particular attribute of the organization, or their dependence on the quality of the people that comprise the organization. While it can be easily agreed that excellent strategies, well-developed and unique organizational capabilities and attributes, and the presence of a high-quality group of members are essential to the success of an organization, it is also true that none are capable of serving as foundational to the organization's long-term durability.

RELIANCE ON STRATEGY

Most organizations would say, upon some reflection, that they are built on a foundation of their institution's strategy. They would also add that their foundation includes a time-tested and battle-hardened ability to effectively execute on those strategic plans. They would likely point to their planning process, the communication plans that operate to advance the understanding around the strategy, and the alignment of personal incentives, as foundational to their long-term success. The language of the strategy would be that of a set of both financial and non-financial goals that form the parameters and measurements around the allocation of resources, and the goals against which success will be measured. Universal acceptance and understanding of the plan within the organization is always a critical part of the process. Some may even say, "We aren't exactly sure where we are going given the tumultuous times, but we know that if we can execute on this agreed-upon strategy that the rest will solve for itself." This is all excellent thinking and the process is critical to any organization's success. Of that I have little question. The unfortunate reality is that it simply does not suffice as a foundation on which to build the long-term durability of a human institution. How can that be? What was just advanced as a successful approach to organizational leadership seems brilliant, no?

I once sat through a whole day of "strategic plans" as presented by the various business unit heads that represented the entire portfolio of businesses within my Company, along with all of the strategies of the internal support units. This was a meeting prior to the end of the year to review the strategic plans with the top one hundred and fifty senior organizational leaders. The meeting's purpose was ostensibly to get "all of us on the same page." We were supposed to be able to walk away from the sessions with a sense of real verve over the plan for the next year. It was clearly foreseeable that at the end of the meeting, the senior-most executive was going to get up and say, "Now that you all know and understand the plan, let's go out and execute." And so it was. And the crowd cheered.

So as an experiment, I planned to do a day-long survey of how many "what-how-when-where" questions were addressed in the strategic plan presentations, versus how many "why" questions were addressed. The experiment was based on the presumption that a "list-of-things-that-we-are-doing" does not a strategy make. After a few hours I just quit. "We are doing X. We will complete it on Y. It will cost us Z. It will deliver XX result." I heard this over and over and over. There was absolutely no context of any kind presented at any point in any of the mini-lectures. I didn't have any basis for understanding why we were doing anything that we were doing. I took away from the meeting a long and detailed inventory of the "things-that-we-are-doing," but no insights as to the rationale. I knew we had an agenda, but I had no idea as to whether we had a strategy.

As a group, most of us didn't know anything more coming out of the meeting than we did going in. Even more unfortunate, I was probably one of the most knowledgeable people in the room given my sales role. I actually sold all this stuff. This was a tremendous example of a faulty foundation built on the over-reliance on a strategy that represented nothing more than a set of unsubstantiated goals and a few related tactics. I have come to call this type of situation a "rice cake strategy": it looks like something to eat, until you bite into it. It is mostly air, has no substance, and clearly has no taste. It does absolutely nothing for the senses.

The true foundation that emerges from finding the answers to the real questions we all have about our environment is immeasurably positive. The banality of strategy is ultimately demoralizing. Worse, strategy is yet another adaptation towards the machine-ism of Post-Sufficiency. There is nothing obviously or inherently wrong with strategies. The problem is that they are not developed in human terms and they do nothing to reflect our human nature. They generally speak to actions and not to relationships. Thus, they can only be very partially understood. They are constructs, even good constructs, but they are not foundations. One good answer that addresses the question "*why* the organization is doing something" is worth more than a hundred strategies and a million tactical plans.

Answers to the "why" questions ultimately lead to community, in that the why questions address values, where the other question-types do not. Yet "what and how" strategies dominate the agendas of far too many Post-Sufficient organizations. A recent song played on the radio contained the words "the simple things in life like when and where." The lyricist recognizes that some questions represent an opportunity to instill deep meaning, and others do not. Show me an organization that is feverishly trying to build upon its To-Do Lists, with all the related what-when-how-where details, and I will show you an organization well on its way to full-blown Post-Sufficiency. If an organization's self-described foundation is strategy, then everyone must be very aware of the related points of failure.

In large and successful organizations the belief systems seem to evolve to a point where "If we identify a problem, we can come up with a *process* to fix it." That is always an interesting conclusion as it appears that with most problems a "process" is actually contra-indicated. What is usually necessary is not a process, but for some individual or group of people to simply make a decision and fix the things that obviously aren't working. Alternatively, we find ourselves in greater need of someone coming up with a creative idea to capitalize on an already existent opportunity. What is needed is not a strategy, or a process that leads to a strategy, but a rich description of the situation on which to build a cohesive narrative that is understood by the entire organization. From cohesive narratives comes the ability to forge a plan.

The idea of a cohesive narrative is just a story that can be retold and understood because the underlying logic is embedded in the story. The notion of strategy has become narrowly defined to include a series of actions being taken to further an even more narrowly defined set of measurable ends. And in that narrowness is the problem. Creating a large number of measurable ends does not solve for the narrowness problem. They are products of processes and the *process* effectively becomes the output. What comes out of the strategy process is the strategy process, as opposed to a coherent and mobilizing narrative.

The English philosopher Francis Bacon once remarked that "Truth emerges more readily from error than from confusion." The word "error" creates the connotation of an intentional act, while "confusion" is almost always a situation that is passively created. We have a tendency, however, to avoid errors of either an intentional or unintentional variety. From the time we are babes, we are systemically punished for error and rewarded for thoughts and actions that are somehow deemed "correct." So the logic would be, if we buy the premise of Mr. Bacon, that we are systematically programmed to avoid the discovery of truth. It might also be concluded that we are natively situated as human beings as prone to error avoidance. And the thought of discovering any level of truth from confusion is very contrary, by definition, to the discovery of truth.

"My goal for this week is to make as many mistakes as possible." I made that comment to my boss on a Monday morning. He was puzzled, even though he knew I was inclined to make comments like that periodically. It then began to dawn on him what I was saying. He knew that I believed we were so inclined to complete "correctness" in our actions, based on our strategy and the associated measurements that we could not get out of our own way. We weren't learning anything of a fundamental nature that would make a difference in the intermediate and long-term future of the organization. Others were out there making mistakes and learning, while we were continually getting straight A's.

G.K. Chesterton once made a comment something to the effect that "Anything worth doing is worth doing poorly." The context created by doing something poorly is invaluable towards the ultimate goal of doing it well . . . or recognizing that it cannot be done. Modern corporate strategies in Post-Sufficient organizations become checklists of the things the organization generally knows it can do. They are generally short on imagination. And they contain no elements of faith. They contain only "stretch goals" which have nothing whatsoever to do with faith.

Strategy attempts to fill a gap, or provide a foundation, that is way too big for its generally shrinking effectiveness in creating the organizational context needed to carry out anything in a far flung enterprise. Strategy is also, at some point, going to be wrong. Insufficient organizations can recover from bad strategies, while Post-Sufficient ones usually cannot. Peter Drucker has commented that strategies are commodities and that execution is a form of art. I do not believe that sentiment at all. I believe that the creation of an organization's strategy is an absolute art form, and that they should be prepared with a much higher level of shared and underlying context. At the same time, it is not the foundation on which organizational performance and durability is built. The point is simply that organizations must dig deeper than strategy in order to form the type of foundation on which they may build. Even if all the why questions are addressed, the result is the same: good strategy, bad foundation.

RELIANCE ON ATTRIBUTES

Many organizations, secondly, would claim a particular attribute of their organizational "capability-set" as the foundation for their existence. Attributes are those elements of any organization that can be singled out as somehow critical to the entity's past success. The list containing attributes which serve as the perceived foundations for the ongoing success of an organization is nearly endless, but includes concepts that have been made popular under labels like "operational effectiveness," "customer-centricity" or "continuous improvement." Organizations will say that "We are exceptionally good at being a fast-follower," or "We are the leaders in supply-chain management within our industry." Popular organizational psycho-babble would have us all believe that an organization can be really good at one thing, and that it is better to build on one's strengths than to work on solving for one's weaknesses. It also wants to sell you on the faulty notion that an enterprise can be built and sustained on a single well-executed strength.

The management consulting profession, like the golf equipment industry, regularly comes out with a "new line" of organizational wizardry (on a rigorously disciplined schedule) that is presented as a fix for whatever malady may be afflicting any human institution. And we have all been reminded since we were five years old that if it looks too good to be true, that it likely is. Attributes fall under this category.

I once asked a golf equipment sales representative about how many generations worth of "new and innovative" golf equipment his organization had stacked up in the warehouse to be subsequently foisted upon us unsuspecting victims. He said to me, "Brian, what you have to recognize is that we are not in the golf equipment business." I said "No?" He then solved the riddle by saying "We don't sell golf equipment, we sell hope." This was exceptionally revealing and seemingly absolutely true. But false hopes remain false hopes, even in their recognition. The unrealized benefits of false hopes weigh heavily on many organizations. And the hope of curing for the organization's ills with a diabolically simple focus on a single attribute of an organization always results in disappointment. The Mind-Head looks at the *engineering* scheme of the proposed solution. The Soul-Head just looks for the scheme.

Attributes are easy targets as "fixes" as they are simple to define and leave much of the real complexity of the fundamental issues on the sidelines. Most attributes are really good things to focus on and implement. The problem with focusing on attributes is, and this is even more so than with strategy, that they are wholly inadequately equipped to meet the foundational needs of an organization. This would be the equivalent of saying that it is absolutely reasonable to assume that if an individual homeowner is very good at keeping their house clean, while at the same time ignoring the core maintenance of the home, that we would be observing a sensible approach. Attributes are exceptionally psychologically dangerous as well, because they are simple and easy things on which to focus the organization's *attention*. "The good news is that we have become very good at X, the bad news is that we have become very bad at everything else."

The Law of Unintended Consequences runs rampant in attribute-focused organizations. Symmetry must be maintained. The other problem with organizations who embrace an attributes-focus is that they have a tendency to shift attributes too frequently, and the organization's members are spun around so fast that they get dizzy and fall down. Rapidly shifting attributes are a sign that no real foundation exists within a human institution, as the frenetic search for a workable and foundational attribute would attest. But attributes are not foundational. You can live with an attribute for a long time, just not forever

An organization can focus its entire energies on creating world-class attributes (operating scale or efficiency, distribution channel control, market intelligence, etc.) and at the same time watch their ship sink to the bottom. The critical question to ask with respect to foundations is, "If we executed on this attribute with brutal effectiveness and prescience, would it represent a path to our continuing success over the long-term?" In the instances of both strategies and attributes, the answer is simply no. And the reason the answer is no is that the approach leaves too many other aspects of the institution to simultaneously fail to guarantee a successful outcome. These would be the human elements that are being left out.. There are just too many fronts in the battle to leave so many important flanks unattended.

The focus on an attribute also narrows the choices that an organization can make. They also often become the object of the organization's attention and serve as a complete replacement-part for actually meeting the real needs of their various constituencies. Attributes tend to start with an external focus and then gradually become an internally-focused faith system.

During my quest for answers to the under-performance and durability question, I spent a lot of time on strategies and attributes. I was convinced that there was a "pony somewhere in that pile of manure." The time and energy that was spent here was, in retrospect, mostly a waste of time. I learned a lot about strategies and attributes and very little about foundations. The fact that both strategies and attributes are subject to significant oversimplification and process-ization should have tipped me off earlier to their inadequacy. The fact that both notions represented very direct answers to the "what" questions (versus the "why" questions) should have been another indication of my research error. And lastly, the ability to conduct these intellectual exercises apart from an understanding of how human nature impacts our ability to effectively assimilate both strategies and attributes was yet another major oversight on my part. Many warning signs were missed.

RELIANCE ON THE BEST PEOPLE

The last of the false foundations looks something like this: "We hire the best people and they get the job done." The best-people strategy is an approach with a focus on liberty and creativity and is thus very challenging for me to categorize as a faulty foundation as such. It is obviously focused on the people side (versus the material and process sides) of the institution and is of tremendous value. A good number of organizations actually follow this practice and many have been very successful over long periods of time. The best people available in the marketplace, like any all-star team, is likely to win a high percentage of the time.

There is a great Far Side cartoon written by Gary Larson that shows an interesting scene. A couple of neighbors are standing in their very heavily fenced backyards, along with their fierce little canines facing off against each other and bearing their teeth. The caption reads, "Those little devils sure are territorial, aren't they?" The irony is wonderfully poetic.

The word "they" could be the most frightening word within the construct of human institutions. "They" connotes some level of difference from "us." As organizations grow, they face the choice of remaining a consistent monolithic mass, or they can break the entity into some number and variety of pieces based on the selection of a functional or "other-derived" set of choices. On one hand, it is exceptionally difficult to manage the massive homogeneity of the monolith. On the other, it is challenging to manage the dysfunctional behavior and segregation-based challenges of all the organizational fragments. The attempt to create an environment where "the best people can get the job done" represents another situation where the ditches on both sides of the road are very deep. When the best people get either lost in the machine or become members of various tribes, they can provide little in the way of collective benefit to the organization. They do not end up working together as a member of a cohesive community and their potential benefits are largely lost. When a particular people group within a system is wronged by another group, the offended party never, ever forgets the fact that they were wronged. And the longer an organization exists, the more "wrongs" that are created by "them."

The other challenge with the "best people" approach, as a foundation on which to build, is that the best people can be compromised in their performance by the strictures and systems in which they are forced to operate. For reasons to be discussed in the next section, the best people often succumb to natural pressures and forces that inflict significant harm on them as individuals and with respect to their ability to contribute to the team. Over time, the best people are no longer interested in participating in a tainted community and the "best people" approach falters. The best people operating in an environment which has lost its soul are generally no better than everybody else. The best people to create organizational durability and positive performance have well developed Mind-Heads and even better developed Soul-Heads. SMUTy environments are no place for the best people to live. Said differently, great people will not perform in a bad environment. The smallest pebbles can knock that train of its tracks, and therein is the weakness.

The overall problem with the collection of strategy-attributes-best-people faux foundations is that it is not possible to establish a solid foundation on that which represents either 1) a part of the machine, or 2) a process on which the machine is programmed to run. Foundations must support the entirety of the institution without contingencies, and the observed problem is that way too much organizational weight is placed on "supports" which were never designed to hold the increasing magnitude of the load. As organizations find themselves standing on the doorstep of Post-Sufficiency, and are finding very few answers to the reversal of their prior good fortunes, the failure to identify and build the right foundations is usually the critical culprit. The organization's faith systems are ultimately compromised as their objects of worship falter, and the certainties of a finely-appointed future home are dashed.

As foundations form a critical base on which to build, the superstructure must also function consistent with the laws of organizational nature which are ever-present. As Mr. Newton described a set of physical laws impacting the material realm, there exists an equally impressive set of human laws invariably impacting human institutions. These forces operate in much the same way as gravity, in that their "overcoming" requires an even greater force. Unlike Newtonian physics, however, there exist no mathematical formulas that drive both certain and predictable results within the human realm. But that does not mean that they do not exert every bit as powerful a force.

NATURAL GRAVITATIONAL FORCES

One of the influences of my youth (and I am very proud of this) was MADD magazine. The magazine was perfectly focused on the mentality of an adolescent male. Irreverent, crude and completely-without-substance were its finer qualities. Of all of the deep impressions created in my pliable mind by this publication, a single picture with a short bit of narrative is the one that endures. The picture was that of a hockey goalie in his complete defensive regalia. The narrative talked extensively about the entire system that was in place to protect the assorted body parts of the goalie. Towards the end of the narrative, the keen insight that was posited was that there was just one area of the goalie's body that was left without defense. The storyline indicated, "The area that is left unprotected is the two inch square right below the facemask." This would effectively leave the area of the goalie's throat unprotected. The punch line came next. It stated: "The goal of the game of hockey: hit the goalie in the throat."

This seemed just hilarious to me. I simply could not help myself. Maybe this was so entirely funny because I grew up in Minnesota, a great hockey state. Or, maybe it was because I had actually paid real money for the magazine and I was trying to justify the entertainment value of my purchase. But I don't think either explanation was actually the case. The reason that it was so funny was that the story matched my teenage male nature so closely. I could not have resisted the humor in that piece if I had tried with all my might. It was a "natural gravitational force" to which I was completely mentally subjected. I also cannot purge my memory of the picture of the goalie after almost four decades.

In the same way, other natural gravitation-like forces act on us as adults and on our adult institutions. We are all subject to them. We are not, as a function of our natures, generally able to resist the forces that they represent. And for the most part, we all understand them pretty well. We just have a tendency to forget about them in our conscious minds, and especially in our organizational minds. So given our subjugation, our choices are to recognize their officious existence and operate accordingly, or ignore them and hope they will magically either go away, or just not apply in our present situation. It is against these forces that all human institutions must relentlessly fight.

The mental picture that might be created is that of a four hundred pound man attempting to do pull-ups. At some point, size trumps all the training and all the preparation that a body can muster. These natural gravitational forces are particularly active in the heavy bodies which are large and successful organizations. It is almost as if Mother Nature somehow imparts to large organizations, "You can get really big, but I am still in-charge, and the bigger you get, the more I am going to weigh you down." The actual burdens of bigness are a set of psychological forces that are ubiquitous and universally applicable. And they are also almost dreadfully powerful.

While the number of these forces is large, and my understanding of them constrained, we will touch on a small group that may be seen as having the most crippling effects on organizations. These forces are, in one sense, absolutely disparate and able to operate completely within their own spheres. At the same time, they are completely comfortable with their essential coexistence. They are in no way, on their merits, either evil or unethical. The gravitational forces serve as the next set of warning signs on the trajectory towards Post-Sufficiency. Additionally, and of greater significance, they represent a set of "habits of the collective mind" that become so incorporated into the ontology of an institution that other important and alternative modes of thinking, those critical to avoiding under-performance and creating durability, are simply lost.

PREDICTABLE OUTCOMES

How many times have each of us heard the line, "People are very averse to change?" Everyone hates change" is stated as if it were a universal and significant truism. Entire consulting organizations and major segments of Human Resources departments in large organizations are devoted to this hackneyed supposition. "Change Management" is now an understandable element of the English language. I have gone to internal courses on managing change, postulated as an art form, where it is intimated that to be a "change manager" is to commit to a painful personal development process that can only be cultivated over one's lifetime and at great personal sacrifice. It is ethereally intimated: "Only for those fully committed to real progress is the spirit and mystical mechanism of 'Change Management' personally available." I went to the last course on change because someone made me go, and I found myself at what I have to assume was reminiscent of a cult meeting. And they were looking for converts to their new organizationally-salvific faith system. The pervasiveness of the word change is, while in some cases justified, almost nauseating. Change, progress and durability, however, are only tangentially related topics.

There is, in my thinking, a large problem from an organizational perspective with the popular notion of change. Not only are people *not* averse to change, we all actually love it. Yes, we all love change. We all love new adventures and new experiences. Our souls long for change and the resultant expansion of our unique portfolios of personal experience. We simultaneously long to have both the security of the sense of being home, while at the same time experiencing the vast and available diversity of life. And this makes complete sense, as the notions of security and acceptance are not compromised by our interests in the entertaining excitement of new experiences.

What we despise is not change, but rather the uncertain outcomes that always accompany change. This is a classic example of seeing an effect and misdiagnosing its real cause. Let me say this again: "People don't mind change. What we all loath are unpredictable outcomes." I refer to this as the Predictability Paradox and it gains intensity within organizations the larger and more successful they become. The reason to refer to it as a paradox is that while everyone knows that the risks of unknown outcomes are involved in accomplishing anything new, the lack of predictability serves as an impediment toward progress with even the most limited set of uncertainties. It is also always challenging to the success of any venture when a premise on which decisions are being made is inconsistent with reality. This we all know to be true. Confusion as to the causes impacting our resistance to an unknowable future is a major source of organizational under-performance.

The idea of unpredictable outcomes as the bane of our existence is very easy to see in our normal everyday lives. Let's say that you have lived in a community for some time and have a favorite pizza place that you have gone to on Friday nights forever. A new pizza place then opens down the street and you conclude that you don't know enough about it, and accordingly decide that you will just keep going to your historically favorite haunt. Your decision is based on a premise that you just don't want to waste a good Friday night pizza experience on what may result in an unknown and potentially bad outcome. Then, a few months later, some friends call and ask you to go with them to the new place. What do you immediately ask? "Is it any good?" They respond that it is the best place for pizza in town, and that they heartily endorse it. So you visit the new place and it ends up being added to your list of approved pizza spots. We don't mind the change of venue as we actually find it rewarding. In retrospect, we may even fault ourselves for being too deep in our former pizza rut. We just didn't know what the outcome was going to be until someone credible tells us that we can expect a predictably good outcome. The trade-off is then acceptable.

This is basically the essence of branding. "I buy X-Brand because, although I know I may be paying more, I know exactly what I am getting. And I will not be the recipient of any ugly and unforeseen surprises." This cost-benefit-risk equation is so deeply embedded in our personal and collective consciences that we hardly stop to think about what is actually happening. And yet the implications for human institutions, emanating from the same force within our natures, are almost alarmingly significant.

Any situation consisting of a set of unpredictable outcomes, especially when the range of likely variants is wide, scares us to death. In the investment management world, the term used to describe the range of potential outcomes is "forecasting risk." Essentially, this term describes the ability of an investment manager to predict the range of potential performance results of the investment under consideration. The greater the level of forecasting risk, the relatively less an investor is willing to pay for the revenue and expected dividend stream that is attached. If we could know exactly the future outcomes of the investment, we would know exactly what we would be willing to pay for it. And if this were the case, equity investments would be priced pretty much the same as government bonds or Certificates of Deposit; those without a "risk premium." If we can live with the lower returns, we will gladly accept the trade-off of smaller forecasting risks.

And what kind of outcomes are we looking for? We are looking for those outcomes that provide for our comfort: physically, materially and aesthetically. We are looking for those outcomes that provide us with both prestige and power. And the reason we want the power closes the loop. We want the power to be able to better control and craft our own little highly-predictable world. We want the power to insure our future comfort. The cause then supports the effects and the effects create a continual amplification of the need to further control the outcomes.

As organizations grow and become more successful, the prayer becomes "Oh please God, let us continue to experience the same outcomes that we have experienced in the past. We desire no turning to the right or to the left. We fervently desire just more of the same. That is all we ask. Really, that is all. And that shouldn't really be *too* much to ask for, is it? Amen." The desire for predictably positive outcomes becomes an overwhelming force, and a bright warning sign that the organization is on the slippery slope of complete risk aversion and Post-Sufficiency.

But this is not just the risk aversion attached to the strategy. It is a level of risk aversion that impacts everything thing that the organization does. The currency used for dialogue within the organization changes and expressions like "We will have to think very long and hard about that" become the ballast in every conversation.

We opt for those decisions that have created the stability of the past. As opposed to the brief prayer that says "We earnestly desire the ability to provide better ongoing value to our customers." the prayer becomes internally focused. We basically decide within our institutional contexts to "keep going to the same pizza place week after week." In so doing, we select only those options that we know are going to pay off with a known and positive reward. But in this case, we don't have the luxury of having friends that have gone before us. We are always on our own. This is especially true of market leaders. And worse yet is the fear that by choosing a new option we may be held accountable for a "dumb decision," logically derived—in retrospect. It is hard to be faulted personally for making the same decision that everyone that has gone before us has made. The new decision is a completely different matter. So we select the paths with the most predictable outcomes, and we select them even though we may know the payoffs are hugely suboptimal. The problem is that the well-worn paths generally lead to an immolation of the senses, which is even more impactful on the soul of an organization than the near-term performance impact of doing nothing new.

One of my favorite examples of the Predictability Paradox is the strategies employed by my organization during the five year period that ended in 2009. We were the market leader in our broker/dealer clearing industry. The industry was changing rapidly and we all knew it. We also knew that we had to make major inroads into the Registered Investment Advisory market. The RIA space was an adjacent market with an established high-growth track record. But what we chose to do was simply to copy the well-entrenched and high-quality competition, and attempt to do what the other heavily branded competitors in the industry had been successfully doing for many years. We had nothing unique to offer. We even hired a known figure in the industry as the President of the subsidiary to make a statement as to our seriousness. But we entered the space where there was not even a reasonable chance that we might be able to generate returns that would approximate or exceed our cost of capital. The value of the strategy was that the outcomes were both very predictable and very poor.

We were clearly able to enter the business on a set of terms that controlled for the predictability of our outcomes at the cost of significant under-performance. But the alternative was to select from a litany of unpredictable strategies, albeit some with tremendous upside and equally significant downside. That, however, simply represented far too broad an array of potentially unpredictable outcomes. A few of those outcomes would have been so bad that some leader might have even lost their job. And when senior leaders can lose their jobs over those types of "gambles," even though the future of the organization may be at stake, little is usually put at risk.

Better to predictably under-perform on "adventures into the new" and lead the organization onto the path of a long-term exit strategy than to do what is necessary to achieve lasting organizational durability. It takes a long time for a leadership group to lose their jobs while on an exit strategy path. With success comes a narrowing of the choices that an organization will find "attractive" or even reasonable, and the narrowing choices represents an array of outcomes that are not in keeping with the past levels of success. The organization's Mind-Head does the calculation and says that the "risk-adjusted return" is too low, while the Soul-Head knows that there is no such thing as a simultaneously low-risk and certain future.

Even if you drop down from the strategic to the operating levels of organizations, the Predictability Paradox looms large. It may even be more significant in that it impacts so many more people and operating functions within the entity. "We only make changes and investments when the result is a high rate of known return on our investment." What that is expressing is that the organization will never do anything that will contain any significant level of risk. When certainty becomes the replacement part for a combination of measured risk-taking and imagination, the future belongs to someone else. No exceptions. And yet, the gravitational force is so strong that the "rut of the certain" is too deep for most large and successful human institutions to avoid. Many times, an organization will recognize the paradox and seek strategic, versus ontological, solutions to their aversions. And that usually does not work out very well. Taking one or two big strategic risks is usually not the substitute for a thousand well-placed and reasonable smaller risks.

The Predictability Paradox is also the reason that individuals who might be best described as innovators or entrepreneurs in Post-Sufficient organizations usually end up leaving the organization. The ongoing process of debate that goes on within the risk-adverse "predictability crowd" is so painful to the "intrepreneur" that it is no longer personally worthwhile to remain a part of the institution. We can all immediately come up with the names of many organizations that have fallen victim to being overtaken by upstart competition. And we can name an even larger group that are still amongst the breathing, but are shadows of their former selves. Look no further than the Predictability Paradox as a root cause.

As organizations predictably take the path of the "known" over long periods of time, their disposition is fundamentally altered such that complete aversion to the unpredictable becomes the new normal. Alternatively, only a very small group of people within the entity is trusted to operate outside of the established and acceptable bounds. When I had asked myself earlier in my career why large and successful organizations did not just bring in more creatively entrepreneurial people if they lacked the needed imagination, I had yet to understand that these people are just machine parts that are marked "reject" by Post-Sufficient organizations. And these parts are not recycled; they are simply discarded onto the top of a big pile.

Imagination is notoriously unreliable. Imagination has in it the potential for great reward and even greater embarrassment. The energy and intelligence that is required to accomplish "just managing the growing complexity of the organization" comes to replace the management of the essential risks that must be evaluated and effectively managed as the driver of success in Post-Sufficient organizations. So, in a quest to stay out of the ditches, the entity stays right in the middle of the road, and gradually slows, until it eventually just stops.

"We are implementing this new but unpopular fee and it is going to increase revenues in the next twelve months by a million dollars." Alternatively, "We are going to cut our budget for customer technical support by a million dollars and all those dollars will make their way to the bottom line." If a current period cost could somehow be added to the impact on the revenues that would have been generated by customers who will leave as a result of either action, the decisions might be different. And while organizations clearly do this kind of thinking, my experience has been that the outcomes are seriously biased by our native human interest in the certain, positive and current outcomes. Our Mind-Head tells us that this is the best course of action, while our Soul-Heads are imploring "You are killing us." The Soul-Head has the ability to measure the opportunity costs and future implications. Mind-Heads just ignore them and tell the Soul-Heads to "keep it down over there."

RULES AND PRINCIPLES

Tacit presuppositions are the tracks on which organizations ride during their period of Insufficiency. These presuppositions might better be described as principles, as they form a vast and complex web of precepts and "mental models" that are developed over time. Principles are very complicated things as they embrace values connected with notions of such things as liberty, decency, equality, equity, fairness, and their relationship with an even broader display of facts and circumstances. Principles derive their power from their applicability opposite any and all situations that might be faced. This would be opposed to the functioning of rules, which are generally narrow and purely situational.

Rules have the advantage of being easy to write and fairly easy to interpret. Rules sit on the fact side of the fact-value divide. Rules require very little thought. Principles sit, alternatively, on the value side of the divide. Principles are subject to a much higher degree of situational interpretation and mental calculus. The gravitational force found in large and successful organizations is seen in the not-so-subtle shift over time from operating on the basis of principles to the continued and enslaving reliance on rules as the basis for both thinking and deciding.

The differences between operating with articulated rules as the core premise versus utilizing inculcated principles can hardly be understated. Rules are required when adequate sources of other authority are lost in an organization. Principles operate in forms that might be described as positively "authoritative," while rules are exhibitions of base power. Principles are, accordingly, much superior to rules in that the context implicit in principles is superior to the non-context that exists with rules. Rules come from "somewhere out there." Principles come from within.

We all have a vested and personal interest in carefully selected sources of authority. Authority creates security and context and is always earned. Power is just the opposite. Power is seized. As organizations grow in success and complexity, the desire for rules becomes almost insatiable. There get to be rules for making rules for making rules. The *language* of organizations actually becomes rules-focused. For me to understand all the rules in my affiliations would have been to consume several lifetimes of study. The rules-makers put out endless "rule-changes" along with new and amplified rules to demonstrate their rule-constructing value. The problem is that rules are like putting a whole bunch of fingers in a very leaky dike. There are just never enough fingers.

The real problem with a rules-based focus is that rules have the very ugly end-result of causing us to focus on our personal and communal "rights," as opposed to doing what is right based on agreed-upon principles. Rules are soulless creations in the minds of the rule-subjects, and are responded to in like fashion. Additionally, as human institutions become more reliant on rules, they become less reliant on thought. We respond individually to the invasion of rules in defiance, as they are hardly ever *our* rules. Someone else just makes them up. And many of them look stupid and are an insult to our intelligence and independence. Principles, on the other hand, can be personally adopted, and in their understanding is much of value to us both personally and for our affiliations.

I was once getting my exercise at the local high school track and was running in the second lane. Some high school kids came to the track and sat in the first three lanes. They knew I was there, but decided to be in my way anyway, even though they had acres of other places to park themselves. The first time I ran by them, I just gave them the look of "You are all pathetic . . . please move." The second time I came through, I literally ran right through the group. They gave me the old "Hey, who let you make the rules? We have the right to sit where we want." I stopped and said, "This isn't about your rights. Yes, you have the right to sit there. This is about acting like decent human beings." They left. This was a bad situation caused by the re-characterization of rules into rights. When the obvious principles were applied, everyone then found the "right" answers.

Rules cannot substitute for right-thinking and right acting, and yet large and successful organizations succumb to rule-proliferation exceeding any ability of the organization to survive the onslaught of the Rule Czars. And all the while, the pre-existing principles are left for moribund. It might be argued that some level of "justice" is attained in the increasing abundance of rules, but it comes at the expense of all personal liberty, and native accountability and imagination. I really doubt the trade-off works towards any positive end.

Rules within large and Post-Sufficient organizations are rarely subjected to any zero-based approaches that allow the rules to be revisited in light of their neoteric environment. They are simply allowed to form a veritable organizational torture chamber without an exit door through which the members have an opportunity to escape. The fact that rules are easy and principles are hard is the core of the problem. Rules can be invented and implemented in minutes. Principles develop and are imbibed over years and decades. Furthermore, it becomes impossible at some point in the rules-assemblage process to dismantle the torture chambers, as the risks in the act of disassembly are higher than the rewards associated with retreating back to the higher and firmer ground of principles. This is a very vicious cycle. The interesting thing is that some believe that there exists an absolute number of rules that once attained will provide for our certain futures. This is foolishness of the foulest magnitude.

VIRTUOUS IDOLS

In answer to a question of a political figure to describe what pornography was, his response was something like "I am not sure I can describe it, but I know it when I see it." Virtue represents a similar definitional problem. It is hard to describe, but we all know it when we see it. Virtuous behaviors are those actions that we consider upright, positive and morally excellent. Virtuous behaviors are those we have come to appreciate as having allowed us to advance our cause and improve our human condition consistent with a definition of "right" behavior.

It is almost universally the case that we are in favor of virtuous thinking and virtuous acting. Without virtue we all know that we end up with chaos and the mess that surrounds chaos. Virtuous behavior is that which is based on our collective notion of right behavior and is the bedrock component of civilized institutions. Without virtue, there can be no trust. Without trust, there can be neither contracts nor enforceable laws. Without trust there is no risk taking, as one can only rely on oneself. That would make virtuous behavior pretty much the center of our moral, organizational and politically practical universe.

Idols, on the other hand, are forged by our own hand, and represent that which we worship. Contrary to the modern notion of a popular idol, think of this kind of idol in the same context as the carved statues inhabiting the pagan temples of the ancient Mediterranean. They are objects that are celebrated, adored and feared. They represent major components of our mental attention in which we invest both a great deal of our hopes and a large percentage of our existential reliance. We point to these things as sources of inveterate strength and protection during times of danger. The great irony, and the associated paradox, is that these idols cannot do anything they promise.

If we combine these two ideas of virtue and idols we end up with something that sounds oxymoronic. And that would be so if it weren't possible for us to abuse virtue. But we have figured out as human beings how to abuse even the most natively good. Amazing as this may seem, even our best instincts can be used against us in our personal and institutional contexts.

In the world of organizations and human institutions, there are a large number of tracks to follow as success is pursued. Some organizations rely on their ability to create life-altering new ideas that will reshape the world. Some organizations rely on just the opposite, as they believe their job is to protect orthodoxy. Depending on the situation, both can be absolutely perfect in meeting the objectives of the group. In some organizations their track to success is that of being highly focused on the customer or some other "outsider needs." On the other hand, a few organizations believe that if they focus on their own internal processes, that victories will continue to mount. Again, both are potentially very valuable and right approaches. But, as has been said in many ways, "One's greatest strength is often one's greatest unguarded weakness." This unguarded weakness is the "Virtuous Idol." It is just another manifestation of how the large and successful can be dragged down the path to Post-Sufficiency by gravitational forces that are inscrutable and that can go completely unrecognized.

To start with, almost anything that the organization lists as a significant source of strength should be viewed with the greatest level of suspicion. Strengths are seeds of future weakness. Every organization does some type of SWOT Analysis (Strength, Weakness, Opportunity, Threat) as part of their planning process. And while this is a good short-term planning tool, the unseen in this analysis is the problem. The reason is that the identified strengths have everything to do with the business, and much less to do with the people. What organizational members view as strengths are often not those ideas that are presented in the analysis. What people usually think about are things like, "We have great processes here that we follow relentlessly and they provide strong momentum." Or, "We are customer-focused to a fault, and we let our customers drive our decision-making and priority-setting, allowing us to constantly meet needs and create value." These types of virtuous statements become the cords that hold the organizational and cultural machinery together at a very fundamental level. And it is easy to see why these threads are very strong, even seemingly unbreakable.

But good notions, those things we lionize, become noxious things when taken to extremes. It is a fallacy to believe that some of us are free and some of us are slaves. We are always slaves to that on which we completely rely. The only question is that which we are slaves to. The classic definition of slavery—that of human beings as the property of others—is one that fits in its own narrow category. The more broad definition is important in that we often fail to recognize the nature of our enslavements. We can even become enslaved by that which we find of such value that we chose it as an object of worship.

In the institutional setting we hear expressions of virtue like, "We are able to deal with incredible complexity—Our ability to listen to customers is second-to-none—We have the best competitive intelligence in the marketplace." These are the expressions of confidence in virtuous behaviors. They are also the birthplace of pertinacity and trouble. This is partly rooted in our desire to want the simplest solutions to the *understanding* of our environment. We boil down "who we are" to a singular set of virtues and then push the application of those virtues to their maximum utility. Then we proceed to push them beyond that point and into negative utility.

The most frightening idol of them all is the "we just work harder than everyone else" idol. To think about this comment for just a moment is to immediately recognize the fallacy. And this is the case with the rest of the Virtuous Idols. We can work harder than everyone else by a factor of three and still die. The idol worship is furthered by an attitude fostered within the organization that drives the personal acceptance by individuals of that person's ability to both speak the language of the chosen virtue, and skillfully practice the virtue's craft.

The results are often sadly comical. Organizations that relentlessly worship complexity end up driving their organizations to a point where the complexity is no longer manageable and the machine is humbled. Those institutions that pride-fully worship their client-centricity often find themselves sans imagination and late to the market as a result of the "listen-to-the-market to the point-of-madness," condition that provides an entrance ramp for their more forward looking competition. And the competitive intelligence cults usually find themselves long on knowledge and short on insight. And insight always wins. Knowing what someone is doing, and understanding why they are doing it are two very different things. This line of thinking is akin to the Grapefruit Diet. Or, for that matter, it resembles the prescription of any diet that consists of the consumptive abuse of any single substance. I don't know who invented this little trap, and I am not sure anyone would claim authorship, but the psychology is always the same: *reductio ad absurdum*

The challenge enters the picture with the practical issue that simply focusing on one thing works really well . . . but for only a limited period of time. It is not a desirable way of life. And we all must ultimately act in a manner consistent with our personal and institutional realities. The virtue that is found in any single mindset or activity can be distorted in ways that create results completely inconsistent with their initial positive intent.

Of all the virtuous idols that I have run into the one that strikes me as potentially the most sinister is the concept of continuous improvement. This one competes with the idol of "We just work harder than everyone else." Continuous improvement hit the shores of America in the early 1990s and was imported from Japan after the Japanese Decade. As a concept, Continuous Improvement has its obvious merits. The sad reality is that organizations adopt continuous improvement as their strategy, or their principle method of market adaptation.

The Continuous Improvement concept is one stolen from evolutionary biology. It would work well if organizational life and evolutionary biology were analogous. However, organizational durability demands either strict adherence to orthodoxy or periodic leaps of faith into an unknown future. Neither of these is consistent with evolutionary biology. Continuous Improvement as a strategy is a form of progressivism that simply fits between two existing realities: orthodoxy and leaps of faith. Of itself, continuous improvement is not a strategy. It is a very good idea, but it can become an idol that *looks* frighteningly like a strategy. Virtuous Idols share one thing in common, and that is found in their substitutionary fallacy. They become substitutes for a foundation, and once again, they are not equipped to handle the load.

Virtuous Idols are mean-spirited and pernicious little devils. They have the entire virtuous lingo down and are very sweet-talkers. They are very good at "guilting us" into believing that they represent a singular righteous voice. They give us all the really good reasons (based in the virtue of simplicity) as to why that is true. They place a blanket of doubt, usually rooted in the fear of having to cope with reality, over any alternative course of action. Unlike the predictable outcome and rules/principles gravitational forces discusses earlier, the Virtuous Idol force is one that feels good to everyone. And that is why it is so incredibly dangerous.

The reliance on predictable outcomes, rules as substitutes for principles, and Virtuous Idols, can create very good perceived advancement in the short-term. It can feel to the organization that these are actually winning strategies. When it is said that we should not let winning "go to our head," that is not exactly the problem, although it is on the right track. The problem with the comment is that it does not adequately define the "destination head." The issue, more specifically, is whether winning goes to the Mind-Head or our Soul-Head. The natural gravitational forces allow the Mind-Head to feel as if victory is occurring. If winning goes into the Soul-Head the outcomes are very different. And it is in the "winning" arriving in the lobes of our Mind-Head where we see the essence and being of the organization beginning to change. The differentiating factor is ultimately the selected head-based home for winning: Mind or Soul.

* * * * *

By way of review, we began our quest by stating that not only do we humans crave a home and communities, but that all human institutions necessitate community as a basis for their performance and durability. We addressed the list of faulty foundations for community that organizations come to rely upon as foundations for success. This list included the fundamental reliance on strategies, selected attributes and hiring the best people as fundamental prescriptions for success. We went on to describe a set of natural gravitational forces that work against the long-term effectiveness of all human institutions including the challenges associated with the need for predictable outcomes, a growing affinity for rules versus principles, and the emergence of Virtuous Idols as objects of collective, but ill-advised, allegiance.

We are working towards an answer to the question of why large and successful organizations under-perform, and for an additional set of answers that address the long-term durability of organizations of all form and variety. What has been suggested thus far is that large and successful organizations are predisposed, as a function of their humanity, to quite naturally position themselves for future failure. It is also suggested that the fear of failure is not sufficient to fend off the failure. The fear of failure can only be successfully motivating if the appropriate sources of the reason for the failure are rightly identified. And this is where all the problems stem. The problem is not in what they, the leaders and members of the institution are doing. The problem is actually "them." And they cannot, or chose not to, adequately see "themselves."

As a tribute to the enduring spirit of mankind, all of the challenges that have been identified thus far can be going on as organizations continue to grow and prosper. Individuals within foundationally failing institutions can prop-up the sagging infrastructure of the machine for quite awhile. You can see the stress of their faces, but they are loyal to their faltering communities, and they will do all they possibly can to keep the organization from collapsing. They do this as they wait in vane for the arrival of the necessary reinforcements. But in most instances, the reinforcements never come, and they simply are forced to give up and let the machine collapse.

At that point, a chain reaction is set-off. The combination of very broadly experienced organizational dysfunctional behavior and a mindset driven by the past success of the organization come together in perfect union. Like most of our un-doings, the proverbial match that launches the conflagration is characterized by unhealthy levels of pride leading to arrogance, which then permeates the leadership of the organization and trickles down quickly into the ranks. This level of pervasive arrogance breeds the rise of the "control virus," which in turn creates an infectious condition referred to as Decision Dysfunction.

Post-Sufficient organizations then begin to assume "the ideology of a cancer cell," as Edward Abbey has commented. It is clearly not a thoughtful ideology, but it is a pervasive ideology. And the rightness of ideologies is always easier to deal with when viewed in terms of their historic renderings, as opposed to abstract theory. Said differently, look at what actually happens, as opposed to what is supposed to happen. We will look at some of the outcroppings of these renderings in the next three chapters. Over the balance of the book we will then turn our attentions back to the topic of "the basics" and foundations, and attempt to reestablish an alternative. In so doing we will directly look for solutions to the problems created by Post-Sufficiency.

* * * * *

Earlier we talked about the fact that we all develop a set of notions that collectively account for our personal worldviews. Our worldviews are comprised of a vast set of values, and it is in the consistency of our value sets that interpersonal relationships are formed. Those relationships are dominantly characterized by trust. The existence of trust (and the elimination of fear) allows for an environment of freedom and liberty that is the necessary basis for imagination. In settings characterized by trust we come to see ourselves as "free-agents." This occurs as the controlling mechanisms that are seen in operation are our values, and not our mandated compliance. Values, as they are generated from within, are the source of all of our personal energy. It is from our personal energies that our imaginations are allowed the flexibility to create the "productivity" that is the essence of our improved existence. Our imaginations effectively are the agents of the creation of betterment, and in betterment is the source of our personal rewards. Betterment is then seen to be derived by our values and imagination and is the progenitor of our rewards systems and personal motivation.

All of this is fairly intuitive and not particularly controversial. What follows from the extension of rewards is what is critical in the evolved existence of a human institution. The reaction to the rewards received by creating betterment in any system follows one of two paths. The first path takes the existing rewards and converts them, or transforms them, into more imagination and sequential positive action. In so doing, another virtuous cycle is begun. Rewards beget more imagination, begetting more actions and the creation of additional betterment leading to yet more rewards.

The second path takes the rewards and converts them into entitlement and arrogance. The second path returns not to imagination, but rather to an emotional response that is unlinked to productive creativity of any kind. They are rather linked to the desire to perpetuate the heretofore successful prior actions. Or to sponsor actions that are simply linked to ego. The former path is a path of humility and is the province of the Soul-Head. This second path is that of the Mind-Head rationalizing its own importance, and artificially protecting itself from any unforeseen downside risk.

The Soul-Head path embraces the future in light of, and despite of, its lack of predictability. The Mind-Head embraces the future in light of its now self-delusional and perfected view of the past. The Mind-Head places its faith in the history of the organization and blindly attempts to have history somehow repeat itself. The Soul-Head places its faith in the community and its ability to adapt to its changing climate. The outlooks and actions that are derived from the choice of responses to the rewards of success are beyond dramatic. They are, however, not essentially opposites. Rather, they are more fundamentally seen as being constituted of essentially different materials. They are of a totally different realm.

The "Second Path" just described is the path leading directly to Post-Sufficiency. It is the path leading to Mutually Assured Destruction. The members, the leaders, the customers, the shareholders, the vendors and suppliers... they all get wiped out. And it begins with a decision to listen only to the Mind-Head. In this case, it is now an arrogantly corpulent Mind-Head. And that is where we will turn in the next chapter.

3

"We Really Are Better!"

> Large and successful organizations gain a sense of superiority. The Mind-Head says "We did this!' while the atrophied Soul-Head begs for some level of continued humility. Arrogance corrupts the character of an organization, thus inducing Post-Sufficiency.

THE NOTEWORTHY BRITISH THEOLOGIAN and historian G.K. Chesterton once said, "If I could preach but one sermon, it would be on humility." Humility is one of the key virtues represented by nearly all the world's great religions and philosophies. This is because pride is a ubiquitous and very observable vice. None of us looks in the face of arrogant pride and proceeds to determine that we like what we see. We natively despise it in others, as we are directly being told by them that *we* are somehow inferior to *them*. We don't care much about the actual nature of the inferiority; the "classist" *sentiment* is what is detestable to us. We become sensitive to the exhibitions of pride very early in our lives. Pride drives all manner of bad behavior and is the tap root of evil.

Post-Sufficiency embraces an excessive level of arrogance that becomes pervasive within an organization. Arrogance is an ill-advised and character-based response to one's situation. It is a radical situational rejoinder driven by false attribution. It effectively and directly links one's positive situation with one's personal contribution or alleged deservedness. Arrogance thrives when the exhilaration of self-affirmation overcomes the other self-meliorating systems of more reflective personal monitoring. It is at the point when an individual determines that their success has been completely earned—and not a function of at least some level of good fortune—that the troubles begin.

The question is asked, "Who owns this success?" The inference is that as an owner of anything, one then has control over it. The answer to the question is obviously that success cannot be owned, and that it is rather a condition, not a piece of chattel or real property. But arrogance claims ownership nonetheless. Arrogance goes on to quantify the contribution and determines that the value of their personal contributions is superior to all other contributions. The superiority then translates into an attitude that "Not only do we have more points-on-the-scoreboard than you, we really *are better* than you."

This sentiment finds its base in the ephemeral effectiveness of faulty foundations and in a perceived set of results for which the true causes are likely misidentified. Arrogance is never earned: it is granted by self and it is always dangerous. The notion that "pride cometh before the fall" does not take a genius to observe. Effectively we say, "Yes, I always knew it, we are better than everyone else. Our current lofty situation is the result of our native betterness. And we deserve the fruits of our labors given our earned superiority. We have rightfully achieved our position . . . and justice has been served."

This is basically a "totem pole" view of the world. It can be observed being played out daily in the lives of both institutions and individuals. We become perceptually aware very early in our lives that there are others who are ostensibly positioned above us on the totem pole. And if we don't somehow figure out how this system works on our own, there are a million sources of this plebian message on which to draw. Said differently, if we don't figure out how the totem pole works, we come to believe that we are destined to live on the bottom of it. The presence of innumerable competitions of all natures, and the even more pervasive presence of modern advertising, creates a personal scorecard for comparisons that go on without end.

It quite naturally becomes our personal mission to move ourselves up the pole. We usually don't care much about, or even notice, those who are below us. But we keep a very keen eye on those who are in the position that *we* should be occupying. We are told that each of us deserves a spot at the high-end of the pole, and that to have missed that opportunity is to be dubbed stupid, a slacker or an unworthy victim. Our natures drive us relentlessly towards both subjective and objective comparisons with others of our kind. We cannot help ourselves. We are slaves to our own frail and fallen egos, and the result is unfortunately highly predictable over the long-term. When we make the determination that we have the game somehow *figured out*, we are asking to be humbled, and often in not very subtle ways. When we live for the applause and accolades of others, as opposed to the satisfaction we find in our accomplishments, the chances of being crushed by some future silence (no applause) goes way up.

In attaining and then reflecting on our acquired institutional success, we imagine that there must have been a certain "success formula" that has been the key ingredient in the instance of our bounteous past. It becomes our organizational "winning strategy." We also imagine that the formula is one of our own making and that it represents a very special and unique gnostic synthesis. In that connection, we determine that we *own* the rights to our formula. At the same time, we discount any notion of simple good fortune or of an historically skillful and nonformulaic adaptation to changing environments leading to our long assent to the top. We come to believe that it is the careful application of this *formula*, along with its attendant genius, which will insure our perennial and sublime position on the totem pole. And it is this article of belief that we worship, and to which we so earnestly desire to be faithful.

The formula, in our estimation, offers the promise of predictably consistent outcomes. As sure as two and two equal four, we suspend our fear of failure, and the associated needed humility, by clinging to Carlyle's "rules slavishly followed without understanding." The desire to "stay on top" overwhelms all of our other self-protective instincts. We tell ourselves that the formula actually insures our continued success and that we must be faithful to none other. We have found (and are now controlling) the forces of the universe and are going to exploit our newfound capabilities to our eternal advantage. We do this even though we know the belief system is not consistent with the observed reality given the dynamic and often random environment in which we exist. We determine it an ethical *constant*, amongst a world otherwise filled with mendacious variables.

While we all intuitively know that things change too quickly for the application of a fixed formula, and that the factors that have impacted the past are all likely to change, we choose to keep "plugging the factor" as long as it *seems* to keep working. Organizations subject to self-identified orthodoxy don't have this problem, as the fundamentals of their environment, their foundations, are by definition static. But for many of the rest of us, the derivation of a success formula is a perceived moment of mastery. It is at those times that the formula is used to project great results well into the future, with nary a comment as to the possibility for non-performance. The "ability to subtract," as Wendell Berry suggests, has been lost. When organizations figure out a formula, it usually prompts them to build a new architecturally magnificent building and to declare the preordained success of their trenchant 'big hairy audacious goal." The knell has been sounded. It is like a big "open house" where the idol of uninterrupted and perpetual progress is unveiled. Mindishness takes over.

It is easy to see why we all love these success formulas so much. They eliminate much of the messiness attached to unpredictable outcomes. The formula is offered as substitutionary atonement for the failures which are found in our institutions. And these success formulas effectively become the home of our arrogance. They are the redoubts in the castles of our addled and fearful minds. They are the "fountains of youth" that allow us to declare our perpetual purposes and ultimate durability. They are the ultimate statement of freedom. We declare ourselves free from the fate that has befallen so many "formula-less" less-fortunates. The top of the totem pole is now our forever-home. And while no organization would ever say, nor claim to actively think about such a thing, it becomes the source of the organization's confidence and an apparition of hope for their future. In a different universe, one's self-determined status may have something to do with a guarantee of future success. In the universe in which we actually live, the opposite is likely the result.

While these formulas represent our fool-hearty confidence, they also represent (in yet another paradox of organizational life) an ontology-changing event that forever impacts who we are. The arrogant mindset takes over large portions of our existence and operates as a warped driver of most everything that we are either invited or forced to address. The desire to stay on top manifests itself in a manic desire to stay right where we are. And we are willing to pay almost any price to maintain our position, even if through synthetic means. The newly acquired sense of invincibility causes us to dismiss the actions and attitudes of others as somehow either second-rate or just irrelevant to anything *we* might be doing. And likely worse than anything, the comparative goodness represented by our deified state releases us from the realities of cause and effect that impact the lowly "formulaically uncertified."

There is a set of lyrics in a recently released Country song that painfully admits, "I knew what I was feeling, but what was I thinking?" Arrogance is a way of thinking that blocks out much of the reality it should be considering. It is a thought process that eliminates most good thinking, as it comes to believe in a sense of artificial entitlement. Arrogance is the immature response to good fortune, and it is followed by equally immature actions, which have even more significant organizational consequences. Arrogance believes that it plays by a different set of rules. And it makes little difference how the entity defines the alternate rule-set, as the mere existence of the difference is sufficient to wreak havoc with the future.

THE CHOICES OF ARROGANCE

There are a couple of varieties of arrogance that are manifest in large and successful organizations. The first is the arrogance that tells itself that it cannot possibly be wrong and then goes out and makes big and irrational bets as a result. Sooner or later the numbers do not come up as planned and the game is over. This is not the type of arrogance to which I am referring. This is a very simple form of arrogance that is easy to spot and can be dealt with in very transparent forums. This first variety of arrogance usually just blows up anything it touches and it does so quite quickly. It is going to Vegas and placing all the chips on a single number on the Roulette table "knowing" that your number will be the winner.

The other arrogance-type is of the quotidian variety that carries itself with more dignity, but subtly reaches into every aspect of an organization's affairs. It is the form of arrogance that says that everything is as it should be, in the face of evidence to the contrary. It is the gradual plaquing of the arteries of the heart that ultimately causes the heart-attack. This latter form has the ability to minimize the amount of effort needed to accomplish the desired objectives as a result of "natural superiority." It minimizes the mental effort, it minimizes the risks, and it minimizes the potency of the other. In many ways, it looks like a form of conservatism, although its rationale is wholly different. This second form believes that it has such a large inventory of accumulated and beneficial success factors that the environment is now "different." Or they believe that they can simply be indifferent to the environment. The idea is seemingly that success can be *stored*. The all-too-obvious subtlety is that success cannot be stored. Community can be inventoried. Success is fleeting, and it always exists in the past tense.

Once planted, arrogance grows like kudzu on steroids. It simply creates too much superior emotional comfort in the short-term for us to "pass" on the experience. It can be planted anywhere: it grows in all manner of soils. Arrogance in large and successful organizations must be intentionally cut down by its leaders and members for the connection between the organization's success and reality to be maintained. The notion that arrogance is somehow motivating for the institution's members is hopelessly naïve, and potentially even evil. Arrogance is a disease whose application in developing anything of lasting worth is wholly ill-suited.

The core problem with arrogance is that as a self-proclamation, it can only be effectively identified by external agents. And to the extent that arrogance is not interested in the assessments of others, by definition, once it gets started, it has no natural end-point other than destruction. In an attempt to help a good friend of mine, now many years ago, I mentioned to him in answer to his question about his own interpersonal effectiveness; "You are having trouble with all these relationships because they perceive you as being arrogant." This would have been a true statement. The people he was talking about told me that he was very irritating because of his arrogance. And they said it with a fair amount of animus attached. Sadly, my old friend and I don't really talk very much anymore after that exchange. That is the way arrogance works.

ARROGANCE AND DETECTION

Success does not dictate pride, and yet it provides the most finely cultivated fields in which to plant the seeds of arrogance. Success is not prideful, nor does it direct its members to be prideful. But it provides a necessary backdrop. And this little article of understanding has been known since the beginning of time. There are many proverbs and idioms that note these furtive dangers: "Success makes a fool seem wise" and "Success consecrates the foulest crimes." Although success is not a guarantee of pride, pride is certainly a guarantee of failure. There is a direct link between arrogance and self-destruction, and the simplest of observations bears this out.

The reality of arrogance is in its impact on decision-making. To the notion of the organization experiencing "detrimental and market-share depleting competition" the answer coming from the arrogant sounds something like, "They are too stupid to come up with something as good as we have!" When challenged, the arrogant don't defend, they accuse and abrogate. To issues of the pricing of the offering (whatever it is that the organization "sells"), the arrogant assume that whatever it is that *they* offer is worth any price that is chosen; by them. When inquiries as to the value of the offering come to the arrogant, the response is delivered as an affront, and the accuser is told that the value is obvious, other than to the mentally inane. To the importance of building additional creativity and innovation into the organization, the response is usually, "What are you talking about?" The arrogant cannot fathom any shortfall in new thinking, as it is contrary to their self-proclaimed status. And on and on it goes.

The lens through which the arrogant view the world impacts every element of everything that is thought, done or discussed. And it is in this all-pervasive effect that the real danger is found. Arrogance is a condition of fundamental disconnection with truth as ascribed by the rest of the world. And no manner of disconnect from reality is more frightening than prideful and immature arrogance. You can instill arrogance in a five year old. It is not a skill that requires advanced age or training.

"We are not about effort around here; we are only about results, baby!" That line came out of the Chief Operating Officer of one of my affiliations. In effect he said, "We don't care about any of the causes, because we're so good, we can just control the effects by the force of our own goodness." If he really believed that, what impact might it have on everything else he might do? What happens when causes cease to be important? In another situation, the President of one of my affiliations decided that our margins had slipped to a level that were unacceptable and increased the charges to our clients (without any increase in services) to compensate for the shortfall. The only problem was that everyone else in the organization knew the increase violated all of our contracts. No matter. When arrogance took over, this guy granted himself the privilege of declaring that we were "entitled" to our margins, and that someone else must pay. "I think, therefore I am . . . right" becomes the derivation of Descartes' famous philosophical observation.

So why does arrogance persist in the face of such obviously detrimental outcomes? Why does it proliferate with such renascent negative social and institutional consequences? The only explanations that seem to exist are 1) that arrogance pays significant dividends, 2) that arrogance is undetected by its purveyors, or 3) that arrogance is mischaracterized as something less pernicious. My belief is that some of each of these is evident in the arrogant and that the psychosis is so deeply engrained that an alternative approach is outside their ability to comprehend. To become a disciple of Machiavelli or Nietzsche is to embrace the laws of power and arrogance as the keys to success. The liberty to pursue arrogance is generally outside the definition of the rights of individuals that most of us will tolerate, or determine to be in any way virtuous. And yet it persists and haunts large and successful organizations. It is a major cause of both their under-performance and lack of durability. It is the seminal root of Post-Sufficiency.

CONFIDENCE VERSUS ARROGANCE

The challenge with identifying arrogance is that it can be easily confused with a healthy sense of confidence. A well-founded sense of confidence is an exceptionally valuable trait found in all of life, and is essential to humanity and to our institutions. We must have some degree of faith in ourselves if we are able to accomplish anything at all. Too much faith, however, is dangerous. And yes, we are once again looking at an interestingly complex paradox. It is a very short drive from Confidence to the next town down the road, Arrogance. We would prefer to think of ourselves as justifiably confident, and to think of the "other guys" as those with the enlarged frontal lobes. And while it is a short drive, the "climate" in Confidence is hugely different from the climate in Arrogance.

The main difference between arrogance and confidence is that confidence retains an element of humility that advises against the unconstrained ability to control outcomes. With confidence there is an air of uncertainty, and an understanding that we should not "boast about tomorrow." Confidence knows that each day represents its own challenges and that while well equipped, our ability to meet the hindrances of tomorrow have not yet been tested. Tomorrow is not here yet. It is when that element of humility erodes away that we slip, inch by inch, into arrogance. That last inch creates the tipping point. Confidence is an expression of preparedness. Arrogance is an expression of entitlement. The two could hardly be any less similar.

During the late 1990s I had an opportunity to represent my organization in a joint venture that we were putting together with American International Group (AIG) and Wachovia Bank. The joint venture never got off the ground mostly as a function of inflated egos that simply overwhelmed the creation of the business plan. I had never run into egos this big before, and they captured my attention by their perversely inflated size. The process was, in retrospect however, very intriguing.

Both AIG and Wachovia senior representatives were part of the planning process. I particularly remember listening to one of the Senior Executive Vice Presidents (note the title) of Wachovia advising the rest of the group as to when it was the best time to buy their company's stock. The answer was, "Whenever you have a dollar in your pocket!" And this was not a statement meant to amuse. It was the statement of a self-assumed birthright. It was apparent to everyone in the group that this man had crossed the line and his display of inward arrogance was nauseating. I remember thinking to myself, "I wonder how long it will be before their arrogant culture will kill them?" It took about ten years. And AIG's plight was even more pronounced. Wells Fargo now owns the remains of Wachovia. The federal government now owns most of the conflated corpse that was AIG. The members of both of these organizations deserved so much better outcomes.

Being proud of one's organizations and institutions is a good thing. The question that emerges is the source of the pride. Being proud of what the organization is, what it produces, and the values that it represents are an admirable set of sources of pride. That the organization determines that it is *better* than the others is the baseline problem. Pride must be based on an absolute value and not on a comparative and subjective set of measures. It is quite simple to hear the relative arrogance level of an organization in listening to how they communicate. Insufficient organizations speak in terms of the value they create, while Post-Sufficient and arrogant organizations speak in terms of comparative superiority. Insufficient organizations talk about what is *outside* the organization. Arrogant organizations focus internally and are self-congratulatory. Arrogance makes "assumption" an operating presupposition. Humility makes "questioning" the premise on which decisions are made.

Show me a group of people that will allow unfounded assumptions to drift aimlessly throughout the dialog and I will show you a picture of decline. Humility is too often mistakenly characterized as an unwillingness to make a decision, all the while arrogance is given a free pass. In reality, humility creates an objective path directly to decisions and is a mindset, not a convention. Alternatively, arrogance represents something far less than objectivity, and any presumption of quality in the decision-making process is frustrated by reality. Worst of all, arrogance completely stifles both communications and creativity.

Ultimately, however, the real damage of arrogance is not the faulty decision-making. The real problem of arrogance is its ability to destroy any sense of community, and this with almost reckless abandon. No one trusts an egomaniac, or an egomaniacal organization, as a result of their tainted views of the world and their disconnected and self-serving value systems. The resultant well-founded and wholly reasonable lack of trust severs the communitarian links, and what follows is a system that is built on the management of chaos.

I was once told that the first rule of organizational management is "You must first get rid of the jerk and pricks!" This was shorthand for the immaturely arrogant. Jerks and pricks impact an organization in two ways with their immature arrogance. Both impacts are the result of a loss of respect. The arrogant are neither respectful of their coworkers, the organization's customers, nor any other constituents. To those who are not respected is little attention paid. When little attention is paid, expanded relational distance is the infinitely knowable result. The distance that is created between the parties results in what you expect when entities are not in contact. The result is just "nothing." Nothing good happens. Nothing bad happens. Just nothing happens. And it all stems directly back to arrogance.

ARROGANCE AND EQUALITY

As I was walking down a shopping mall one day I saw a family with a couple of late-single-digit-age boys. One of them had a t-shirt that said, "Winning isn't everything. Seeing you lose is everything." Call me sentimental, but the sight of a kid displaying this approach to the world made me very sad. In my simple-minded way, I said to myself, "That is essentially what is wrong with the world . . . and we are teaching it to nine year olds!" I suppose it was intended to be funny, but that was of little consolation. Messaging is important, and this one was a really bad one.

Bringing down the other guy is not a morally-neutral proposition. Everyone basically loses in that scenario. The nature of the soul is to look for win-win situations. The difference between wanting your team to win and wanting the other team to lose is massively significant to the success of a human institution. It is a defect of the Mind-Head that results in a desire to see someone else suffer. The sight of suffering of any kind always causes harm to the soul. Look no further than modern on-screen "entertainment" to determine the extent to which we are willing to view the demise of the other. When one is a party to the suffering of another, the impact should be that of shame. To the extent that it is anything else, it borders on the diabolical. Permanent harm is being inflicted. Soul-Heads always see this, and they see it with great clarity.

I worked with a senior sales manager at one point in my career whose central philosophy in life seemed to be "the other guys suck!" No matter what the topic, this guy's approach was never based in any form of absolute; it was always based in arrogance-driven comparison. The impact on his audience was always predictably the same. "Yeah, you are right, they do suck!" And their mother's, I have to suppose, also wear army boots. The impact on the organization was tangibly negative. The other guys really didn't suck. But the entire marketing and sales organization was suffused with his arrogant and unrealistic views. Is it possible that the "other guys" have a psychological and tactical advantage if you think they are pathetic?

Arrogance ultimately kills two important attributes of the institution: one is the organization's relation to its clients; the other is within the institution and in its relationship with itself. Some notion of *equality* of condition must be maintained for organizations to remain grounded.

ARROGANCE AND GOODWILL

Post-Sufficient organizations forget that life creates and necessitates the need for a balance of giving and receiving. All healthy relationships create a balance that is noble and enabling to the participants. When arrogance takes over, the willingness to "give" is relatively compromised by the perceived and excessive right to receive. This imbalance makes Post-Sufficient organizations untrustworthy partners, who appear equally predatory and self-serving.

All human institutions are built on the fundamental truth that what one gives and what one receives are to be held in almost complete balance, with a small amount of "profit" emerging in one form or another by both parties. As I am using the terms, giving is simply the product or output of the individual or the institution. Receiving is the reward that is given in return for the output. When the giving and receiving formula gets out of balance, our Soul-Heads immediately cry "foul" and look for the reappearance of equity. The orderliness of this formula is seen everywhere we look. International free-trade agreements are built on natural laws for the need to equate giving and receiving. The exchange of Christmas gifts between related families is often denominated in a limit on the value of the gifts. And the limit is often based on what the least affluent members can afford, such as to avoid any ill-will. Our relationships with our friends are giving-receiving neutral, if they are to endure and thrive over time. Our relationships with our spouses are full of the giving and receiving theme. Even our relationships with our children are based on the same balancing act, although it may sometimes *appear* to be more heavily weighted toward the giving side as parents. But if parents didn't receive adequate compensation for having children, the end of the race would be rapidly upon us. When arrogance is present, however, the formula is manipulated and contorted and the result is always negative for the collective good.

Arrogance values the giving side of the equation with an increased weighting that is inconsistent with the evaluation of the gift by the receiving side. Arrogant organizations and institutions come to see what they do in a more favorable light than what would be seen by the dispassionate observer. They see themselves as superior, and thus worthy of more compensation for their gifts than comports with reality. The inflated price the client pays is a direct result of the organizations inflated arrogance. "They pay us for the privilege of doing business with us." As a result, the "pricing formula" becomes the thing of wishes and ideals and the rope with which the organization is ultimately hung. The act of "selling" a product is not necessary to get the pricing formula wrong. We see this played out in our social lives all the time. We see it in the girls who continue to take abuse because the "popular girls" seemingly have the right to give it. We observe it in the actions of the "privileged" who refuse to give the appropriate respect to those who provide them service. The unfaithful husband who expects his wife to deal with his philandering overstates the worth of his gifts. And on and on the saga goes.

The basic notion of capitalism and trade and "specialization-of-function" is to create win-win situations. The Ricardian economic notion of *comparative advantage* is noteworthy here. David Ricardo figured out that different entities (in his example, nations) have advantages in producing desirable goods and services. It is easier and less costly to grow wheat in Kansas, and bananas in Costa Rico. It therefore makes sense for the two to trade between themselves, such that the outcomes of both their abundance can be shared and expanded. It makes very little sense for Kansas to build greenhouses and for Costa Rica to put a big tarp over their fields to keep all the rain off. Arrogance sees the value of the wheat, but discounts the value of the bananas. And everyone becomes a relative loser.

Arrogance promises gifts of exceptional value. In the short-term, this strategy is always one hundred percent effective. But you can't fool all the people forever and in the end, the soul of the organization is burdened by the inability to make the giving and receiving formula balance. In the latter stages of Post-Sufficiency, the organization cannot comprehend that they might actually owe something to their clients or other constituents. They will continue to operate in arrogance, treating their clients at arms-length, believing that the clients are privileged even to be associated with them. They will do this until their faulty reality is shattered, and the organization is left customer-less and confused. They will do this until all the goodwill in the sum total of their relationships has vanished. An inequitable organizational life is truly a sad life. When others look upon you with disdain for your inflated view of yourself, it simply reinforces what is already known.

ARROGANCE AND INSIGHT

Post-Sufficient organizations create tremendous amounts of knowledge and a relative inability to utilize that knowledge to advance their organizations. When arrogance takes center stage, the willingness to pragmatically assess the real and effective intellectual capital abilities of the organization is stultified. The situation becomes mentally tainted and it results in a shortfall opposite the requirements of organizational durability. This makes Post-Sufficient organizations vulnerable to their environments, as they are unable to convert a large absolute amount of knowledge into high-value and marketable offerings.

I have come to believe that there are three levels of "knowing" within human institutions. The first of the levels is "common sense" which serves as the basis for almost all of the decisions that go along with an organization. The second level is that of "knowledge," or simply that which is cumulatively known. Unlike common sense, it does not discriminate, it just is; it has no *sense*. Knowledge has the advantage of being impressive in its acquirement, and in its supposed scalability. Those who possess knowledge have a massive arsenal at their disposal, or so it would seem. The third level of knowing is something that might be best described as "insight." Insight is that which takes common sense and knowledge and forges from them into an elevated and improved view of the future. And in that view of the future is much value.

The critical point of difference along this knowledge continuum is that point where information moves from the category of data and knowledge into the realm of insight. Insight is difficult to describe, but easy to identify. Insight is the ability to contextualize data, to see the big picture, and to make decisions which incorporate the less tangible and quantifiable factors. The problem is that organizations usually end up with a bunch of really smart people, with large amounts of knowledge, most of them so lacking in overall context that they are unfortunately rendered almost useless in pushing the organization forward. The organization ends up with exceptionally large amounts of "absolute" intellectual capital. If you add up what everyone knows, it is a very healthy sized pile of knowledge indeed.

On the other hand, the "relevant" or actually *useable* intellectual capital is, in many large organizations, often decreasing with the passage of time. This is especially true when the standard is a measurement against the increased need for useable capital as the organization grows in size and complexity. The absolute and relevant intellectual capital is frequently "separated" in an organization. It is as if the ingredients to the best meal ever prepared are all in the house, but they are situated in different rooms and cannot be brought together to create the feast. As a matter of fact, the people in one room don't even know of the "ingredients" in the other room. As a result, the organization is long on knowledge and short on the insights into the situation that are the keys to driving real progress. Arrogance prevents a human institution from seeing anything other than the levels of absolute, versus useable, knowledge.

I have also come to believe that common sense and insight are the critical elements in the development of human institutions, and that knowledge, simply of itself, is nearly worthless. Knowledge may actually be a detriment, except to the extent that it contributes to insight. Common sense allows an organization to make most of the decisions that it needs to make. Only as common sense is stifled is it not allowed to be a major contributor to success. Insight allows the organization to glimpse the future, even if darkly, and claim a stake in that future. Knowing a lot about something and knowing what is important to the future are two very different things.

Arrogant successful organizations frequently place a high level of value on collecting data and attaining knowledge, but have no real ability to make meaningful decisions with all their information. And they often discount the value of common sense, as it is not consistent with the notion of being "better." That which is *common* cannot, by definition, be superior. Knowledge too, often masquerades as insight, and always looks down its nose on common sense. Knowledge exists. Insights act. T.S. Eliot wrote "Where is the wisdom we have lost in knowledge? Where is the knowledge we have lost in information?" And he wrote these words long before the Information Revolution. The problem is now infinitely magnified.

In the wake of the Great Recession, Ben Bernanke was Chairman of the Federal Reserve. Asked if low interests rates, in retrospect, might have had something to do with the asset bubble created in residential real estate, he basically said that they were only a small factor. This is an example of a ton of knowledge and very little common sense. Let's think, "If we give away free money, and tell people they need to put up nothing in exchange for the free money, do we think the demand for the assets that might be bought with that money might be high?" This might have been not-so-true for institutional borrowers who might have passed on acquiring the cheap money if they had no way to profitably invest it. But individual people are not investing in a productive asset; they are buying a home, for free, as defined by the required payments. Common sense would tell us that interest rates had to be a major factor in the asset bubble. Mr. Bernanke, for all his brilliance, is lost in his large house full of knowledge. Knowledge, to the intellectually arrogant, occupies huge amounts of brain-power that is often used for nothing other than the support of itself.

When I was promoted to the "executive level" of one of my organizations, I received a letter that ostensibly was designed to direct my path in my newly appointed and "heady" role. One of the most interesting parts of that letter said the following: "Personal bias is set aside. The facts drive our decisions." My only response to that was: "What? We are not to have opinions?" I immediately thought to myself: "Am I not, as a human being, but simply a vast collection of personal values and biases? Is there some great pool of data in the sky to which I need to be connected?"

The organization was confusing a number of topics here which included both ethics and insights. Insights are "biased" by their very nature. The facts of history could be said to be almost literally "known," and yet we all express a wide variety of opinions as to their meaning and their lessons. Facts do not speak, only people do. The problem is that we have come to believe that objective facts and the resultant knowledge automatically lead to "objective" and high-quality decisions. But the world is rarely that simple, or that knowable.

We don't always have all the data. And even if we did, it is unlikely that two people will arrive at the same decision based on the grand data-set. No real decisions are truly objective. And wishing the situation to be different does not make it so. Their very nature is subjective. We see this frequently in the political arena. A political conservative and a political liberal will access the same data, but the decisions they make based on that data are very different. Arrogance enables an organization the luxury of worshiping the input, without troubling itself with the untidy nature of determining what those inputs actually mean. My organization was, in its mandate to make decisions based on the facts, simply singing the praises of knowledge, without any notion as to its real meaning. It was the Mind-Head making itself very clear.

Arrogance breeds a reliance on the numbers, as the numbers are generally very reinforcing within a Post-Sufficient organization. Numbers are thought the ultimate in objectivity. When the numbers begin to drive the business, the business is in trouble. The difference between the numbers and the real economics is a real threat to all organizations. We simply measure the wrong long-term indicators of success. And we don't even attempt to measure the ability of the organization to utilize the types of common sense and insights that are the real drivers of the future. If balance sheets could capture the asset-value of insights and common sense, and the future burden of the liabilities represented by arrogance, the market capitalization of those organizations would be very different.

High operating margins are a classic problem amongst the Post-Sufficient. You can always starve your way to short-term prosperity. And you can do it for years. While the other guys are said to "stink, just look at their crummy margins!" they are also potentially investing in their business in ways that the arrogant margin-misers do not. I was asked one time why I was so hard on the numbers that come out of the accounting department. My comment was, "I really like the Accounting Department. The problem is that the accounting numbers always lie." Alternatively, and more accurately, it is not so much that the accounting numbers lie, but rather that they tell half-truths, and they don't address so much of what is critical. Accounting, broadly defined, can be contorted to meet the interests of whoever is managing them. At the University level, Accounting Majors think Economics Majors are stupid and vice versa. In reality they both have something very valuable to offer. But leaving the numbers solely to the accountants is very dangerous sport. Big organizations prefer the exactitude of accounting over the plenary, but confusing (and controversial), nature of economics. Numbers have in them the semblance of knowledge. Numbers and theories together are sharper and more deadly than the best two-edged sword. But they are worthless in most efforts as they contain none of the values of common sense, and none of the sagacity of insight.

"With all this knowledge, we must be in a position to rule the world!" is the sentiment of the arrogant. But I have continued to witness these knowledgeable people being brought together and watched their conversations, so lacking in common sense, common context and insight that little communication is actually taking place. Different languages are being spoken and no one even recognizes it. Knowledge is being spewed, polyglot is the format, and "intellectual terrorism" is the result. Frustration simply grows at the lack of ability to understand one another. Arrogance can't believe this is happening or doesn't see it. Or is just chooses to look the other way.

It is always interesting to me when a senior executive does a presentation for a group of internal people and they write out the comments in advance and then *read* them to the group. Knowledge lacks a sense of internal cohesion, and sadly renders its inhabitant incapable of contemporaneous speech. Knowledge, by its nature, is in the business of de-construction. It takes things apart to better understand them. Common sense and insight are just the opposite. They take the disparate pieces and assemble them in new and better ways. The differences in the dialectic could not be more striking.

I came face to face with my own personal arrogance when I was a kid. One of my most famous lines came as a twelve year old while on vacation in a state park in Minnesota. We were in our camper at night and my parents, sisters and I were all in our comfy little Styrofoam beds when a relatively loud noise came from right outside the door. As I was best positioned to see outside the camper in the direction of the noise, it fell to me to be brave and play pet detective. I was the one designated to open the "zipper window" and discern the nature of the menace. The expression that came out of me at that point continues to live large in the annals of my family. I said, "It's either a bear or a chipmunk, but it is too dark to tell." I guess the suggestion was that if I couldn't tell the difference between something the size of a bear and something the size of a chipmunk that I really didn't have any clue as to what I was assessing. And the truth was that I didn't.

Sometimes an answer is urgently needed but we just can't see it because the environment we are peering into is just too "dark." We might actually know the difference between a one pound creature and a three hundred pound creature, but it is of little value. Arrogance says that we must come up with something anyway. The problem is that everyone around us knows that we have no clue. But arrogance demands an answer. Humility asks more questions and seeks more input. Humility recognizes the darkness. Humility may answer the question but simultaneously acknowledge its risks. As a twelve year old male I was doing what so many do while in positions of needing an answer: I just made one up. The problem is not so much that I made up the answer. Whatever the source of the noise outside the camper, it didn't create a major catastrophe. The problem was that I had compromised my integrity in pursuit of the naturally unknowable. I should have said, "It's too dark, I can't tell what is out there" and then directed my dad to go out and check it out. When an organization can no longer admit to the darkness, calamity ensues. Mind-heads have a tendency to make up answers and spit them out, unless the Soul-Head counteracts and counsels otherwise. The analytic Mind-Head needs answers. Soul-Heads understand that in many instances ambiguity reigns supreme.

When an arrogant mindset takes over, the way we assess the current environment, the way we assess the prospects for the future, and the way we assess the nature of all our relationships changes. Rather than acknowledging the unknowable, we become deceptively and harmfully creative. In many ways arrogance is just a simple response to and a method of shielding ourselves from a frightening unknown. Better to boast in the face of danger than to wince in the face of fear. At the time when the organization should be seeking to find its home, it launches off in an opposite direction.

As arrogance is not trustworthy, it is also not trusting. To the extent that our Soul-Head is no longer functional, there exists no check on the trust equation. The lack of trust is seen both with respect to relationships outside the organization and those on the inside. It is hard to tell which audience is most impacted, but it is easy to see the impact internally. The impact of arrogance is manifest in seizing complete control of the machine. "The machine can be trusted, but the people cannot." The quest for truth is abandoned as the quest for complete control of all parts of the machine is commenced.

Arrogance is naturally inclined towards control. If one has all the right answers, it makes sense to inflict those views on everyone else . . . those "without the answers." And in the progressive destiny of Post-Sufficiency, that is where we will turn next.

4

Controlling the Uncontrollable

> Large and successful organizations look to their glorious past and develop a success formula to guarantee its repetition. They believe they have mastered the future, which is now under their direct control. Control stifles the imagination and propels Post-Sufficiency.

OUR NINETEENTH CENTURY PSYCHOLOGIST friend, Mr. Freud, once indicated that he believed that "Neurosis is the inability to tolerate ambiguity." Ambiguity infers the lack of defined choices in our environment and an associated lack of control of the desired outcomes. Given that we all live in a world of significant ambiguity and randomness, we must all, therefore, be neurotic. When we concern ourselves inordinately with maximizing the "knowable impact" that we have on our surroundings, we unknowingly destroy the essential control we were seeking to gain. As opposed to "Boldly going where no man has gone before!" we revert to the cowardice of control.

It is very interesting that at a point in history when we have collectively exhibited a greater level of control of almost everything around us than ever before (from the control of diseases to the temperatures in our cars), we are simultaneously the most alienated and anxiety-riddled. A friend of mine referred to this condition as "learned helplessness." We are fundamentally helpless as it relates to the control over our own lives, and we are essentially skilled at it. We reject the inevitability of unpredictable outcomes and seek to compensate through our attempts at control over our circumstances. Control is the domain of the Mind-Head and is an attractive, yet horrifically dangerous illusion that permeates Post-Sufficient organizations.

The result of the control illusion is that organizations find themselves in a position where no one within the organization can trust anyone else, either inside or outside the organization. Trust is, by definition, something that remains, by an exercise of faith, in the hands of someone else. Trust and control are inconsistent with one another. Trust and faith occupy a vast middle ground on a continuum bounded by control on the one end, and chaos on the other. Our desire to flee the countless ambiguities we find in our personal and collective lives emboldens a natural longing to migrate towards the *control* end of the continuum. Chaos is perceived as just a completely unacceptable outcome. But in our organizational lives, we overreact in the direction of control. We come to see any lack of control over every aspect of the organization as a lapse of major proportion.

The only way to successfully gain any semblance of personal control of the future is to recognize one's own limited ability to control that same future. To assume "control" is to embrace a false presupposition that fundamentally thwarts efforts aimed in its direction. The only way to realize a dream is to simultaneously cling to it, while at the same time emotionally holding onto it very loosely. To abjectly fear the non-realization of a dream is to place it further from reach. This should not be confused with our interests in planning and building for the future, as those are positive and important aspects of each of our lives. It is our energies directed at *controlling* the future that form the basis for our institutional mental illness. Alternatively, our energies directed at *facilitating* positive future outcomes through the establishment of a set of *conditions* where the desired state can actually emerge is the true beginning of their actual realization.

The exhibition of a considerable level of trust and faith, which occupies a large section of the middle of the continuum, is the zone within the control-chaos continuum where the Soul-Head recognizes the organization must exist. The connection between faith and trust, and the direct impact on the ability of organizations to create meaningful imagination forms an inviolable link for the Soul-Head. Mr. Tolkien was likely very accurate in his belief that all wonderers are not lost. The same would be true of institutions. Institutions that wonder, as a result of their faith in themselves, are prone to finding some very interesting places. And in so doing they are also prone to experiencing much richness. But a problem exists for wonderers. And it is the same old "ditch-on-both-sides-of-the-road problem."

The very deep ditch on the right side of an organization's path is the control ditch. The equally deep ditch on the left side of the road is the chaos ditch. The more Post-Sufficient an organization becomes, the more it fears the loss of control. It is also often times the case that the second or third generation of leaders in an organization actually grew up *controlling* aspects of the business, as opposed to growing them, and for them, control is a naturally good and virtuous thing. And they are now in-charge. As the pendulum swings towards control, and as the balance of control and organized chaos shifts, the organizational pliability that is required for long-term durability is exsiccated. If an organization flirts with operating too close to the control ditch, their likelihood of falling into it goes up commensurately.

On one cold January day, we got an e-mail from the CEO with his New Year's Message. I thought that it might be interesting to see what he had to say, so I opened the three minute video. His first comment was that he was glad that the prior year was over. With that comment, we could all empathize and agree. And we all understood his perspective and opinion. At that point he started into his discussion of the high-level strategic priorities for the upcoming year. The first of three adumbrated priorities was that we needed to better control expenses (read: reduce them) while maintaining high levels of customer service. The second strategy was that we needed to better manage and control the risks in the business (read: take no risks). And the third priority was that we must control the use of our capital wisely (read: no investments). While I really wanted to interpret these priorities in terms that left open the possibility of any sort of advancement or growth of the business, I could find none.

The strongly delivered message seemed to be simply, "Go back to your offices and provide good customer service with a smaller budget. Don't take any risks on anything and don't even think about making any investments for the future with the company's resources." This message was absolutely stunning to me. I sat at my desk and said, "Is this for real?" I thought that the appropriate response might be that I should just hide underneath my desk in a fetal position. These were frightening times, but it seemed that ordering everyone under their desks was excessive and completely devoid of hope. This guy was a former Chief Financial Officer, and this was the voice of the Mind-Head.

Could it really be the case that the CEO wanted to tell us to do nothing other than inflict higher levels of *control* on our business? Is it possible that all he wanted us to do was to go back to our desks and provide good service to our current customers? There was absolutely no mention in his video of looking for opportunities to strategically grow the business, nor was there any mention of using our imaginations to advance our longer-term interests during a challenging environment. He didn't even want us to use our creativity to manufacture better controls, or so it would seem. Any notion of inspiring the associates to create a brighter future for the team and its shareholders was seemingly put on indefinite hold. To the Mind-Head, this was completely rational.

When the CEO of a company with tens of thousands of employees makes a statement to all the associates as to its priorities, many people will pay attention (although no one else in my department bothered to listen to the message). If associates were actually paying attention to this message, it was unfortunate. The message was so troublingly Post-Sufficient that, in one short three minute video message, the cause of the organization was almost unalterably altered in a negative direction. There was no balancing of emotions and interests in the statement. There was no sense of any level of adventure in the statement. There was no sense of any humanity. It was just a "dead message" and was plainly sad.

Interestingly, a couple of weeks later the CEO released another little video clip in which he talked about some of the opportunities that the Company was pursuing. It was almost an apology for his earlier message. Maybe someone got to him and told him that he had left his troops with little hope, and that his earlier message was extremely dispiriting. I once heard someone say that optimism doesn't cost anything. I strongly disagree with that comment. On the contrary, pessimism is free, as indicated by its abundance.

Pessimism is the default option when a lack of imagination limits our ability to see an optimistic future. And control is the language of the pessimist. It looks backward and honors the known past. It stifles the organization's passions and depresses the "controlled." Controls are a necessary evil, as opposed to any sort of legitimate organizational imperative. But they come to be viewed as facilitators and even the drivers of continuing success. As we come to think about the concept of control in any other terms (other than as a "necessary negative"), we have then lost track of its rightful place in the life of any human institution. Controls might be strategic and mindish, but they speak directly and pessimistically to the soul of an organization.

WELCOME TO THE WORLD OF CONTROL

The dual notions of being long on personal and collective virtue and short on prescription and regulation are the foundation on which the United States was built. In a theoretical sense, all laws and rules and their associated enforcement are systemic non-value-adding wastes of energy, time and money. Rules and their enforcement would not be necessary in the presence of a commonly ascribed and universally motivating set of values and proscriptions for virtuous behavior: those behaviors that operate in complete harmony with the organization's agreed upon collective ethic. But the world never operates within the bounds of reasoned and virtuous behavior, so rules and laws must emerge as a means of control. These rules are put in place such as to maintain personal security and a sense of perpetually reliable personal justice within the community. The rules and related punishments must be operational in order to retain a belief in the systemic order that is required for the reasonable functioning of the system. Unfortunately, the polarity of most large and successful organizations shifts over time and this relationship becomes exactly reversed. The system becomes the oppressor and not the protector.

As the effective management of organizational values and principles becomes more challenging, the establishment of rules and laws, processes and procedures (and a steadily increasing body of "this-is-exactly-how-we-must-do-stuff-around-here") becomes the first and only organizational response to any "control weakness" that is spotted. Policies substitute for values based on principles. The principles then become evanescent. Policies don't support values, they mutilate them. And, as we will see later in this chapter, the number of violation "spotters" increases as the organizational polarity is changing as well.

The operating premise of the Post-Sufficient organization effectively becomes a set of rules-based prescriptions for all behavior. Any residual virtuous or values-driven behavior is left to squeeze out between the cracks. The "Power of the Rules" becomes the replacement for legitimate and needed institutional moral authority. And they are the replacement for most other original thought as well.

If the desire is to destroy an organization's soul, then develop and enforce a set of rules that are linked to every situation in the subject-member's life. Put the subject in a cage and monitor and control every aspect of their existence. The number and scope of rules necessary to fit every conceivable situation is so vast that the soul of the controlled will be immediately overcome. "I just cannot possibly keep track of all these rules and I am in fear of the consequences of my inability to keep track of all of them." Watching people try to follow rules as a substitute for using their brains is both comical and tragic.

If the desire is to build a soul, create an environment where values are allowed to emerge over time based on shared experience and the common lessons learned over time. It is possible to *share* values, but they are not subject to *implementation,* as are rules. Humans cannot be re-wired to drive behaviors that nicely comport with the rules-infused hokum. What they need are systems of faith, based on values and common experience. The situation is analogous to exercising as we get older. The time needed to get in shape becomes more protracted, and the cessation of the exercise program results in very rapid decline. The same is true in Post-Sufficient organizations. It can be observed that as values and principles are replaced by a constantly expanding set of rules and regulations, the system declines very rapidly.

We are all intractably drawn towards those elements of our lives that create security through predictability. Virtues and values are not widely believed or thought to be sources of security. Rules and procedures are all-to-commonly held in much higher regard as sources of ballast. The opposite is actually the case, and most of us would agree with this if presented the case in our everyday experience. Do you want to erect an electric fence around your house to keep bad people out, or create an environment where no one desires to break in and steal or harm? We all know that we cannot build fences that are high enough to keep the ingenious felons out. And yet our actions proclaim the virtue of rules, and the non-virtue, or lack of situational applicability, of virtue.

The problem in Post-Sufficient institutions, however, does not come from the erection of a single fence. One or two fences actually might be a good thing. The problem is in the labyrinth of fences that not only fail to keep the bad guys out, but that are remarkably effective of keeping the good guys "in" and "contained." Contact with the real outside world is forever compromised. We all recognize these organizations when we come in contact with them. They simply cannot get out of their own way, as the fences block their every move. It is as if they are operating in a maze of their own making. The overall fence-building effort is one of those insidious processes that have no "Warning: Construction Zone" signs. No hard hats are required, thus resulting in significant Soul-Head injuries.

I got a call on a Friday afternoon from the Chief Administrative Officer of one of my multi-billion dollar affiliations regarding one of my subordinates. Apparently Eddie had not completed his mandatory California Sexual Harassment training on time. While we subsequently found out that he had never been *notified* that he was in need of the training, the resulting story is indicative of the fence-building problem. This is an exhibit of Post-Sufficiency that is emblematic of so much of the condition.

As it turns out, what had happened was that a Human Resources bureaucrat at the parent company called our CEO, who called the CAO, who called the Head of Sales, who notified me of our massive (and likely conspiratorial) lack of attention to this detail. This story might have actually ended well if we had found out that this process of escalation and notification was actually a mistake, and would therefore not be repeated. To have learned that the CEO would not be contacted in the future, and that I, as Eddie's boss, would be the first point of contact, would have been a good outcome. It might even have been good to first determine if Eddie had actually been notified of the requirement before the febrile alarms were sounded. At the end of the story, however, I found out that the process was "as it should be" and that it would continue.

So let me get this right. They don't call Eddie and they don't call me, his boss. No, they have to call the CEO of a billion dollar subsidiary to report a *potential* pending violation of a Human Resource, albeit state-mandated, legal policy, without even validating that anything was amiss. If one simply does the practical mental exercise of multiplying this situation by a couple thousand control policies, and thousands of employees, we have totally redefined the role of the CEO. The CEO should have been *at least* highly annoyed about the process, mostly as a result of the noise coming from the five-alarm fire over something that should clearly not have been escalated. But the results were just the opposite. We had a control-based "worship experience" that was once again transformational for the organization's soul. The process was actually confirmed and the excessively mind-numbing controls were substantiated and maintained. If you don't see anything wrong with this picture, you are clearly a part of the problem. Just like the CEO in this example.

UNFUNDED MANDATES AND UNFUNDED IMAGINATION

In the world of state government in the United States, there exists a phenomenon known as "unfunded mandates." Effectively the federal government tells the states that they have to follow some new rule or process, but that they, the Feds, are not willing to provide any funding for the administration or execution of the new mandate. The message being communicated is "*You* figure out how to pay for this. We just make the rules." The same protocol exists in all organizations that lack any sense for accountability for these types of progressively weighty mandates. When control becomes a virtue, it is carried in the wind.

The other message that is simultaneously being communicated with unfunded mandates is that whatever the new mandate, *it* is now more important than anything else that was previously being doing. *It* is more important, and *it* results in a complete re-prioritization of time, unless the "mandatee" was sitting around with idle time. And to accuse the mandatee of sitting on their thumbs just adds to the insult. The mandators create a level of pressure that screams for control without the slightest understanding of its actual environmental impact.

I was in an organization where the senior management team met monthly in a setting referred to as "Business Review." These sessions were ostensibly designed to allow the organization's Relationship Managers (the key intermediaries and sales people that operated in the space between the organization and its institutional clients) to provide reports on the state of the organization's relationships, additional revenue opportunities, and any other significant strategic issues impacting the current and future state of our clients. The meetings generally went on for about three hours, with several clients being reviewed at each meeting. All the meetings were run by the firm's most senior executives.

In a particularly memorable meeting, I decided to do a little informal survey. I wondered how many questions coming from the CEO would relate to driving revenue and looking for additional profit and development opportunities, and how many would be related to controlling the business. I had a suspicion the answer would be heavily weighted toward the latter.

The survey results were fascinating in that they reflected, as was no surprise to me, the sentiments of this leader, and the sentiments of many a Mind-Head. On this particular afternoon, the CEO asked eight questions of the presenters. Five of the questions were specifically directed towards compliance, control and the management of risks. The other three questions were directed towards managing expenses. There were *no* questions or comments that in any way spoke to sales effectiveness, customer value, strategic ambition, or the future direction of the organization. There were none that were even *close*. No interpretive skills were needed in the evaluation of this brief qualitative survey.

This was the periodic meeting in the life of the organization where many of the organization's other leaders got their best sense of what was actually happening in the lives of our customers. And yet, if you just landed on the planet as an alien from Mars, and were asked what this company did based on your first experience, you would say "It does not seem to do anything . . . It just controls its activities and expenses." And that would be an apt observation. It would be different if the setting was with the Risk Management Committee. But this was a meeting with the sales and customer relationship people. It was easy to see that this organization was driven by a desire to control. The Post-Sufficiency oozed out of every pore of this organization with the imposition of one unfunded mandate after another.

SURPRISES AND ASSUMPTIONS

While the control creature is born of a million mothers, we are all students of a couple of idioms that have come to dominate much of organizational thinking. They each contain a grain of truth and several grains of falsity. We are all trained within hierarchical human institutions in the Rule of the Unexpected Surprise. This rule says that almost anything can be tolerated except the unexpected. To think about the rule for just a moment is to begin to address its absurdity. "No surprises" is a value system whose tentacles reach ever outward. It is universally assumed that the no-surprise ethic is a completely positive approach and is universally applicable. It fits in with the equally idiotic axiom regarding "assuming" of which we are all familiar.

"You know what 'assuming' stands for? It makes an A-- out of 'u' and me." The problem is that our whole lives are comprised of big sets of assumptions and the only way to avoid surprises of the *commission* variety is to make nothing happen. The only thing unique about any particular assumption is that someone decides to make it unique. The original assumption around the "no-surprises" dictum was focused on effective communications. The surprise was not the actual event, but rather the lack of communication around the event. It has now been radicalized into a version that speaks to the actual creation of the surprise itself.

You and I make hundreds of assumptions before we ever arrive at work in the morning. And to interact is to create surprise. For instance, I assume the floor is next to the bed when I get up in the morning, that the ferry is running on time, and that boats still float like they did yesterday. I assume that the Diet Coke machine at my breakfast sandwich place will be adequately stocked and that I will enjoy my preferred breakfast beverage as much today as I have everyday for the last thirty years. The point is that there is a premise working here that is inconsistent with the realities in which we inhabit. The world is full of surprises and we can't help it. And the costs to make-it-no-so are huge, and the opportunity costs are usually even larger.

We all have to make assumptions in order to interact with a world where those interactions create unknowable outcomes. Controls operate under the no-surprise rubric with little sense of their costs. Just because someone comes up with at trite little expression doesn't mean that is universally operable and effective. It may be truly dangerous. So a natural and very personal operating conundrum follows for anyone in this situation.

The question for each of us is then what we do in response to the "no-assumption no-surprise" value system. The answer is that we spend massive amounts of otherwise productive time doing "nothing that can create or allow a surprise, based on someone else's definition of what a surprise or a bad assumption actually is." All this basically means is that we are being told that sins of commission are much greater than sins of omission. It also says "We do not, or cannot, trust you." The personal downside risk created by allowing something bad to happen are greater than the risks we absorb by doing nothing of any added value.

As fear-avoiding creatures, the dually powerful messages of no-assumptions and no-surprises permeate deep into the fabric of an organization. When one constantly hears the message "control, control, control," it overwhelms all other messaging, as it becomes clear that a failure to control may be fatal. I remember hearing Walter Wriston, the former Chairman of Citigroup, make a comment to the effect that "Without risk, there is no future." Apparently not all of us agree with that, and are on a path to prove that wisdom invalid. This issue does not speak to chaos. Rather, it speaks to our organizational natures.

The alternative to cultures of control and no-surprises is not a binary insistence on something that would equate to a culture of "out-of-control." It would look more like a culture of independence and both rational and balanced accountability. The alternative is to live in the middle of the control-chaos continuum and to create an environment characterized by significant elements of trust and faith. The reason that Tocqueville was so impressed with the US is that we had, for the first time in history, said to ourselves as a civilized people that "We are going to give the control to the people, and we are going to trust them to do the right thing (my words)." That type of statement makes the French Revolution look like another boring and uneventful time in history. The revolution in France was just another version of "who controls what?" and was simply a change in *who* was doing the controlling. America was a radically different change in the world's history.

Ultimate control of one's destiny and durability is gained, and even then only in its potential form, through the ability to give up control. If the desired outcome is out-performance and durability, then excessive control is contra-indicated. It has to be. Excessive control does not kill the organization; it just provides it with a significant disability. In attempting to control, organizations essentially get what they are asking for, along with a bonus. The bonus is that they get no *positive* surprises either. They get control over some relatively modest percentage of what they are actually attempting to control, and for that they give up the things they can't control anyway. Plus, they give up most of the opportunities that would have been realized in the process. Every organization needs various types of controls; the pertinent questions are simply those of degree and approach.

Giving up personal control as a leader is very different from shifting the control to well-trained and carefully selected fiduciary agents of the organization who are significantly better representatives of the entity than the often distracted leaders. The problem gets to be that most senior people in large and successful organizations neither *can* trust (for legal and liability reasons, as a result of our often erratic regulatory and judiciary systems), nor are they *inclined* to trust individuals who they neither know, nor have they even personally met. Without trust, and with a large dose of control, nothing bad is *supposed* to happen. And if something bad does happen, the control focus often provides a reasonable alibi.

If an organization fails to invest the time and energy to both select and educate the group's members on the nature of the controls, the system will not work. And most organizations are unwilling to invest the resources to create a system where the citizens of the organization can be self-ruling. As organizations grow, the challenge becomes even more grand scale. In Post-Sufficiency, the gap between the trust that is needed and the trust that can or is granted continues to expand. We effectively create a slave state in which the charges stand and wait for the Politburo to create orders. And then we wonder why control processes proliferate to the point of organizational strangulation.

My organization was responding to a Request for Proposal (RFP) from a large institutional prospect, as was the normal practice within our industry. An RFP is just a long set of questions around which to provide the buyer a set of answers as a basis for their making a selection from a group of potential providers. The thing that was interesting about this potential RFP was its required communications protocols. Effectively, we were told that we could have no contact about this buying decision with the requesting RFP organization, other than the rigid method that was defined in the RFP. The inference was obviously that the "right" decision might be somehow adversely swayed by the dreaded intrusion of any biased or self-serving communications. The only communications that were allowed were in written form and directed through their "Procurement Office." Apparently, if the human interaction could be kept to a minimum, that would then insure the best outcome.

The pity in this situation was that the network of people in the industry was such that the decision-makers all knew each other and the trust levels were very high. The best answer would likely have been driven by a handful of phone calls. But that was not "objective" enough for an organization focused on control. This type of "human interaction" solution would have taken one percent as much time and energy, and would have rendered a better basis on which to make a decision. This was a sad state of affairs. The Mind-Head said, "You can't talk with them. They might lie to you. And besides, if they lie to you in writing we can sue their butts off." The Soul-Head responds, "Yes, but these are some of the most knowledgeable people in the business, and I have worked with them very successfully for two decades." No matter: Mind-Head 1, Soul-Head 0.

We all know that no one walks around as a leader pronouncing themselves as control-freaks, or that they are attempting to move the organization ahead through the implementation of a series of bureaucracy-building and organizationally stultifying control tactics. No leaders of any organization announce that the path to future prosperity is paved with more heavy-handedness from the center. And therein we find another root of the problem. Everyone sees the efforts at control in the same light. Controls are generally viewed as either good, or at worst, as proper and necessary. So they accumulate and the fences proliferate and then engulf.

CARRIERS OF THE CONTROL VIRUS

Controls never come from the bottom; they always come from the top of any organization. Very few member-level people in any organization say "Hey, it's Tuesday, so let's figure out a way to shine a larger light on the possibility of us doing something dreadfully wrong or entirely stupid. Something illegal might really get their attention. And let's especially focus our efforts on ways that will allow our superiors to immediately know when it happens, such as to create a simultaneous and negative feedback loop that will result in our looking really bad and likely get us fired. Then we can all suffer with the associated ugly consequences. What do you think?"

Controls are accepted as necessary, but are an insult to everyone who has to endure them. "We really don't know what it is that we want you to do, and we don't really know what it is that you are deciding, so why don't you just not do anything, and if you do, ask us before you do, and then report what you did before you do it." Really? And this is totally acceptable within Post-Sufficiency. We find ourselves on a pathologically debilitating course, that if left unchecked, leads to everyone tracking the fact that nothing is getting done. Post-Sufficient organizations are unwilling to invest in an environment where people can be trusted to make good decisions, and then attempt to solve for the underinvestment with the more "cost-effective implementation of a whole raft of rules and procedures." I have literally watched this happen. We all know that the consequences of lack of control are bad and that leadership has a right to know that certain procedures are being followed and followed well. But some organizations worship controls and other do not. The question becomes why that is so.

Our Mind-Head screams, "We have to keep this thing under complete control." Concomitantly, our Soul-Head responds, "We have to seize the future." It appears that some heads are more inclined towards this triumph over the soul than others. It also appears that the personality types that tend toward control are identifiable. One of the greatest discoveries of my life was the introduction I received to a lady by the name of Kathy Kolbe. I will do little justice to her theories, but even the rough outline of her approach to understanding the "people dynamics" within human institutions is extremely powerful.

Kolbe looked at the world in terms of a concept that she referred to as "Conative Energies." The notion is that we are individually predisposed to a set of affinities and a matching set of *energies* around four areas of endeavor. The classification system has each of us divided by the personal levels of energy we have around 1) finding and accumulating facts, 2) following through on activities, 3) coming up with new ideas, or 4) working with tangible objects. In most organizational settings the first three are applicable, while the last is generally not, except in the engineering and construction world. The first three are applicable to our discussion of controls.

We all know people who have a relentless desire and seemingly endless amount of energy attached to acquiring more information. More data is always better than less, and no amount is too much, regardless of its cost to obtain. Ask a "Fact-Finder" a question, and they will ask you for more information. Ask a Fact-Finder to make a decision and they will ask you for more information before they can make the decision. Ask a Fact-Finder to do a presentation and they will provide you with lots of data points. I once worked with a guy whose every communication ended with the same thought. Arthur ended every memo and e-mail with "... as we gather more data, we will then be in a position to make a decision." Guess how many decisions ever got made? Jack Webb was a detective in a television series in the 1960s called *Dragnet*. He was a pure Fact-Finder. "Just the facts, Ma'am" became a household expression and is the standard salute among these kindred spirits.

Those with the second set of interests and associated energies, the "Follow-Throughs," live with an energy set around following through on their task lists. And again, we all know people who fit neatly into this category. My wife is an "off-the-chart" Follow-Through. She loves having a list of things to do, and then neatly checking them off as "completed." She is a highly-trained professional. Ask a Follow-Through to get something done and they will create a list. Ask a Follow-Through to tell you how things are going, and they will pull out their lists and provide a thorough and current accounting. Ask a Follow-Through about how effective they have been in the last week, and they will tell you what percentage of the stuff on their lists got checked off. I call these people "Listees." If we stick with nineteen-sixties television shows as places to find prototypes, Jane Hathaway on the *Beverly Hillbillies* was a perfect Follow-Through. Her life was built on the notion of letting nothing fall through the cracks, and to complete all assigned tasks with brutal efficiency. My German-ancestored wife is just the same.

The third set of applicable energies as classified by Kolbe is "Quick Start." These are people stricken with a set of driving forces that compel them to come up with new and better ways to do everything. They are always thinking about the new and the different. Ask a Quick-Start to solve a problem and they will give you three potential approaches and how they came up with them. Ask a Quick-Start to look into an opportunity and they will ask you if there are any constraints around the solution, and if they can start right away. Ask a Quick-Start to actually get something *done* and they will likely run away screaming. Quick-Starts are born of ideas and that is where they must live. They are likely either your best resource or your worst nightmare. Lucille Ball, in her role as Lucy, in *I Love Lucy* is a great example of a Quick-Start. She had an idea, or likely a scheme, for every situation. You could literally see her thinking about the object of her current fascination. And poor Ricky was likely going to be negatively impacted as a result. Her example is not of a particularly positive Quick-Start, but you get the idea.

Looking at these three energy sets (and ignoring the fourth), it is Kolbe's thesis that we all possess some of each of these elements. At the same time, the amount of a particular energy associated with any of the elements may be so low that we are actually *resistant* to that element. For instance, many follow-throughs are very low on quick-start, so it is challenging for them to actually make up something new, as it simply adds to the list-of-things-to-do, and is therefore a negative contributor to getting the list completed. The implications of this theory of personal energies for organizations are myriad and profound.

To the extent that the organization's leadership is in the Fact-Finder or Follow-Through categories (and they often are seen together as a closely linked pair of energies) they are inclined by nature to move their organizations towards greater levels of control. They truly cannot help themselves, as it is literally who they are. As an antidote, they either must surround themselves with people who are more Quick-Start, or somehow otherwise compensate for their native leanings.. If you want control, find a person with Fact-Finder-Follow-Through conative energy profile. And they are literally everywhere.

Organizations with leaders and associated cultures (and organizations always take on the disposition of their leaders—and they do it very quickly) that are in the Fact-Finder and Follow-Through (FFTs) classes are especially prone to becoming Post-Sufficient. The control impulse within organizations points at those who are FFTs as a safeguard against the concern over veering into the chaos ditch. How many seasoned Chief Financial Officers become good CEOs? The answer is very few. They became a CFO (and a financial person in general) because they were Fact-Finder Follow-Throughs in the first place. Their FFT is what moved them into their field of study and vocation earlier in their life. When you find the combination of a large and successful organization and a leader in the Fact-Finder Follow-Through class, you are very likely looking at an exit strategy.

The number of mistakes that many a Corporate Board of Directors have made by exhibiting a lack of recognition of this fundamental first principle are legendary. The Boards, usually coming off a good stretch of leadership, decide to substitute *control,* as the sacrifice to the gods, for the pattern of *predictability positive outcomes* that had been established by the prior leader. But the predictability they are seeking is not what they are about to receive. They are going to get the predictable outcome of excessive levels of crippling control. Fundamentally, what the Board is saying is that they do not believe that the prior leader can be adequately replaced, and their only choice is to attempt to somehow cling to the past. Without an identified source of senior level imagination (and having seen no demonstration that the organization has within itself any abilities in this regard), they decide that they should just attempt to hold on to what they have, which is only possible in a world were causes and effects are only randomly associated.

In the real world, life is not so simple. So within a few years the mistake is obvious to everyone. Then another few years go by waiting to see if something different happens, and then another leadership change is made. All this takes a tremendous toll on both the soul of the organization and on the perception of the organization in the eyes of its publics. It took Coca Cola ten years to recover their soul when the Company lost Roberto Goizueta, and replaced him with their former CFO. I blame the Board of Directors of Home Depot for destroying their corporate soul by placing an overpaid Six Sigma guy from GE to run a formerly soulish company lead by a dynamic and visionary leader by the name of Arthur Blank. The new leader nearly killed Home Depot within a few short years, and the resulting damage is now easily seen many years after he was asked to leave. Everyone wants to blame the former leader for his faulty strategy moves. I simply "fault" him for being a FFT.

As FFT leaders are enamored with both data and lists, they tend to rely on those tools as the instruments of their future success. The reality of the situation is that data, in and of itself, does not create any imagination, and lists don't create any meaningful prioritization. But data and lists feel very good in the hands of an FFT. They are all the FFT can hope for. In assembling the data, the goal of the FFT is not to decide, but rather to know and understand . . . and thereby avoid "list-breaks." In making lists, the goal of the FFT is not to evaluate, but to complete. Data and lists are very sterile and neat. And if you are an FFT, those are real virtues. Data and lists, on the other hand, do not inspire the hopes of an organization; they have a tendency to do just the opposite.

Post-Sufficient institutions believe *everyone* is a potential source of a control problem and that supposition drives their actions. Like liberal politics, Post-Sufficiency seeks to punish the many for the sins of the few. The oft false notion of a rat amongst us contaminates the whole environment. Instead of seeking out and killing the rat, they treat the rest of the group for rabies. I used to say that we needed a ceremonial hanging once-in-awhile just to make a statement about our value systems. This was not a message to the bad amongst us; it was a message directed at the good. Effectively, I was communicating that we punish the bad guys around here and let everyone else do the stuff we hired them to do. And for which we have confidence in their ability to do. More important is the real statement that we trust them to do it. Excessive controls are the punishment of the many for the sins of the few.

Insufficient organizations start with passion and then use common sense and insights as a basis for the development of creative solutions. Post-Sufficient organizations start with a proclivity for safety and complete predictability and use the tool of compliance to manifest environments of control. The endless loops that are created based on the chosen starting points are highly predictive. And no progressions are linear. They are all exponential . . . both going up and going down. As a result, the selections of FFTs as leaders create a set of results that are more dramatically negative than otherwise be expected: and they happen quickly.

SEPARATION OF MIND AND THE IMAGINATION

Post-Sufficient cultures see Mindishness and creating the "right answers" as master. In the Land of Large and Successful Organizations, more is being asked to be "reported up," than vision and inspiration is being "communicated down." The leadership of Post-Sufficient organizations yells down at the organization, "Is everything under control?" The question should be, "Are we taking advantage of our opportunities?" Or, "What new ideas do you have to make us a better organization?" The under-control question is one that is always looking backwards. Effectively the question becomes "Have we done anything in the past, including both our decisions and actions, that will come back to bite us?" It is hard to control that which has not yet occurred. On the other side, the opportunities and "ideas" questions are forward-looking.

Looking backward, by definition, creates no new sense of hopefulness. Looking forward at least provides the opportunity.

I was taking one of the many compliance and ethics training courses mandated by my organization when I came upon the following that was embedded in some anti-money laundering training:

"The liability imposed upon you as an individual is daunting. *The prospect of a prison sentence for doing nothing may seem unfair* (my italics added). However, if we are to reduce money laundering and terrorist financing, the prompt reporting of suspicions is vital." Just pause and reflect on the italicized portion of that message for a moment.

This message was being read and inflicted on people making forty thousand dollars a year. And we wonder why people don't provide excellent service or venture into using their brains. If I think I might have to go to jail if someone slips something past me, does the organization actually think I might give a rip about providing good service? "The prospect of a prison sentence for doing nothing may seem unfair." No kidding. Is this our home? No, this is just a "welcome message" to Post-Sufficiency-Land.

This message essentially communicates that the crimes of the system are so significant, that *you* cannot be trusted to simply do a good and responsible job without being threatened with a new piece for your wardrobe that says "inmate" on the back. The organization was forcing its associates at gun-point to police the negative actions of others. Might this cause the death of the soul of an individual or an organization? I got a "Certificate of Completion" for finishing the course. I guess that was supposed to make me feel better. Seems I forgot to get it framed. The real problem in this scenario, like so many others, represents one where the emotional and human price of this control-based action is immediately paid. The bill has just not yet arrived in the mail.

The bottom line is that organizations sacrifice their imaginations on the altar of control and then fail to recognize the impact of the sacrifice of their new mindset. They force themselves to live completely apart from faith and trust and their Soul-Heads become brain dead. The messaging sometimes looks like this: "The Manager's *Toolkit* is a reference for managers on Human Resources *processes* and management *practices*, including a wide variety of links to the enterprise's *policies* and *procedures*. It has been developed to support managers across the organization by providing *tools* to help *manage* people effectively.

The *toolkit* addresses *processes* and *procedures* for new managers as they acclimate into their new roles, as well as to refresh knowledge and skills for experienced managers (all italics are my additions)." I did not make this up. This is the language of control. In three sentences the notions of "tools and policies" were mentioned eight times. Note also the reference to "across the organization." This "thing" is being centralized and spread across the organization in a uniform fashion which some consider a marvelous mindish advancement. It is also interesting the use of the word "manage." Manage is a control word, amongst so many others that could have better described our human interactions. Even in attempts to mobilize people for action within control-based organizations, the words come out in the language of rigidity and oppression. This one came out of Human Resources.

When organizations get to the point where judgment is put in the hands of the *system*, humans are degraded and so is the resulting output. When IBM's' Deep Blue beat the world chess champion, Gary Kasporov, the world rejoiced. From my standpoint, it was a sad day in the life of the world. Committees, approval processes, algorithms, codes and policies creep into the life of the organization and they become either the replacement or excuse for making sound judgments. "What does the data say?" is the question. The data never says anything! The data is only just data until judgment is applied. Post-Sufficient organizations forget that last fairly important application step.

The control system grows in a ratchet-like mechanism, with each new layer being supported from retraction, while others are added. The system of fences grows, and the fence-designers and fence-builders and fence-menders grow in their officious influence. Fence People are usually very nice people and are always very proud of their children. And they come by their craft naturally and with significant support. And the Labyrinth of fences is expanded.

Alexis de Tocqueville summarized very eloquently the impact of the control fences in human institutions (focusing specifically on governments, but the implication is clearly broader) in a way that will likely never be repeated in such a forceful way:

> "The will of man is not shattered, but softened, bent, and guided: men are seldom forced by it to act, but they are constantly restrained from acting: such a power does not destroy, but it prevents existence; it does not tyrannize, but it compresses, en-

ervates, extinguishes, and stupefies a people till each nation is reduced to be nothing better than a flock of timid and industrious animals, of which the government is the shepherd."

The methods change over time and in different circumstances, but the psychology remains a fixed element in our organizational lives. The "compression and enervation" occur in a variety of forms. But the eventual death of the organization is what Tocqueville was predicting. In human institutions around the world, this challenge is created by the will of the fence builders. The first of these contractors are the specialists. The second are the tacticians, and the third are the minimizers. We will start with the specialists.

DEATH BY SPECIALIZATION

As a ten year old child growing up Northern Minnesota, my family went over to the Mesabi Iron Range in Northeastern Minnesota for a summer vacation. While some amongst us may not see this as a dream vacation, I thought it was great. We toured some of the big open pit iron ore mines and a few mining museums. We also did a tour of an underground mine that I thought was very frightening. It was from that underground mine experience that I derived "Nygaard's Allegory of the Cave."

What I learned that day was a few things about the utility of canaries and donkeys. The canary story made sense, but caused me no palpable feelings of injustice or gloom. The donkey story, however, haunts me to this day. What they told me was that once a donkey was lowered into the mine, that it would never come out alive. The little devil would work pulling iron ore along a set of tracks until it died, and then they would hoist its lifeless body up the mine shaft. But that wasn't even the sad part. The sad part—the tour guide told me—was that after a few months, the donkey, having been exposed to very limited light for a long period of time, would go blind. That just didn't seem right to me. How was it that this particular animal's capabilities and potential contribution could be so narrowed that other capabilities had to be jettisoned? Seeing the tremendous sacrifice of these little beasts made me sad. It was the same reaction that I had to the kid who wore the "seeing you lose" t-shirt.

When I walk into many large organizations today, I see the same thing. I observe high-utility individuals walking around without their sight. They are operating within a narrow range of specialization of function that has rendered them blind to the rest of what is going on around them. They are contributing to the team, and yet have no idea in what direction they are pulling, or what happens to the load when it gets to the end of the line. The problems are two-fold. The first is that of the dispiriting impact of being a cog in the wheel. The second is even worse. The second arises when the blind decide they know where it is that we are collectively going, or should be going, and quite naturally seek to take us all there. Even blind donkeys have pride, and they have goals, and they have a will to power. We should expect nothing less. We even admire the character and perseverance of anyone who has but little hope doing the best they can. And it is in this set of emotions and their impact on organizations that we see Death by Specialization.

"Our goal is to be as thorough as possible." This line came out of William Haley, Compliance Department, in response to a question in a meeting about the upcoming initiative to review our client base to determine if we had any additional financial exposure heretofore undiscovered. He was a control-person. I couldn't help but think of a man with a similar name, William Paley, who wrote *The Blind Watchmaker* and was, at least for a moment, amused. Of course, this was the only answer that was likely acceptable in terms of his role. This was his new job and he was going to do it well: "To be as thorough as possible."

But was this *really* the goal? Really . . . seriously . . . was that the goal? The problem was there was no end in his mind as to the amount of work that could be envisaged with his new-found responsibilities. And there really wasn't. This was just one gaping Black Hole. He knew what all good bureaucrats know and that is how to expand their little world of authority. I felt very sorry for the guy. He was now in-charge of our new "Know Your Customer" requirements, and he was going exhaust the task. Or, exhaust himself in pursuit of his now noble endeavor.

He didn't recognize that his "thorough as possible" goal was very misguided. In his mind, it was not. If we *were* going to be as thorough as possible, it would kill our business. Our clients simply wouldn't put up with an additional stream of interrogation and surveillance. The goal should have been to be as effective as possible at reducing our exposure, while balancing the risks and potential rewards. And if you asked Bill if that was his goal, to be balanced, he would quickly agree. But what else would you expect him to say. Specialists do what specialists are asked to do. Specialists have a tendency to torture that which they do not understand and cannot control. The functionalization has the tendency to reduce the size of the playing field. And the relative span of control of the functionaries goes up accordingly.

The problem within large and successful organizations, given the interest in the control of everything, is that the pendulum of power shifts consistently over time in favor of the specialists, who are ill-equipped to handle it. They are also ill-equipped to relinquish it. Rather than continuing to invest the power to make decisions with those who are in constant contact with the value created by the organization, the cynical nature of leadership unknowingly shifts the locus of power towards those with the "special knowledge", the *gnosis* that is required to *objectively* handle the issues and to make the right and informed decisions. The fact that many specialists are completely lacking in a broad enough view to make any sort of informed decisions is subsumed by their alleged objectivity and lack of "conflict of interest." The complexity of the world screams out for the need for deep specialists to create and solve for complex equations. The complexity of the world does not cry out to have these same people make all the decisions.

Specialization is one of those insidious factors within a mature business that feels very good to everyone, but creates massive long-term downside risk. Specialization becomes a surrogate for creativity and imagination in the view of the Mind-Head. The question that must be continually asked as the organization gets bigger is "What percentage of the thoughts and activities of the total enterprise is being performed by the internal and semi-blind activities of the specialists (particularly those with control functions), versus those involved in the "real business" of serving the various constituencies?" The short-term demands for productivity result in large percentages of what is being done within the institution coming from people with very little understanding of what their efforts produce. At some juncture the hinge point is reached where additional efforts by these people is very counter-productive. And we basically beg for this to be true.

It was relayed to me one day that I had became an "M" in the Global Pay Structure. Oh happy day. I was required to attend a mandatory training class on my new status and the implications of the new grading system in my management role. I guess I could now be classified by my genus, species and placement in the Global Pay Structure. And everyone on this particular conference call (and there were dozens of us), thought this new compensation structure and the related evaluation process was in the category of the sacrosanct. The participants were simply gushy with praise in the plenitude of our organizational accomplishment. "This is such a wonderful thing for the organization, and I am glad we finally got it done" expressed the sentiment of the group. I could have chimed in with "I see this as the less-than-worthless further de-humanization of an egalitarian and control-focused entity that has totally lost touch with what it takes to be effective in a world where real human beings live." But I decided it might not have been an appropriate end to the call.

We all want to know others and to be known by them. My goal was not to be an "M". I wanted to add a question at the end of the call, "Why do we think that being labeled with a coding strip, akin to the one on my laptop, should make me feel like anything other than an insignificant and lost sheep out in some endless pasture?" Was the perceived equity or systemization that was to be potentially gained in this system worthy of the dehumanizing effect? Is our quest for cosmic order and justice so strong that we would rather be treated somehow more "fairly" than being acknowledged as a unique contributor?

"If we can specialize it, centralize it, codify it, and formulize it, then we can control it" becomes the mantra of the specialist. More critically, the lack of technical understanding of broad-based generalists puts them at a disadvantage in organizations that come to prize technical ability, and the associated exactitudes, over general leadership and strategic abilities. And the result is that we end up with very technical, but effectively blind and soul-less organizations. If you hear more than three acronyms are used in single sentences within an enterprise, be concerned.

The truth of the expression that "five minutes of experience is worth five years of study" is evident within human institutions. Experiential training is contextual, whereas study lacks a framework on which to connect the trappings of the newly acquired knowledge. If life divided itself up into nice little manageable pieces, excessive specialization would make more sense. But life is not like otolaryngology, it is more like general practice.

DEATH BY TACTICS

The story is told of a scene in the US Civil War where the infamous Southern General, Nathan Bedford Forrest (a subsequent founder of the Klu Klux Klan) was in the midst of a heated battle. At one point in the exchange of gunfire, one of his Lieutenants approached him and said, "General, we are in real trouble. We are surrounded on all sides." The General, it is said, looked at the Lieutenant with fire in his eyes and said "Excellent. Then we can attack in all directions." And apparently he meant it. In a military strategy—in any situation with few alternatives—that approach may make sense. In the real world, it is almost universally a less-than-desirable strategic conclusion.

In a world of control, dominated by the impact of specialists, one of the endearing palliatives is an endless list of tactics. When all else is looking challenging, a good and long list of tactics is often just what we are looking for. Tactics are defined as activities with a limited time frame and a measurable set of outcomes, often binary as to disposition. Either they get done or they don't. We either completed the tactic or we did not, thus making measurement infinitely simple. Tactics are always attractive in a world where the outcomes of our actions often take years and even decades to unfold (and often with uncertain correlations as to causation), and where it is required that each individual participant in the organization can demonstrate that they are currently getting something of value done.

"If we cannot watch them, then the only alternative is to measure their output. And we will measure the output that is measurable, whatever that happens to be." And large lists of tactics often fit that bill very nicely. Or they are the best solution that can be found. It is usually a safe course of action to get twenty relatively useless things done within most large and successful organizations, than to discover the cure for cancer. The lack of finding the cure will not even be noticed, but the completed list of twenty tactics will get you promoted.

It is always amusing to engage in conversations with individuals within Post-Sufficient cultures as they usually begin with the greeting "I am just swamped. I can't tell you whether I am coming or going. But, hey, that sure beats the alternatives!" The last part of that statement is rather dubious. And the more distant the individual contributors are from the organization's leadership, the more important the expression of personal control over an unfathomable list of tactics becomes. Lists are good things. Lists-as-gods are an evil of the first order.

In its advanced form, this pendulum shift towards tactics and lists ultimately can take over the strategic process. The organization's strategy simply *becomes* the list. If the biggest abdication of leadership is telling the organization to "just do everything" (as leadership can't really decide on and prioritize any specific courses of action), then lists are the manifestation of that strategic fecklessness. Often times the progression of the career of a leader has seen them being rewarded for their ability to "manage their list." "Nothing ever falls through the cracks when John is involved . . . the guy really keeps all his ducks in a row." But who cares if the ducks are in a row and walking right down the middle of Interstate 95 just outside of Jersey City at five PM on a Friday afternoon?

In *Barbarians at the Gate*, written by Bryan Burrough and John Helyar, the story is told of what was ultimately the largest leveraged buyout at that time. Ross Johnson, the protagonist, had just taken over the leadership role at American Brands. He is staring at piles of strategic planning documents representing the management's plans to continue the long skein of very modest, but consistently increased earnings, of which they were very proud. As the story goes, Mr. Johnson pushes the documents to the side of the table and says something to effect: "This is not business planning. Just tell me the two are three things we are going to do that are going to make a significant difference."

He was dealing with an organization that had lost its imagination and had "resigned itself" to creating reams and reams of incredibly accurate but totally worthless planning documentation. It was a million little tactics all strung end to end. This was "planning by stapler." He was also saying that the *organization* needed to be the source of imagination, and that it was not his job to come up with all the big and important ideas. He needed more than tactics. He needed important ideas and he needed priorities, and he needed the rationale for both.

The Personal Management Development Form that I needed to complete for one of my subordinates, to help them better develop their skills, interestingly had a "Date Completed" column next to the various articulated developmental needs. So I submitted (for one of my star associates) an entry indicating a strategy to "further development of an executive leadership framework and philosophy." This was a person with tremendous energy and drive, and a wealth of technical skills that were the envy of the whole company. What she needed was to develop a set of inter-personal and strategic skills that would allow her to effectively move into senior leadership. My plan was to work closely with her over the course of the next few years to challenge her to think at a broader level.

On the Development Form under the column for "Date completed" I indicated "ongoing." The form soon came back to me from Human Resources and what was indicated was that I needed to place a "completion date" on the form. I had not apparently followed the instructions appropriately and someone in Human Resources couldn't "check that form off" as being completed. The assumption, I guess, was that one can effectively develop into an executive on a schedule, and that it should be ultimately discernable when the process had been completed. They were indicating that we should put a date next to her name, or maybe on her forehead, when we were *done*. In doing with great efficiency that which shouldn't be done, it can easily be concluded that we are truly not making any progress.

DEATH BY ORGANIZATION

The first time I saw Abbott and Costello's *Who's on First* I thought I had died and gone to comedy-heaven. I almost couldn't believe how anyone could have come up with something as stunningly humorous as that skit. The "disconnect" between the meaning of the words being spoken and those being comprehended represented a magical microcosm of so much of human interaction. The question of "Who's on first?" often comes to mind as we watch organizations struggle to figure out how to orchestrate and organize themselves around their need to advance. When an organization has seven people, the number of organizational options is, by definition, quite limited. At a few hundred people, the number of choices outnumbers the quantity of people by many times. As you get to tens-of-thousands, you need a staff of a few thousand just to keep track of the whole affair. What is it that is being organized and for what purpose? If ten or twenty thousand people out there doing-their-own-thing (without any structure or organization), is not the right choice, then what is the best answer? And on what basis could one create the maximal orchestration?

There are some very obvious ends to be met in organizational structures. Fostering good internal communications is a starting point. Creating an effective decision-making process is another. Developing functional aspects of the organization in an optimal way is yet a third. And the list goes on. I would suggest, however, the control virus seeps into the organizational design aspect of large and successful organizations in ways that undermine their future stability and success. Any and all organizational structures can be effectively undone by attempts to utilize them to control for all outcomes.

So the simple question is asked: "How does the organizational structure and our leadership team further our control and related control-based communications agenda?" versus, "How does our organizational structure and our leadership contingent further our creative ends, and our needs to provide the flexibility and freedom that allows our people to maximize their contributions." Post-Sufficient organizations rely heavily on the first as the basis for their structures and very little on the second.

Who invented matrix reporting? Undoubtedly, it was the same person who decided that belts and suspenders were somehow fashionable. The culture of control simply uses the mechanism of this organizational approach to steal the life from the victim, which happens to be itself. The same logic is applied in assembling large groups of disparately backgrounded people to come up with solutions to issues where both everyone and no one has an understood role. The message looks something like: "We really don't trust any individuals within the organization to do anything on their own. So we are hedging our bets by bringing a structure into play that will create absolute mediocrity, but with a much better sense of control." The question is not whether more ideas coming from a group are better than those coming from a single individual, as that is likely, in most cases true. The question is a function of the confusion as to priorities, the associated gridlock, and the organizational ossification that sets in as a result of the reliance on groups versus individuals. Two heads are better than one, only when in-fact two heads are shown to be better than one, and not by definition.

The question of organizational effectiveness becomes one of the loci of decisions. As organizations get bigger, they have a tendency to move the locus up the organizational chart. And to the extent that the decisions are moved down, they are moved down with "strings of controls" attached. The need is to constantly push it back down, but without the strings, and with the needed level of context and authority. The problem is that most organizations don't make the investment in the decision-making support, both technical and human, of those who are the closest to the customer. Rather, many organizations will invest in a layer of jobs whose function it is simply to tell the people above them what the people below them are doing. These people don't have real jobs.

The cost of communications within all the layers creates a huge opportunity cost, the magnitude of which is rarely grasped by the Post-Sufficient. The "tweeners" are also filters that sanitize and distort. Rather than investing in people, such that spans of control can be very broad, we see just the opposite. Empowerment without mobilization is comical and disastrous. Management from on-high is the alternative and is equally disastrous. Mobilization with adequate priority setting and resourcing, training and trust is magic.

Political thinking in organizations can also lead to the pretext that the only knowledge level to sufficiently manage the whole of the enterprise is at the center. The result is that the answer to almost any number of organizational ailments is to centralize the function. "If we brought all of this stuff into a single location, under a single leader, the problems would all just melt away." Didn't we just recently experience the twentieth century? My belief and experience is that most centralization efforts fail. And they fail for the same reasons over and over again. The primary reason for the consistent failure is that the people in the center lose contact with both the broader organization and the value the organization brings to its customers. They develop unique and non-complimentary worldviews which drive tribalism and chaos. They simply become the observable universe, at least to themselves. Whenever I hear the cry go out for centralization, I immediately ask myself how many years it will last before the function is once again decentralized.

Centralization to the human ear sounds to us about five times better than it actually is, and yet we listen to the same story again and again, and fall victims to its pretentiousness. The reasons are always the same. On paper, the advantages of centralization from a purely mechanistic standpoint are immense. When you add the element of humanity, the spreadsheets can all be better used to line a bird cage. Control has value, as do scale economics. They just have much *less* value than we usually construe. Unless scale through centralization is *the* strategy, it is usually an elusive and generally effete goal. To the Mind-Head, centralization is eye-candy.

"Escalation Cultures," alternatively, may represent the epitome of decision and organizational control. When everything has to escalate its way up through the hierarchy to get attention, then the management comes to see themselves as heroes, and they begin to define their personal value propositions by how many "big problems" they can solve. This would be as opposed to viewing their functions as seeking ways to avoid the problems in the first place, or to actually drive the organization forward in some strategically positive way.

At H&R Block Financial Advisors I had a heart-to-heart with many of the senior operations leaders. I said to them, "I want you all to be totally transparent (unseen) to the organization!" I was asking them to step away from their direct problem solving roles. I was asking them to quit talking with customers who had service issues. This was asking more of the group than one might imagine. They were all superheroes in the organization, as they could fix absolutely anything, even at significant personal cost. They were revered for their commitment to quality. The problem was they were not doing their jobs. I loved them all, but told them they really had to go back to building their people, so as to avoid the problems in the first place. I asked them to work on positioning our organization for improvement through the use of a more personally engaged group of associates who could then contribute to better meeting the future needs of our clients. At a core level, their direct reports needed to be shown more respect and dignity. And that is what they did. And everyone was happier. Someone just had to ask. When the cannons are rolling on the deck, it is important to praise the heroes who secure them. But it is more important is to find out why they were rolling around in the first place.

I gather that the reason we refer to "organizations" is that their goal is to organize something. When the goal becomes sequentially more one of controlling as opposed to organizing and optimizing, the effect of the effort is sub-optimized. When organizational decisions are made with a pretext of making certain that something is kept under control, it should be determined first why the *something* is a problem in the first place. Organizational structures and the associated communications and relational protocols are very soulish things. When we treat them in a utilitarian fashion, and use our Mind-Heads to determine how to best organize the entire scheme, we de-humanize and demoralize the institution.

DEATH BY BUDGETS

The problem with budgets is legendary and the reason is easy to see. The lack of perceived connection between the budget and the observed realities of those subject to the budget has a dramatic impact on organizations. Post-Sufficient management comes to think of managing revenues and managing expenses as if they were moral equivalents. The problem with that line of thinking is that while the math is right (a dollar of top line and a dollar of expenses impact the bottom line the same, at least mathematically), the focus is wrong. What happens is that because expenses are susceptible to a choke-chain approach to management, they get a disproportional focus.

"When we get through this next round of expense management, we are going to shift the focus back to revenues." And that day rarely if ever shows up. Post-Sufficient companies just come to love expenses relatively more than they love revenue. They evolve to a point where they take their revenues for granted. Expenses act more like machines, while revenues act more like people. Expenses are subject to math calculations. Revenues are subject to the vicissitudes of the market place. Expenses are infinitely more predictable and they don't, or cannot, fight back. When you have more to lose in not managing expenses than you have to gain in driving additional revenue, you reach an inflection point that marks one of the signposts of Post-Sufficiency.

I was sitting in a meeting where the organization's Chief Information Officer was discussing a twenty-million dollar savings that had been wrought by his staff. This was a good thing. He then asked the group of sales people, "And what level of revenue do we need to produce to generate twenty-million dollars of bottom-line savings?" The dutiful answer was "A hundred million dollars," as we had twenty percent margins. The problem with this is that while we did have twenty percent overall profit margins, we were operating at a scale that allowed eighty percent of all additional revenues to fall to the bottom-line. So the real answer should have been twenty-five million dollars of revenue. And yet the organization glamorized the expense savings at the expense of a revenue focus, simply as the result of a bad view of the economics, and a very bad expense theology.

Cost containment can morph itself into an organization's most core value. It can attain the status of an organizational virtue; a first-principle. The presence of existing and significant revenues (subliminally impacted the thinking of management), coupled with a large percentage of associates within the organization that have no contact with anything related to revenue, provides a climate where the "needle moves" from a state of some level of the balanced importance of revenues and expense management, towards a state where expense management becomes *the* game. The contrast with small and Insufficient businesses could not be more stark.

In a small business, every effort of the organization is focused on finding the next customer and driving the next sale. Minimizing expenses in Insufficient organizations is simply a given. In these organizations, everyone knows if money is being needlessly wasted. In Post-Sufficient organizations, one gets the sense that the machine is greased with expense management, not additional revenues.

The real issue becomes the basis on which expense management is created. The experience of most managers within large companies is that the senior leadership looks at the revenue projections, subtracts the projected expenses, finds a gap between that result and the "needs of the business" and then subtracts yet another level of expense support. The logic of the expense reductions then becomes "to make the numbers work." Making the numbers work, and making the business work are only tangentially related. And they might be correlated at a "minus one" correlation coefficient level. But the isolation of senior leaders makes the process more clinically neat, and much less perceptually bloody.

In many organizations, the budget lays claim to being master of all. Budgets, even if they could be done perfectly (and they cannot), only reflect the thinking of one point in time, which would be fine except for the fact that tomorrow comes. Budgets are control mechanisms and should be viewed as such. They are also substitutes for ongoing judgment. Budgets are very significant and valuable until they become disconnected and the object of coercive passions. What is needed is some process that allows organizations to determine at what level of expense management is the enterprise moving into a "zone of negative marginal utility."

In any situation, with perfect foreknowledge, there is an inherent support level that will maximize the future outcomes. Most in management don't know at what point the marginal utility curve goes negative. They are just not close enough to what is going on to know. By the curve, think of a matrix with the horizontal access representing increasing pressure on expense management, and vertical access being organizational financial results as measured over the long-term. Both of these measures, albeit challenging to quantify, represent a real set of trade-offs for leadership. When expense management is "pushed too far," the first level of organizational reaction might be described as "expense management stress." The second level is "brand image destruction." The third level is "irrevocable damage to the entity."

Associates become increasingly demoralized as they slide down the curve and their souls are scarred because that is what their reaction should be. They see the damage being created and have no ability to fix it. While it is possible to effectively manage the organization somewhere near the first level, the problem is that levels two and three are reached very quickly, and no one in authority is willing to effectively push back before it is too late. I once heard a very senior leader for "The Americas Region" (representing billions of dollars of financial service revenues), when asked about a concern that we had pushed expense management to the point where it was hurting the long-term prospects for the business say in response, "Isn't that what you get paid to do?" This was to infer that irrespective of the level of expense reductions, a highly-paid leader should be able to figure out how to effectively deal with it. What an idiotic statement. Why not just reduce expenses to zero using that logic. Additionally what was being said was, "Don't ever ask that stupid question again, as *I* will make the determination as to our expense levels . . . and I will also make the decisions as to your future within the organization."

Most people within large organizations think about "managing within the budget". And they simply prioritize projects within the construct of the budget. This is as opposed to looking at opportunities in terms of returns on investment, or even thinking about how to manage expenses within a framework of increasing revenues and managing margin levels. We do not exist in a capital constrained world, but it seems we often act like it. Budgets should clarify and ratify a set of *principles* being deployed to make the organization better. Instead they often end up clarifying and ratifying that the organization's leaders are completely disconnected from reality. This is very tough stuff to deal with. But the Post-Sufficient deal with it very poorly.

The very imperfect connection between the investment in expenses and the financial results experienced over time is a problem for every human institution. "We make X investment today and we anticipate Y result tomorrow" is repeated a million times a minute in the world we live in. The challenge is that the "regression analysis," which attempts to strip out the non-correlated variables and drive causal connections is hard to do in the best situations. The complexities of the processes, the number of factors working in those processes, and the shear enormity of data points renders the correlation analysis mute. As a result, less investment in expense support is the default. "We really don't know what the right answer is, so let's just lower the expenses." And this is not necessarily a stupid decision. Rather, it is the only logical decision given a lack of any concrete evidence, insight, or incentive, to act otherwise.

The insanity of expense management efforts in large and successful organizations is universally known. But one example will comprise enough of what messages are being sent in these situations as to suffice for our purposes. A friend of mine told me that an AT&T Vice President was called by the AT&T Expense Police and asked whether four-dollar lattes were really necessary and why the individual did not stop for gas in Oakland to refill his rental car versus paying the rental car company to fill the tank. The messaging can be summarized fairly simply: 1) You are not an adult and we are not going to treat you like one, 2) Spending an hour of Expense Police time to "save" a few dollars is worth the investment of our time, 3) We truly lack context around managing our business expenses and investments, 4) The expense inmates are running the asylum, 5) Expenses are more important than revenues, 6) We don't appreciate your 16 hour days, nor your concern about stopping for gas in Oakland at 2 AM.

Even a saner example of this problem was evidenced by my company's sincere request for me to limit my travel expenses to ninety percent of the prior year's budget. Everyone on the sales team was asked to do the same. The problems were obvious. I had already gone to great personal inconvenience the year before to limit my expenses, so the opportunities were already limited. But more significantly, it is undoubtedly the case that the company should have asked me to travel more to generate more revenues during the tough times. The problem again, was that there was no ability to link expenses with future income. But we *could* link travel expenses with current period profits. So, as a result, ninety percent was my new target. Of interest, the sales team was applauded for saving three million dollars in expenses that year, the equivalent of acquiring just *one* new client. One.

The government is the perfect example of control-laced Post-Sufficiency. They have almost no incentive to do anything other than control. The relative percentage of control activities within the various elements of government, versus activities that actually produce something of value, is the standard against which all organizations might manage themselves. In any sort of competitive situation, if the control activities represent more than forty percent (and I am just making these numbers up) of what the government ratio is, it is a real problem. The risking of capital to produce future gains is not seemingly relevant to the function of government. So we end up creating universal client and member experiences like the Department of Motor Vehicles, the Post Office or the IRS. And these are the *customer-centric* parts of the government. As organizations, we should ask ourselves "How much are we beginning to look like the government?" The sad truth is, however, that the bigger human organizations get, the more they begin to look like the government. And one needs look no further than the rampant desire to control as the cause of the dysfunction.

* * * * *

We are now brought back to the questions of under-performance and durability. The linkages are direct. As organizations build their formulas for success and vow to limit their forecasting risk, the control seeds are planted and flourish as if growing in a well-watered and sunlit garden. More and more energy is deployed against the control goals and less and less energy is directed towards doing things that actually create value. And this would include value both internal and external to the organization. The choice is effectively being made that the organization is going to die slowly as opposed to immediately. Controls are the weapon-of-choice of those looking to assassinate the soul of a human institution. Nothing can match the soul-destroying, anger creating, and purpose-destroying power of inflicting a pogrom of rules on a person or a system. In the absence of liberty, there is an absence of creativity and risk-assumption. In the absence of the latter two notions, all progress ceases. Controls are an ineffective substitute for a whole raft of desperately needed organizational capabilities and attitudes. They are like morphine in a very painfully hurt person. The pain is removed, but nothing is fundamentally improving.

The control-chaos continuum causes organizations to seek comfort in control to a degree that destroys their ability to manage their futures. The imposition of FFT leaders and a raft of specialists within organizations results in a hyperkinetic focus on elements of the organization that are not foundational to their ongoing success. The control virus attaches itself to the organization's strategy and manifests itself in simply a strategy made up of disparate lists. The virus inflicts the core organizational functions of managing scarce resources via the human design of the organization. The organization's Mind-Heads observe their perceived control as a work of art. The Soul-Heads observe it as devoid of trust and faith. They see the impact of the chaos-avoidance mechanism of an organization broken into tiny, functionally-controlled pieces and loath its complete lack of imagination and resultant and complete loss of hope.

5

"It Just Runs"

> Large and successful organizations struggle to make the "success formula" and the controls work in the absence of a Soul-Head. The result is a complete break-down in the cohesion of the community. Decision Dysfunction confounds even the Mind-Head and ultimately destroys the human institution. Post-Sufficiency has now run its course.

THE STORY IS TOLD of an exhibit at the World's Fair held in Chicago in the early part of the twentieth century which drew much attention. As the story goes, the exhibitor assembled a massive and impressive collection of pulleys and levers, bells and whistles, and assorted other moving parts that gathered the fairgoer's attention quite readily. The "machine" was an impressive collection of technology and apparent innovation, with an attached sense of mystery. It was not, however, readily apparent what the function of the machine was. At one point, the inventor of the machine was addressed by an onlooker: "That thing is really impressive, but what does it actually do?" The answer to the question by its inventor: "It really doesn't *do* anything; *it just runs.*"

The logical next question to ask is why anyone would intentionally assemble a machine that doesn't do anything, or serve any particular function. The only reason that I can come up with (outside of creating something considered "art") is to make a point. In the case of the exhibitor at the World's Fair it was, I can only presume, an intentional act designed to make a point. Unfortunately, in many analogous replications of this exhibit as seen in large and successful organizations, the intentionality is absent. And so is any art form. The reality of "it just runs" is too often observed.

All organizations are a function of a collective set of decisions that have been made over the organization's past. Insufficient organizations have a very thorough understanding of the impact of those decisions and the implications for their future. Post-Sufficient organizations are not as fortunate. It is just much harder in a large institutional framework to see the impact of one's decisions. The lack of understanding of the organizations' roots, its historic trajectory, and the associated implications on the rest of the organization create a void in large organizations that is very debilitating. I often see organizations advertising how long they have been in existence and I wonder if that is supposed to be a good thing or a bad thing. History is only as good as memory and the ability to effectively synthesize those historic learnings in the current context. History is only good in its ability to drive better decisions going forward. And many large organizations are long on history and short on the positive application of the institutional memory.

When Chase Bank moved into California, they advertised themselves proudly as having "two-hundred years of banking experience." They were telling us they have been around long enough to have learned a bunch of lessons and they were inferring that they would craftily use those learnings to serve their clients' needs. I had to laugh. This was the same two-hundred year old bank that had literally just received billions of dollars in US government bailout money. How smart were they again? Chase may have been the best run bank in America at the time of the government bailouts. I really don't know. It was just interesting to me that they would attempt to use *experience* as their market penetration driver in the wake of the government bailout.

The connection between the machine at the World's Fair and many large organizations is that the decision processes become so stilted that they begin to create an arc that bends ever more steadily in the direction of "it just runs." And not only are the machine's outputs lowered in terms of their ultimate functionality, the machine actually slows over time. Clearly, the machine doesn't slow to a stop, or quit producing outputs of any value. Rather, it is just sub-optimizes its effectiveness to the point where it is replaced by a new machine (owned and directed and staffed by someone else), that is in some way more effective. And ineffective machinery gets sent to the landfill housing once proud organizations. The reasons are linked specifically to the organizations devolving and obdurate decision-making capabilities.

But why would old, established, large and successful organizations *not* continue to improve in their ability to make decisions over time and over their organizational expansion? Wouldn't the addition of all those new brains into the organization, on top of the accumulated organizational memory, most naturally make them an unstoppable force within whatever sphere they operate? And doesn't enough momentum get established at some point in an organization's life that it keeps going indefinitely without additional decision-making and positive intellectual forces being applied to it?

All individuals within an organization represent some level and direction of "force." The question is whether those forces are complementary, or whether they represent a form of vector mathematics. More important than the relative intensity or magnitude of the application of those forces is whether they are operating in harmony. Bad decisions can be effectively responded to by organizations that have the ability to operate in reasonable lock-step. Good strategies can, alternatively, be destroyed by organizations whose decisioning mechanisms are impaired or non-functional.

Well-functioning decisioning mechanisms require a set of fundamentals that appear to get lost in the bigness of the Post-Sufficient. Those fundamentals fall under the category of sharing a common mind.

COMMON MINDS

I have now heard the word "Diversity" used over the course of my entire organizational life. The personal problem that I have with this concept is that I am yet to understand what the word truly means. The source of my confusion may be that the word has a whole raft of definitions and intended consequences, and I have yet to grasp them all. I cannot tell if the focus of diversity is on making sure that 1) everyone in the organization has an equal opportunity to succeed, 2) the organization has a defense against discrimination lawsuits, 3) there is an improved opportunity for the development of creative solutions to problems, or 4) everyone in the Human Resource Department has something to do. As best I can determine, diversity is one of the most confusing words that I have ever heard.

On one hand, I am pleased that the inference seems to be that we should all respect each other, and on the other hand I am chagrined that we have gotten to the point that such a basic notion as respect has to be made into an organizational program. What I do know for certain, however, is that it is hard to get anything collectively done when people address any set of issues with both opposing points of reference and divergent opinions. It is a grand and lofty notion that people with varied backgrounds, histories and opinion sets will magically (upon seeing the value of the ideas of others) form an intellectual synthesis that will somehow transform the world, or even advance it slightly. The realities of life are usually far-removed from that generally useless panacea.

A good thing to keep in mind is that the history of the world is one of disagreement and conflict over what might be considered the smallest of differences of opinion. My reason for mentioning history is to reinforce the fact that human nature does not naturally respond well to differences of opinion. We would all like to see the better angels of our natures in others. But blindness to the realities of humanity of the challenges represented by "differentness" is a large source of organizational instability and pathetic decision-making.

Every time the word diversity comes before me, I think of another word: sameness. Sameness is an alternative to diversity that focuses on those areas of our existence where we are actually similar, as opposed to different. And this seems to be a very good thing. It seems infinitely more logical that most of "who we are" is the same, so why is it that we focus on our differences? My point is that progress is only made when people are working together in a way that facilitates imagination and with the result being harmonization of direction and effort. The essence of any effective team is a coordinated and passionately executed set of actions. The most cursory review of most big organizations reveals something less effective than that for a reason that I refer to as the "lack of a common mind."

The sharing of a common mind is very easy to understand in concept, and yet difficult to create in the context of large organizations. It also flies directly in the face of my limited understanding of the notion of diversity. Simply stated, a common mind is accomplished when the members of the organization have established some level of agreement as to 1) how the world works, 2) what forces are acting upon it, 3) the truth of the current situation, 4) where the organization should be going from here, and 5) how it should proceed to get there. The first three of these questions are presumed to be so basic as to not be addressed at all by most large organizations. This would be a very bad presumption. The last two questions are usually addressed at such a shallow level, again with an assumption the answers are obvious to all, such as to lack the associated and necessary synthesizing effects on the organization.

A common mind is the best answer to the incredible communications problems that exist within large organizations. There are not enough hours in the day to keep everyone with the appropriate level of information to operate in a cohesive fashion. The number of hours spent on not actually doing anything, but rather just absorbing what in smaller organizations is obvious, is enough to result in a tremendous competitive disadvantage.

As the effort to establish a common mind is either dismissed as wrong in its orientation or an overly-Herculean task, a set of substitutes emerge within organizations designed to fill the gap. To prove my point, ask a group of managers whether the organization is well-positioned to meet its long-term challenges and see how far you get in coming to a workable and consistent solution. They will immediately get into an argument. Given no solution to the question, these substitutes form the basis of a workable, yet wholly suboptimal, operating-environment that serves as the basis for the demise of the organization's decisioning. In order to get along with one another, surrogate solutions that are designed to bridge the gaps in the various opinion sets emerge that frighteningly create the semblance of function, without the substance, and in so doing, create a very bad decision environment. Effectively we compromise on the equation that one plus one equals two, and come to agree that it equals about one point five. It doesn't add up, but we can all agree to the *same* fallacy.

Democracies have been established for the purpose of getting nearly nothing done. Forced compromise is well-designed to slow all change. On the other hand, democracies are established to give people a say. We see this happening everyday, and this is a very good thing. Or more simply, democracies are designed to keep us from fighting with each other leading to the point of bloodshed. If we got "what the people wanted", we would blow ourselves up within a few years. Will Rogers once commented "Be thankful we're not getting all the government we are paying for." We are continually disappointed with the functioning of our government because we seem to believe our problem is that we "cannot set aside the partisan politics and simply make the decisions that are in the obvious best interests of the American people."

This notion of putting aside partisanship is beyond massively naïve for a broad array of reasons. The issues are not about partisanship, they are about deeply held views and values and worldviews as to how the world can and should work. It is incredibly arrogant and naïve when a politician says the reason that their views were not accepted by the people was that they "just did not understand it clearly enough." No, the problem was that they understood it and just did not like it.

It is also very dangerous as it assumes there is an end-state that can be approached which somehow "naturally maximizes" our *collective* interests. So all that is substantively left for the politicians to do is to go out and find those falsely-illusive answers. But this is clearly not going to happen as long as we forestall the collective and wholesale lobotomy of the human race. We natively disagree unless something pulls us together. And in most human institutions, that something is missing.

In democracies, unlike our other institutional affiliations, we do not "opt-in" to the system. We are a part of the system by virtue of being a citizen, most likely because we were born into the system. Unlike other institutions where we associate ourselves with others of like-mind or interest, in democracies one is made a part of the system simply by being alive and a citizen. Insufficient organizations are akin to institutions of desired association. Post-Sufficient organizations are more like democracies. The larger and more successful institutions become, the more likely they are to have members with broadly divergent opinions. And while it is interesting to think of the possibilities of a wonderfully congealing strategic plan that merges all divergent opinions, the realities are that it is easier to get five people to understand, cooperate, agree, and operate in concert as a function of shared values and outlooks, than five thousand.

My experience in corporate life is that the time and effort required in building an appropriate level of mind-consensus in Post-Sufficient organizations represents an almost insurmountable problem. One of two situations exists in Post-Sufficiency. Either the group is made up of people who are not *thinking* and thus not able to contribute, but are willing to blindly follow. Or, strategies are tacitly agreed to but not embraced, particularly in their execution. Both situations lead to underperformance and reduced durability. It is not that fights break out in the hallways. Rather, the lack of a common mind just dilutes the efforts of the group in ways that cause increasing amounts of wasted effort. The scene becomes simply political and the outcomes a function of political and organizational power. In most cases, less quality decision-making gets done than in smaller organizations on a per-capita basis.

In the absence of a common view of the world, the ability to make effective decisions impacting both the current environment and the future vision are severely limited. The lack of a common mind manifests itself in a variety of ways including an inability to understand the various "starting and ending points." Without the right reference points, organizations begin to "fill-in-the-blanks" with substitutes for decisions that would have been much simpler during their period of Insufficiency. The results begin to look like organizational gridlock, but the genesis is an inability to figure out the correct starting points.

FIRST AND SECOND ORDER CAUSES

Of the two seemingly inviolable and universally agreed-upon truths in this world (including the fact that one plus one equals two, and that causes create effects), the first is all too readily embraced by human institutions and the latter is generally ignored. Or, maybe more accurately stated, effects are often confused with causes, and the resultant decisions are based on flimsy or completely inaccurate premises. Organizations spend excessive amounts of time and energy on efforts that, in the end, don't solve for their intended utility. Then they shake their heads and wonder what went wrong. Of all the common mind issues, the inability to establish a commonality of opinion around root causes is the most dramatically disparate between the large and the small. And it is the most pronounced in terms of the relative competencies and effectiveness in Post-Sufficient organizations, as compared with their Insufficient brethren.

As a very simple example of the causation problem we can take a problem that plagues almost every organization: "Our sales results are just not what they should be." The first suggested response that comes from the group whose mission it is to solve for the problem is that the amount of current marketing support is ineffective . . . and that its focus must be refined. The second idea offered is that there has been an historic lack of investment in the product line. The third and final last-ditch response to the issue is to create a better defined target marketing strategy supported by better database technology. After five years, the problems of poor sales continue and everyone in the system is completely exasperated. It may be that all of the suggested responses may have been warranted, but they all potentially fall under the category of what might be called "second-order causes." While they each represent a partial cause of the issue, they are not the "first-order cause" that represents the real heart of the problem.

For purposes of this argument, let's assume that the real problem that was generating the poor sales results was a completely worthless sales process and equally poor sales management. If we assume that this was the real root cause, it can easily be seen that the solutions attached to the responses noted above would do little to meliorate the problem. It is in this inability to disaggregate problems down to the level of first-order causes that allow large and successful organizations to waste massive amounts of money and relative effectiveness. Post-Sufficiency almost always fails to understand the true root causes.

Additionally, misdirected efforts as a function of misunderstood causes have a tendency to further blur the path towards effective solutions going forward. The frustration of past mistakes, the pressure created by being "even further behind the competition," and the self-doubt that results from "failures-to-solve." inevitably makes the future even more difficult to discern. As a point of contrast, where failures in execution (doing the right thing, but executing poorly) often create a positive learning curve which is beneficial on a going-forward basis. The failures emanating from the lack of ability to accurately identify root causes, alternatively, create little in the way of learning. What is not known has a strong tendency to remain unknown. The root cause issue is not self-identifying. The problem perpetuates itself and the condition results in the development of more bad decisions and more confusion. Poor *execution* is usually readily seen and understood by the participants. The frustration attached to ineffective solutions stemming from the lack of identifying the essence of the issue, on the other hand, leads to a simultaneously occurring demoralizing apathy and panic. But why do we solve for second-order causes first? Alternatively, why do we often fail in many instances to see the root causes?

The first reason we tend to migrate in the direction of second-order causes is that they are usually much less emotionally painful to address. Blaming a process for a problem is much less fraught with potential distress than blaming a person or group of people. It is much easier to be a victim-of-circumstances than a personal contributor to any problem or lost opportunity. The process of identifying systemic or process deficiencies is much less traumatic than identifying human and very personal deficiencies. And the less personally engaged in the institution, the easier it is to error towards the former.

I was once sitting in a small group meeting of six or seven of us talking about retooling one of our strategies that had clearly not worked as well as anyone had anticipated. At one point in the meeting, someone asked me "Why are you being so negative? We need to look forward, not backward." And it was apparent that the sentiment being expressed by my detractor (and pretty good friend) was shared by several others. I was looking for a first order cause. What I came to recognize was that while none of us in the room were personally responsible for the past decisions, the group wanted to divert the energies off the problem represented by the real causes and onto something more immediately identifiable and fixable. I was unwilling to "look forward" to solving for our issues until I had a reason in my head that was shared by others as to what the nature of our issue actually was. The group simply did not want to "dig in the dirt" to unearth the grubby reasons for our past failures. Communities can rally around the need to get deep enough to get to the core sources of the challenges. This is in light of the fact that the challenges may be very personal. Mind-Heads will work hard to stay away from the soulishness appended to affixing root causes.

Facts, especially those of the quantifiable nature, are much easier to deal with than anything we would put in a non-fact category. The second reason we tend away from dealing with first order causes is that we restrict the intellectual playing field to the analysis of the causes which are expressible in terms that are, by nature, "known and verifiable", as opposed to those which might be subject to an interpretation or a dreaded opinion. In the scientific age in which we live, we have seemingly come to believe that if we can circumscribe a problem with a large enough set of facts, then some kind of mystical and non-personal algorithm will appear and solve for all of the issues. Henry Clay once made the point, "Statistics are no substitute for judgment." That would be a true statement. We would much rather listen to our Mind-Heads in searching for first-order causes, but we often need to defer to our Souls-Heads.

In another small group meeting, this fact versus opinion conundrum was equally in evidence. We had been gathering market research around the issues at hand for many weeks and the research was now wonderfully arrayed for all to see. The discussion quickly moved from the market research section of our documents into the "Strategic Choices" section. Effectively we had spent no time on the market research. I stopped the group and asked why we weren't having more discussion as to the interpretation of the research. My question was, "Aren't we going to spend some time interpreting the data, and allow ourselves the opportunity to provide some insights into what we think the data is telling us?" Again, we had an uncomfortable few moments. The assumption of the group was that "data is data" and that it speaks for itself. They also indicated that "Everybody knows what this data means already." Apparently that was true of everyone but me. At that point in the meeting I said, "By some projections forty million Americans do not have health insurance. Does that data point suggest an obvious answer to the problem?" These were my friends and I could get away with challenging their approach, but the difference in the decision-making coming out of an uneasiness with opinions as to data are readily seen. We often just don't want to go to the hard and very personal work of assessing the true first-order causes. And in so doing, we end up with answers to issues and opportunities that are off-point too many times.

Beliefs are personal and intimate. Facts are banal and innocuous. Beliefs are subject to the analysis of one's character and intelligence by others. Facts can be made lifeless and utilitarian. On a continuum where the poles represent opinions on one end and pure data on the other end, large and successful human institutions seem to want to move irretrievably towards the data end. Facts are friendly, while people can be prickly. And in focusing on the data we end up making bad decisions of both the omission and commission variety. We address second-order causes and then wonder why the decisions are less-than-effective. Facts are great and invaluable. They do not represent the universe, however.

I am, in the case of causation, not inferring that all decisions within large and successful organizations are of the second-order variety. At the same time, it does seem at least remotely possible from my observations that the causality problem in big organizations is one of the biggest differentiators with their Insufficient friends. Rather than addressing the first order questions as to past failures and missed opportunities, the response is to attempt to make the dysfunctional machine just go faster. So the machine doesn't do anything any better, it just makes more noise. I have heard throughout the entirety of my career the question, "Can you believe how stupid that decision was?" This is often an expression of divergent notions of causality.

So decision dysfunction begins with a set of disparate notions as the result of an inability of the organization to share a common mind, and continues and is enabled with an inability to identify root causes. These could be considered the starting points. To these are added the problem associated with a lack of commonality as to what the future looks like: the ending points.

DESTINATION AND "END POINTS"

"Heaven help us!" was the only thing I could conclude coming out of the experience I had just endured. I had just finished adding some thoughts to a "white paper" commissioned by my organization called "Our Industry: the Future and its Implications." Besides the relatively arrogant tone of the title was an even larger underlying problem. As a group of senior leaders, we had absolutely no ability to craft any common view of the future of the industry, short of the sun coming up again tomorrow. I actually think that one got nixed as well. At the end of the proverbial day, what came out in the report was an embarrassment to everyone. Each trip through the discussion gauntlet would ultimately lead to more anodyne consensus, less creativity, and thus, no real content. I guess we finally concluded that the industry would continue to exist. We also were able to agree that "the only constant is change," and a few other tawdry platitudes. The entire process rendered the outputs of the project woebegone and meaningless. As has been said, "If you don't know where you are going, any road will take you there." Lewis Carroll's Cheshire Cat is the master of understanding the need for a *consolidated and agreed-upon* view of the future. If you don't know where you are going, no decision is right, or wrong, or anything. It is just a decision that leads to somewhere and anywhere.

Let me underline the word "consolidated" and set it opposite the word "accurate." No one knows what the future will bring. That might have been another thing my white paper group could have agreed on. At the same time, the roads we travel in our institutional lives are always subject to being off-course and confusing. The notion of a common mind as to the future is a direct corollary of the notion of a common mind about the organization's starting point ... the truth of its current existence. If we know Point A and we know Point B, we can much more clearly assess if we are staying on the course we have set for ourselves.

Going back to the story of our White Paper, the question that has to be asked is, "If we can not as a management group agree on the direction of the industry, how in the world is it possible for us to develop a cohesive strategy that everyone within the organization will understand?" More importantly, "If we disagree on where the industry is going, how can we make decisions in any sort of cohesive and productive fashion?" The answer was as simple as the question: we could not. Or it might be said differently. The only things that could be agreed upon were at such a high level that they made no difference in our decision-making. And we were all ostensibly working off the same prescribed "strategy." Every member of the management team was supposedly working from the same strategy, and yet we could get almost no agreement on the future of the industry in which we operated.

The two options available to organizations in aligning their views of the future might be expressed as either ends-specified, or cause-specified. The ends-specified approach implies a broad and defined set of destination descriptors. The cause-specified model is more complicated and suggests an "if-then" approach to the future that allows for more flexibility, but requires significantly more core understanding of the issues and the landscape. The cause-specified approach to the future attempts to identify those factors that will impact the future. The ends-specified approach makes assumptions as to the causes and goes on to predict a definable and explainable end-point. Both approaches have their place, but the choice of option causes decisions to be made in very different fashions. Some people, as a matter of their values, prefer one and some the other. But organizations absolutely need one or the other, or both, in order to drive good decision-making.

John Wooden never specified an NCAA national championship as the goal for his great UCLA basketball teams. He simply talked about every member of the team doing the best they could possibly do, execute on the best basketball they could play, and then "let the chips just fall where they may." John Wooden was the classic cause-specified leader. He said that the cause was "Everyone being the best basketball player they could be." And that is what they worked on in practice and in their games. On the other side of the ledger, the military is the classic example of ends-specified thinking. The objectives and the mission are all laid out in great detail in advance, and "victory" is just as carefully and thoughtfully defined and communicated.

I had dinner with the Chief Information Officer of a billion dollar company while his organization was at a very important juncture in its existence. This was a man who had won multiple "CIO of the Year" awards over his twenty year career. He looked at me and dolefully said, "I have no idea as to what we collectively believe the future of this industry or our enterprise is. So I am being forced to just make it up as I go." He seemed hopelessly resigned to simply waking up in the morning, showing up at work, and making *something* happen.

Decision dysfunction begins with a lack of context and depth that essentially foregoes the opportunity to understand the root and first-order causes to the issues that are faced. In this situation, many "solutions" are created for problems (and opportunities) that just do not exist. The natural migration of this lack of context is then projected "forward." Without an agreed-upon view of what is to come, the context needed for effective and coherent decision-making that exists with current issues (and the associated first-order causes) are simply extended into those that have implications based on the future. Lacking overall context in both the present and the future tense, the starting and ending points, the organization is then forced into making decisions that are based on *something*. That something represents a variety of substitutes for the kind of decision-making that is necessary for long-term durability.

DECISION SUBSTITUTES

When an organization gets to the point where it can no longer determine the essential root causes of their problems, nor agree as to where they are strategically going, they quite naturally begin looking for substitute-logic in order to make the needed decisions. They don't "go-random," Their Mind-Heads will not allow it. The organizational response is then to develop a set of "Decision Substitutes" whose mission in life is to *compensate for,* or simply *live with,* the damage done by the lack of a cohesive and agreed upon set of causes and ends-descriptors. As is the case with most everything else we have discussed, these conditions can act in isolation or they can act in concert. But whatever their configuration, they represent a set of responses that could be described as just frenetic reactions to a rapidly petrifying common soul. After having lost the organization's soul, derived from the need to master the future through the imposition of excessive controls, the only remaining thing the organization has to rely on is its mind. And in the following description of substitutes for a common mind, we see the institution loosing its mind as well.

DECISION SUBSTITUTES—GOALS

If all else fails, attach a number to it. And then, after having tagged and numbered it, everyone can feel as if the world is in order and the cosmos has been rescued from capricious randomness. It is a good thing—to be a goal-setter. Goals are reflective of discipline and determination. But goals have there place. And they serve but a limited function in relationship to the long-term interests of an organization. Goals do not make decisions. And they can distort the "ends" in unintended ways that actually make matters worse.

Fifteen years ago I established an event that is referred to as the Nygaard Pentathlon. The event includes a 400 meter run, a bench press event, throwing a twelve pound shot put, and the standing broad jump. The event concludes with a 1500 meter run. There are two-hundred possible points to be earned in each event and the only rule for the event is that Nygaard makes up all the rules. I tell the group "If you don't like the event, or the scoring system, you can just make up your own!" But everybody likes the program and they all laugh when I tell them that the only rule is that I am the only authority on all the rules. The reason I put the event together was to provide some accountability to myself for staying in shape, and to plot the course of my aging body over time.

Tallying the scores of the participants after the conclusion of the running of The Pentathlon is always great sport. "Who won and how many points did they score? How did I do versus last year? Were any records set?" Goals placed in numerical form are fascinating, and they deserve to be. Goals can be soulish things as they speak to the results of tests of personal capability and willfulness. More significant than the annual scores in the event is the evaluation of the individual and personal commitment to the spirit and intention of the event. Said differently, the goals of the system align with the interests of the object of attention, and in so doing provide for the significant focus of energy. The Pentathlon represents a simple situation where the goals of the system and the related objectives of the participants are very tightly aligned.

To shift to a analogous setting, but one much less personally interesting than The Pentathlon, I had joined one of my affiliations later in my career and was attending a meeting where we were reviewing the results of the November edition of the company's Focus Goals. This was a set of broad-based goals (likely a hundred measurable outcomes ranging from Company revenues to the number of Human Resources training events that were attended) that were allegedly the list of quantifiable outcomes for which the organization was to have been laboring over the prior many months. The charts and graphs were very nice and every goal result was given a designation as "Green—Yellow—Red" as an indicator of the progress-to-date that had been made towards meeting those goals. This was a positive exercise for the group as it cast significant light on the outcomes experienced in the recent past.

The problem was that the goals seemed to have alarmingly little to do with the intentions and interests of the organization. That was not my assessment; it was the assessment of the group. It did seem, however, that that group was at least entertained by seeing the scores.

The Focus Goals looked like a random sampling taken from a list of several thousand possible goal-candidates. Some of them were very good goals, and some of them were literally throw-aways. You could see that some of the goals were included so that each department had a goal "on the board." Some of the goals were there because they represented something that could be measured, but said little about actual progress. Some were there so that some *one* could get up and *speak* to the progress. There were goals on the list representing situations over which the organization had literally no control. We had goals on the list that were stated in ways that sent distortive messages given the nature of the objectives. Most of the goals represented but a partial picture of the real objective. And the challenges went on.

The core problem with the goals was not that they were a completely misdirected set of goals. They were all good things. The problem was in the messaging that the goals sent and, more importantly, the strategic disconnects between the goals and what actually needed to be done. The goal set represented a very hardscrabble setting in which to eek out a good set of associated decisions. Given this organization's limited ability to talk about its strategy, the goals took on even more importance. This set of goals drove a large amount of decision-making within the organization. As a result, much of decision-making process was actually compromised, and not fundamentally aided, by the randomness and partiality of the goal set.

Goals must flow out of a well-defined set of collective intentions, or they end up doing more harm than good. Misdirected goals create the opportunity for more bad decisions than having no goals at all. Without the goals, common sense is the hoped-for guide. Goals have the ability to create great personal and organizational focus, given their simplicity, and in that is the problem. The correct role of a goal is to exactly measure that which is desired. Without an adequate grasp on that which is desired, the setting of goals is an exercise in futility.

A couple of examples from the situation just described will suffice to clarify the impact of misplaced goals on organizational decision-making. The Human Resources area of the company was very pleased with their ability to create "learning events." I actually think the department did a pretty good job with the events and they were both well-intended and well-attended. The problem with the goal was that it failed to measure whether anyone actually *learned* anything, which I assume was the real goal. The goal that was measured was the number of "Learning Events" that had been sponsored multiplied by the average attendance in each event. So the focus of the effort, as driven by the goal, was always just "more." To have been determined to have been more effective in advancing the intellectual capital of the organization was a completely *different* goal. But that goal wasn't on the list. In this particular case, the results was not likely very harmful. Others on the list, however, were nearly diabolical in their ability to contort the decision-making process.

The second example fits in the category of truly distortive. One of the expressed goals was to increase the amount of lending that was being done. We made more money, at least in theory, if we did more lending. The problem with the goal was that no one was looking to change anything opposite the willingness of the organization to actually do anything to encourage or facilitate more lending than we were currently doing. The economic environment was going to be completely responsible for any changes that would be experienced in our level of lending. Anything the organization did to move the needle was then unintended. The pursuit of "making the number" was in no way correlated with anything that could actually be controlled. By definition, this creates a very bad goal. The internal "thrashing" that went on within the organization directed at meeting this misguided goal was frightening. A lot of time was wasted. But the soul-destroying "fights" were the real issue.

At the end of the meeting the session was concluded by the CEO with, "So let's get out and turn those 'reds' to 'green' by the end of the year." Irrespective of what the organization really needed to do, the focus was now on two colors. With respect to decision-making, the obvious connection with goal-setting is that the goals create a set of points of attention. To the extent that the points of attention are inconsistent with what the members of the organization know are what really needs to be measured, dysfunction is created. Alternatively, and to the extent that the members do not know the difference, it creates an even larger problem. The sentiment seems to be "Better to focus on a few things that we have identified, even though they may be the wrong ones, than have nothing to definitely report on in terms of progress." Without goals that truly reflect the sentiments of the entire organization as to the real measures of success, decisioning is always challenging. Mindless drones will always follow the goals. Mindless drones are great if it is the desire of the organization to operate a machine that just runs. Goals can come to completely replace thought.

Goals cannot fill the role of a common mind, but can only *support* the already existing commonality. Goals can create as large a set of negative outcomes as positive, given a lack of alignment with the organization's true objectives. And it becomes obvious that the more complex the environment, the more challenging it is to gain the achievement of the relative alignment of the organization's goals with their objectives. When goals are forced as a substitute for more fundamental conditions of understanding, the level of Post-Sufficiency grows. To complicate matters, the organizational focus that is supposed to be gained by the creation of goals is made even more difficult by a lack of willingness to make the difficult decisions that actually drive focus. The default decision is to default to doing everything.

DECISION SUBSTITUTES—JUST DO EVERYTHING

With the myriad choices available in large and successful organizations, it is often a path of least resistance to just not decide *against* doing anything. The conclusion effectively becomes: "We cannot really decide what to do, so we are going to just do everything" and in so doing cure for the disparate mind problem. We can all agree that everything on the list is important. If we can avoid the messiness of prioritization, life will infinitely simpler. This approach rests on an overly optimistic notion that an organization can effectively pour a gallon of fluid into a quart jar without spilling anything. I once had a conversation with a guy who was one of my favorite bosses. It went something like this:

> Eddie: Why aren't you guys doing call reports? (Written reports of our client visits)
>
> Brian: Because we have too much else to do.
>
> Eddie: Why can't you do them on the plane?
>
> Brian: Because we are using that time to work on keeping up on e-mails.
>
> Eddie: Aren't internal reporting needs more important than e-mails?
>
> Brian: No . . . those reports can wait. Client demands are a higher priority.
>
> Eddie: Can't we be more productive?
>
> Brian: No . . . we can't.
>
> Eddie: Can't we . . .
>
> Brian: (interrupting) Just do everything . . . no.

In a frighteningly memorable scene from the movie *Silence of the Lambs*, Anthony Hopkins' character is describing to Jody Foster's character the nature of human desire. The rough translation of Hopkins' comment is that "we want what we see." In our organizational lives, the amount of things that we can see (and that we then want) is always more than the plate can handle. And yet we operate as if everything that gets added is "just another two drachma tax." Overwhelming the best people in an organization with too much work and too few priorities is cancerous to the soul. I was in the office of one of my co-workers one day and as I walked in her comment (before saying hello) was, "I do everything half-assed." She was an exceptionally talented person and the reason for the self-assessment was simply that she had so much to do that everything she did was suffering. And it was easy to observe that this situation hurt her to the core. Her soul was wounded.

One of the biggest cop-outs of leadership is the failure to avoid a strategy of "Please just do everything." The strategy is really no strategy at all. It is simply a default mechanism. Unlike the challenges that exist in the world of the excessive reliance on lists, the "just-do-everything" strategy is focused on a broad set of intended outcomes, and not on the mobilization necessary to achieve those outcomes. The problem is often compounded as budgets are being cut; complexity is increasing, and the communications demands are growing faster than the complexity. I refer to this as the "cut and hope" strategy. The demands are increasing so much faster than resources are being applied that all focus is lost. The only remaining choice is to simply attempt, as best as possible, to manage the whole unruly hoard of issues, and the associated execution challenges.

Organizations often recognize that the just-do-everything strategy is taking its toll on their people. So they try to help by offering all manner of emollients, including things like time management and work-life-balance classes. And while most people are happy that the company is trying to help, they would rather have the Company make up its mind as to what is important (and what isn't) and resource the efforts accordingly. I refer to the measurement of the "time and work tax" inflicted on people within an organization as a result of attempting to do everything as the "Implicit Quality of Life Deflator." And what is deflated is the soul of the people within the organization.

Instead of work-life balance discussions, it would be better for organizations just to be honest. "What we need is productivity. Productivity drives what we do. To the extent that you provide more productivity we can promote you or pay you more, or both. So, if you decide that your family is important, and that you can only work forty hours a week, that is fine with us. Just expect to be treated accordingly." I think that is what is actually meant by work-life balance. People appreciate honesty more than they do lip-service to that which is a chimerical.

The "just-do-everything" strategy, as a substitute for the development of a common mind, is the expression of exasperation. It is also an expression of misplaced and illogical confidence. I once heard an executive say, "We are very pleased that we just got the big new contract. But we are not going to be adding to staff to meet the needs of the new client, so I want to make sure that none of current customers ever hears that their priorities might be subsumed by the interests of our new business. Make sure that none of your people ever tell any of our customers that we are going to be reprioritizing their priorities." The problem with the obviously unethical sentiment is related to its soul-destroying nature. Everyone knew that the trade-offs were going to have to be made, and that work for the existing clients was going to be put off. Everyone also knew that the clients would be justifiably angry and confused. What were we supposed to say to clients had actually happened to their projects and priorities? We were going to have to make up a lie, or expose the CEO's deception. It was deception based on a lack of willingness to accept that the just-do-everything strategy is impossible to implement without massive damage.

*****

By way of review, we find that Post-Sufficiency begins with an attitude that attempts to control for successful outcomes through the use of a formula that represents a level of arrogance in its notion that the future can somehow be controlled. That formula, and the resulting controls placed on the organization, result in massive strains on the organization's ability to think and grow and adapt. At the same time, the growth of the machine clears a path to an inability to identify both the causes of the organizations challenges and the route that will be taken to foster continued success. In the failures to identify the crucial elements of their existence, there follows a number of non-foundational substitutes for the thinking and decision-making which represent attempts at re-creating the past.

What emerges from this malaise is the Post-Sufficient Organization in perfect form. They have come to believe that their abilities are sufficient to conquer for all challenges, and that this pristine situation will be a reflection of the truth for as far as the eye can see. Yet they fail to recognize that what they have actually *become* is so far removed from their needed reality that they are completely incapable of that which they claim. What they have become so dominates what they do, irrespective of their choices, that their results are always consistent with their being, as opposed to their actions. And those results are predictably both under-performance and lack of organizational durability.

These Post-Sufficient organizations all look alike. They all embrace the SMUTy approach to organizational development. They expect much of their people and yet collectively fail to understand the human needs of those same associates. They provide lip-service to the importance of people, but their actions are usually unrelated to that notion. They are control-focused and un-trusting in their approach to leadership, but claim otherwise. They have lost their humanity. They have lost their souls. And their members are without community or home. When you ask a member of a Post-Sufficient organization about their job you often get the response, "Well, it's a place to work." A place to work is a long way from a place called home.

The reason that large and successful organizations under-perform their smaller peers is not that they do everything a little less efficiently and effectively. They do many things, and have many attributes, which are infinitely *superior* to the little guys. Even in Post-Sufficiency, these advantages remain in place and are very valuable. The relative superiority of many of these attributes creates, at least in a vacuum, hugely better results than their Insufficient competitors. The significance of being large can hardly be understated. At the same time, the problem they have is in what they have become. They have become soul-less, and as a human institution made up of human beings they are tremendously *inferior*. The effect of these very large absolute discrepancies is a net negative. The little guys win.

As a result, the idea of focusing on the organization's strengths as a strategy is rendered of little use. Most large organizations are already doing well in the things that big organizations do well. They just do not realize how the things that they do poorly, resulting from their ontology, are so large. The price of carrying these humanly denominated and very large millstones is too significant for most to bear. And the Post-Sufficient usually fail to make this connection until very late in the game. And that assumes they ever figure it out. They need to remove their own injurious hands from their own tender throats.

Carol King wrote and sang one of my favorite songs. It is one of those tunes that continues to play over and over in my head, as it has for over three decades. The music and melody are outstanding, but it is the words that have always held my attention. At the end of the first verse which speaks to being in a state of depression over a broken relationship, the verse says "or maybe we've just quit trying." The chorus then begins with, "And it's too late baby, now it's too late, though we really did try to make it. Something inside has died and I can't hide it; I just can't fake it . . . no, no, no." This is the national anthem of Post-Sufficiency. Hardly a thing needs to be added.

* * * * *

We turn next to the question of whether the Post-Sufficient organization is capable of recovery. The question is whether a group of refugees can find their way home. As mentioned in the Introduction, my sentiment is guardedly positive. Changing what you do is easy. Changing who you are is problematic. Like psychoanalysis and counseling, the results are usually seen over very long periods of time, and then, positive results still may be fleeting. It is just another version of leopards and their spots. In the case of institutions, the challenges are even greater than with individuals. The good news is that to the extent an organization can develop an accurate understanding of the impact of the loss of community, the power and interest found in the group's members to rebuild community is almost irrationally and inconceivably strong.

6

Back to the Basics

> Large and successful organizations can only be rescued with the establishment of durable foundations. These foundations are found in the nature of the organization, and not in their processes. Foundations are the province and responsibility of the Soul-Head, and represent the cure for the under-performance and durability of human institutions.

"Back to the Basics" was the message that came out of one the world's premier financial institutions which had just been financially bailed out by a group of European governments. The worldwide financial services industry had been rocked by the impact of excessive risk-taking during the period of 2003 through 2008, and global financial services organizations were attempting to sate the market's interests in their viability and strategies by indicating publicly their plans. One of these institutions said that they were going back to doing business by returning to something they considered "basic."

I found the summary of ING's strategic intent very troubling in its presumptive use of the word "basic." While the words themselves sounded reassuring, the expression "back to basics" is both overused, and in this case potentially very revealing.

What were the "basics" in their definition? Assuming the inference was that they had not been executing on the basics before, what *were* they doing during the several years prior? Asked differently, what were they *now* going to be doing differently? Was it that they formerly had come to think the "basics" were somehow no longer necessary for an organization of their stature, scale and prescience? Or, were they saying that the world had mystically changed and that "basics" were, at least at this uniquely revealing juncture, now once again applicable? Obviously,

I have no idea as to their actual intent or meaning. But the comment as to their new strategy was fascinating.

I wondered if the statement came from an attitude of contrition and humility. Were they admitting to the massive carnage that they had both participated in and created, or was it just another "We continue to be masters of our own universe" strategic and ontological declaration. Were they entering a plea of guilty, or a plea of innocent by reasons of temporary insanity? Or, were they just victims of a set of cosmically uncontrollable circumstances, and were now just proceeding to simply turn a page in their long and glorious history? As I considered the ING headline, I was reminded of a conversation between parents and a rebellious teenager after the youngster's first semester away at college. The youngster says, "Yes, I have learned my lesson. I promise that I will party less and study more next semester. Really, I have learned that the party-focused "extra-curricular" activities have to go. Really, truly, I have. It is going to be different going forward."

It makes no difference whether ING had been well-managed before the melt-down or whether they managed the organization with the skill of a highly focused group of protozoa. The result of the government bailout, and the associated need to tell the world what they planned to do, created a set of fairly detailed strategic choices as to which of their business units would be retained and which ones would be spun off. Additionally, the Company did a bunch of restructuring of governance and management, and obviously emerged with a very different balance sheet. But those things are largely irrelevant as compared with the issue of what had really happened in the organization at an ontological level that had lead to the problems, and what then fundamentally needed to change.

Were they the same organization as before, or were they now something different? The inference of the announcements was that the combination of business unit portfolio changes, governance modifications, and balance sheet "enhancements" was their new "basics." Of more interest would be the question of the type of institutional attitudes and values that would emerge as a result of their near-death experience. What were the real set of lessons that were actually learned or inculcated here, and what "basics" *should* form the foundation of the new enterprise?

The word "basics" is challenging to deal with as there seems to be no natural bottom to the enquiry. In this sense, the term basics and the idea of "that which is foundational" are similarly situated. Both terms are attempting to express the notion of some set of core concepts, attitudes, precepts, or "somethings" on which all future advancements are to be built. But it is very difficult to know how far *down* one has to go to get to something that is in fact foundational.

Is the poured concrete under my house the foundational concept on which my house stands, or are the composition of atoms and the functioning of gravity the baseline on which all structures are built? Or, does the question rest on a metaphysical theory? I clearly don't know the answer to this question, but what I do know, coming from my observations within large and successful organizations, is that many either fail to ask the question, or define the answer as something that would be determined less than truly foundational.

We talked earlier about false foundations, and virtuous anchors. We also discussed some of the natural gravitational forces that act on human institutions. We considered the impact of an arrogant mindset and the downstream effects on the organization's control and decision mechanisms. And it is against the backdrop of those existing and observable phenomenon that the issue of foundations must fundamentally interact. It is unfortunately very easy to simply avoid addressing the "foundation question" as the success, scale and established brand of the institution creates a false level of confidence in the supportive existence, albeit not defined, of a true foundation.

What ends up happening is that large and successful organizations effectively say, "We don't know what the foundation really looks like. As a matter of fact, we never go to the basement because we are a little afraid of what we might find inhabiting or evolving into life down there. But our house continues to grow, and rooms and floors are being added on, and the support seems pretty strong, so we are not going to do the engineering studies until later. That's it! We are actually *committed* to doing the investigative work, but we are going to do it *later*." Was it Mark Twain that asked whether it made any sense to wait until tomorrow to do something that could just as easily be done the day after tomorrow?

Foundation, as a concept, is also a very hard thing to objectify. And therein lies the problem. The real issue behind the definition problem is that *foundations* are cosmological or metaphysical concepts that can become very personal, and way too spiritual, for most organizational leaders to advance, or to even explore. Basics and foundations represent the answers to the really emotionally-hard, politically-charged and spiritually-laden questions that can be completely irreconcilable within the walls of an institution. Basics, in this sense, are a veritable snake pit for management. This is not a Mind-Head discussion. Without a Soul-Head, no serious conversations can occur.

The establishment of marketing schemes and their associated budgets is an infinitely easier exercise than addressing what it is that the organization actually thinks, and more importantly feels, about its offerings and about itself. I was once in a meeting where it was announced that recent surveys of the organization's customers indicated that "we really stink, but we were better than the other guys." We remarkably just walked away from that meeting . . . just like we walked away from any other meeting. "All this hard work and dedication and the overview comment from the survey was that we 'stink'?" Shouldn't we pause to address that "little question" before we move on?

The problem is that the issue is thought to be hopelessly ontological, and organizations in Post-Sufficiency really want to stay away from any notion of being and essence and meaning. I was in another management session where the question was asked as to how well the organization was fundamentally situated to effectively "compete" over the next ten years. On a scale of one through ten, the responses of this very bright group of leaders varied from three to eight. This informal survey represented a disparity in the definition of the nature and strength of the organization's foundations, as opposed to its current performance. Post-Sufficient organizations are awash in ontological questions for which no answers exist, and towards which no energy is being directed.

The *back to basics* concept is incredibly powerful and important. To both answer the question and to act on the answer is the only cure for the disease of Post-Sufficiency. The basics and foundations of any human institution are the essential ingredients in the creation of long-term durability. It is impossible to continue to build infrastructure and scale, broadly defined, on a faulty foundation. And it is in the failure of organizations to continually address the fundamental human foundations of the organization that they stumble. If organizational strategies, mergers and divestitures and corporate governance are not the fundamentals, as ING would have seemingly suggested, what are the fundamentals? How far does one have to dig to get to the bottom?

Over the next four chapters we will be looking at set of answers to the "Where is the bottom?" question. It is in the answer to *that* question where we will also find what I believe to be the answers to the broader questions of the under-performance and durability of all human institutions. Each foundational element represents a paradoxical situation that grows in magnitude as the human institutions grow. And as the paradox grows, so grows the need for the organization to come to an understanding of it.

The foundational elements are all rooted in our human natures. The individual foundational elements represent "agreements" or informal contracts that the institution has with its members that form the basis on which everything else that goes on within the institution are predicated. As organizations themselves, *per se*, do nothing, and the members' individual attitudes and activities constitute the entirety of what an organization both is and does, the foundations are focused on the members, and not on any notion of the whole. They represent a foundation, in this definition, in that they start and end with the people who make up the human institution.

Included in the list of foundational elements are four core concepts that point in the direction of home and a community. The first of the core concepts, or foundational elements, is represented by the informal agreements that the *individual members* of the institution have with the institution *itself*. Effectively this agreement memorializes the relational understanding of what the member will provide the organization and what the member will expect to receive in return. Without this agreement, the organization's members are just atomistic "free radicals."

The second foundational element is the informal agreement the members of the organization have with respect to the relationship the organization has with its environment. This agreement is a set of opinions and judgments that represent the relationship the organization and its members have with the world in which it operates. The agreement includes both objective and subjective inputs that create a picture to the organization's members as to "how we view the world." It is essentially a statement of the deeply imprinted values of the organization. Added to this list are the third and fourth foundational element that represents agreement among the organization's members as to desired outcomes and the trust levels that accompany those outcomes.

The foundational elements, accordingly, represents a tapestry on which is printed the network of intra-personal and interpersonal relationships within a human institution. The tapestry creates a picture for the members of the nature of the relationship of the member with the organization, a picture of what the organization stands for in relationship to the member and the world, and a picture of the reasons why the organization is in existence. That summary of relationships then allows an environment of trust to emerge and form the basis for progress. In total, the agreements form the basis for all communities and create the definition as to what it means for each of us to be *at home* within our institutional affiliations.

When home as a concept is expanded to include larger groups of people than that live under a single roof, but consist of people with the same needs, values, and goals, they are a community. Without an effective community, people just get in each other's way or begin to fight. It is well-documented that the enemy within any well-established setting is almost always represented by forces from within. In large and successful organizations the underlying enemy is the loss of the soul of the community.

Small and Insufficient organizations possess large doses of community. And they exploit it to their advantage. It *is* their advantage. Insufficient organizations maintain the foundational elements either by design or by default, but they retain a foundation on which future growth and success can be built. Large and successful organizations become that which is consistent with the loss of the foundational elements, and everything else that is built on top is directly tied to that singular core frailty. Every member of every institution sits on, and is supported by, these human foundations. For better or worse, the institution's long-term outcomes are determined as a result of the soundness of the foundations.

It is in providing an adumbration of the elements of the foundations of Insufficiency that I will dedicate the rest of this book. The focus will be on the development of a soulish and enduring community. The discussion will be around the appropriate maintenance and nourishment of the souls that comprise a home. It is the description of an organization with both of its heads, their Mind-Head and their Soul-Head, operating in concert.

7

"Here's the Deal"

Large and successful organizations must create foundations that establish a virtuous growth cycle that begins with belief systems and ends in trust. Organizational foundations are falsely presumed to be in solidly in place by the Post-Sufficient. While the Mind-Head builds the outputs of the institution, the Soul-Head is the builder and sustainer of the organization's foundations.

WHEN OUR DAUGHTER WAS a teenager she made the occasional mistake of addressing her mother with the opening line, "Here's the deal." No matter what followed that precedent clause, the result was not going to work out well for her. She learned that pretty quickly. The problem with "Here's the deal" was that it was the ultimate "red flag" for her mother. Whatever it was that was to come out of our daughter's mouth next was going to be in direct violation of the heretofore existing "deal." To the extent the old deal was somehow flawed, her mother was completely unaware. And that was the problem. Until the deal was altered or changed, based on some newfound rationale, her mother was just not going to be a buyer. The informal contract that existed between mother and daughter was long-since established, and was working well, at least in Mom's mind.

The better the contracts are both agreed-to and understood, the better the working of the relationships. Otherwise, mistrust and disagreements reign. The contract has to be understood and the terms have to be met by all of the parties all of the time. Harmony emanates from such contracts. Progress can only be found in environments where the terms of the deal are agreed to and honored. The alternative is frustration. The alternative is also soul-destroying and riddled with personal heart-ache.

In the comment "Here's the deal" we find the basics of our human existence. There is nothing more fundamental to our individual and collective prosperity, defined both materially and emotionally, than the terms that were inferred in this conversation between mother and daughter. Only the players change. Every relationship we have with every other human being on the planet, whether we personally know them or not, is subject to a set of terms. "The Deal" comprises the entirety of the set of terms on which our inter-human lives are built. Our abilities to both acquire and to protect are subject to the terms of The Deal. When The Deal changes, our lives are altered: for better or for worse.

The institutional affiliations in which we participate have all established a set of deal-terms that are, to some degree, consistent with who we are as individuals. Our families, our groups of friends, our families of faith, our corporate "families" and our governmental affiliations, all comprise a set of these terms. The deal terms set out our obligations and rewards as members, and more importantly, the frameworks within which we can freely and rightly act. They are the foundations on which all of our "affiliational" security and engagement is built. In the terms of The Deal we find the source of a foundational substance, the strength of which is sufficient on which to build all human affiliations.

We have defined the condition of Post-Sufficiency as the situation where our Mind-Heads become dominant and our Soul-Heads become unusable. It is the highly important job of the Mind-Head to speak to the issues of analyzing inputs, creating processes and developing courses of action. It is the equally important job of the Soul-Head to develop the terms of The Deal. Without a Soul-Head to create and monitor the ongoing effectiveness of the deal terms, organizations lose their souls. Without the deal-terms, the community has no foundation on which to build... anything. The Soul-Heads are subterranean operators: their job is always below ground. Their job is in building the real foundations on which all human enterprise can flourish.

Mind-Heads can be understood as building the organizational structure that is built *above* ground. What is above ground is the more tangible, and that which is the result of *process*, broadly defined. The processes of thinking, analyzing, calculating and directing are what appear to us as the aesthetically appealing and usable components of the structure. The structures may be either well constructed, or just a badly configured hodge-podge of building materials, but the Mind-Heads role is the same: The use of the mind is to build something that works well. Mind-Heads should get all the credit for the above-ground structure, as it truly is their creation.

Our subterranean Soul-Heads have a different role. They deal with the intangibles that come not from our processes, but from our *being*. In their foundation-building role, the materials that Soul-Heads use are a raft of mental abstractions that work very hard to avoid strict definition. Mind-Heads apply their trade with materials that can all be neatly weighed and measured. The materials of the Soul-Head, conversely, are much more amorphous. The paradox is that the amorphous is the stuff of foundations. It is also true that the building materials of the Soul-Head are those that protect the work of the Mind-Head from eventual decay. The abstract building materials of the Soul-Head protect large and successful organizations from the arrogance, and control and decision dysfunctions that characterize Post-Sufficiency.

The actual building materials that are the province of the Soul-Head, and those that create the substance of The Deal, are those that are used in building the organization's foundation. The foundational materials include the elements of 1) beliefs, 2) meaning, 3) growth, and, 4) trust. It is in the correlations and the interactions of these materials that The Deal is assembled. And The Deal literally sustains and supports everything the Mind-Head can think to build on top of it.

BELIEFS

Some of us believe in the Tooth Fairy and some us do not. Some of us believe in the existence of worldwide conspiracies and some us do not. Some of us believe in the eternal existence of the human soul, while others do not. Most of us believe that barns should be painted red, while a few of us think they should be white. The vast majority of us believe that we are subject to gravity, and yet some of us have jumped off buildings in an effort to prove that at least *they* were not. Belief systems are literally everywhere we look.

Our belief systems create within each of us a prioritization as to the relative significance of the elements of our beliefs. Those are the things we determine to put on a sliding scale of importance. We say to ourselves, "This is how the word works (based on my beliefs), and accordingly, this is what I will determine is important." So whether the issue is the foremost preparation of candied yams or the preferred method of political organization, our belief systems dictate our thoughts and actions. Of greatest significance, however, is not the relative importance of our beliefs-derived systems of prioritization. What is significant, at least with respect to our participation in human institutions, is that we are no more willing to suspend our belief systems opposite our institutional participation than we are to venture off a ledge from forty stories above the pavement. We just will not violate those belief systems. The textures and dimensions of our lives are essentially based on those things in which we believe.

MEANING

I never play Backgammon with my wife anymore. It is just too humiliating. No one should be forced to deal with *never* getting to win. The Backgammon board is an interesting looking pattern. To look at it without any context, it would just look like a piece of art. If, however, the game is actually understood, it takes on meaning. The board is now actually good for something.

Our belief systems form the "boards" of our lives. But they just sit there until we infuse them with *meaning*. It is in meaning that we seek our material and emotional fulfillment. We actually design a game, through the defining of meaning, where we develop the ideas of winning and losing. The board simply creates the context for the definition of the game and its associated meaning. Without the board we have no basis for understanding the game and its implications. We would only have a bunch of game-pieces, but without a real game.

The implication in our institutional lives is that the meaning we attach to our experiences is that which provides our incentives for action. All action. Unlike our belief systems, however, the problem with operating outside our natural zones of meaning is that we just fail to understand the game. With that lack of understanding comes a lack of interest in participation. Or worse, the complete unwillingness of the members to participate.

GROWTH

That something exists and *is* creates a set of mysteries. But we generally don't spend a lot of time marveling over the simple existence of something. Things that are physical are thought both explainable and common. That something changes and actually *grows* creates something that is very different. The existence of growth is the validation of life. Growth is not explainable and common. It is rather, transcendental. It is as close as we get to seeing something created from nothing. In that connection, growth is the demonstration of real genius. It represents our strongest connection with that which is outside of us.

As belief systems and their associated meanings create the "board and the game," the presence of an opportunity for growth creates the incentive for us to become a better player. The nature of the game is self-defined, but the desire to be "better at it" is universal. We all want to grow personally, so as to better participate in the growth that we can experience within us and around us. To grow and experience growth is to be human. It is to be alive. And we experience life as both individuals and as members of human institutions.

To be neither growing personally, nor experiencing the growth in our affiliations, is to become a rock in a stream. We are not alive, just an inanimate object, and the elements are literally wearing us down. Meaning, as a concept, literally creates the demand for growth. Beliefs beget meaning, and meaning begets the need for growth. To divorce this notion from our institutional lives is to be estranged from our essential *raison d'etre*. The path of growth is the path of hope. Without hope, we would each be better off as a rock in a stream.

TRUST

It has been commented that the definition of Hell is a place where reason ceases to exist. Without reason, we are left with nothing other than expectations of randomness. If causes don't create a reasonable set of expected outcomes, we would seek after no causes. And in so doing we would replace Hell with nothing, which is just about as bad. The good news is that we are allowed to come to a point where we can trust in things as a result of reason. The amplified version of that good news is that we can also come to trust one another. And as two-heads-are-better-than-one, our opportunities for growth are improved as we can trust one another.

One of the core questions in the political arena is that which we choose do with the fact that we are born with varying types and degrees of native giftedness. Some of us are better looking than others. Some of us are smarter. Some are more artistic. Some are physically stronger. In the political realm, this is a problem. It forms the basis for most of our societal dilemmas. In the organizational, it is a massive opportunity for betterment. We can use our varying areas of giftedness (not to be confused with "specialization") to improve our collective lot, but only in the event that we can trust one another to fulfill our promises to one another.

In the notion of trust we see the completion and synthesis of the foundation. We only trust those whose belief systems are consistent with our own. We are only inspired towards action as a result of the meaning that comes from our beliefs. And we are interested in growing as a direct function of our established meanings. Lastly, we are mobilized to trust as a natural offshoot of our interest in growth, assisted by the maximization of our unequal giftedness. It is this set of distinctly human factors the foundation blocks that drive and sustain the successful development of all communities. Without these factors, communities simply do not exist.

Organizations who attempt to build themselves on foundations other than these are fighting a loosing battle against our native humanness. With these foundations in place, an organization can place a very large burden of "process." Without these foundations, the processes of the Mind-Head are simply overwhelmed by the same forces of entropy that polish rocks in streams. The reasons are many, but the organizational stability provided by the Soul-Head built foundations is the antidote to the destabilizing effects of Post-Sufficiency.

More specifically, Beliefs and Meaning are very weighty offsets to *arrogance*. Growth and Trust naturally police the implementation of unwanted *controls*. And the collection of all four of the "foundational building materials" provides the Polestar towards which the organization can point and *decision-dysfunction* can be overcome.

Mind-Heads are an organization's engineers. Soul-Heads are the organization's artists. The Hoover Dam and the Human Genome Project are great works of engineering. They also took a lot of very hard work and tremendous skill and knowledge. Michelangelo's *David* and Tolkien's *Lord of the Rings* are great feats of art. They also took a lot of very hard work and tremendous skill and knowledge. The inputs are similar, but the crafts are different. Most of us think of ourselves as more engineer than artist. The challenge in organizational life is that we need to be both. The artistry found in human institutions is often found where one might not expect . . . in the basement. It is in the basement that we will find the foundations of belief, meaning, growth and trust. And that is where we will find our Soul-Head.

8

The Values Delusion

Large and successful organizations understand the importance of values, but fail to understand their magnitude and nature. Values are built on broadly understood belief systems that form the absolute basis for all the institution's actions. The Mind-Head sees the importance of "stating" values, as the Soul-Head works to make them personal, profound, and actionable.

Our son came home from the second grade one afternoon and declared that math was both stupid and, from his youthfully enlightened point of view, completely unnecessary. He was therefore going to take a "pass" on math for the rest of his life. "Let others pursue that dismal science, as for me, I will pursue that which possesses things of much greater intrinsic value." was essentially his message. As our seven year old was very verbal, he made his case in quite dramatic fashion. But for one minor detail, this communiqué would be of no consequence. The little detail was that there were two people within his immediate sphere of influence who did not agree with his newfound belief system. His views of how the world worked, and his associated value systems, were already in full bloom as a fifty pounder.

The word "belief" is shorthand for that which we believe both worthy of trust and in which we vest importance. More dramatically, it contains the notion of some underlying rationale for those priorities. We establish our beliefs and values as we experience the world, are taught in the ways of beliefs, and as a function of the unique methods that our minds and souls use to process all of the various inputs. Beliefs represent our essential humanity.

Our belief systems manifest themselves in the "values," or "what's important" expressions. No two of us have the identical set of beliefs-

centered values. We can be grouped as to like-thinking and sensing, but none of us is exactly the same as another. In this disparity comes a great deal of the fullness of life, and a very large percentage of the relational and organizational pain. Disparate value systems are natural prescriptions for disaster. In small doses, these value system differences result in the simple loss of organization effectiveness.

Beliefs are literally infused into every facet of our lives. When we open our mouths to speak, it is beliefs and values that proceed. We cannot talk about the score of the most recent football game without some element of personal beliefs-driven values coming out. This applies whether we are deciding on a destination for a dinner out, or a discussion on geopolitics. It applies to our thoughts and reactions to the sight of a newborn baby or in a debate over the topic of abortion. Beliefs are the prisms through which we observe and interact with the world. There are no values-less interactions between human beings. Beliefs are the screens through which everything we do and think is sifted. Our essential essence is the collection of a very large and intricately assembled set of personal beliefs. Beliefs and their expressed values and worldviews are literally who we are.

The range of issues impacted by our worldviews is as broad as the range of issues itself. Whether we see our lives through a worldview that understands the existence of evil as a function of 1) sinfully fallen humanity, 2) the random and undesired interjection by the gods, or 3) as the result of an endemic system of institutional oppression, the view is altogether different. Discussions as to things as simple as the definition of "successful outcomes" (with respect to any topic) often create a relationally debilitating exercise. There may be agreement as to the desired *outcomes*, but massive disagreement as to the *means* by which those outcomes can or should be accomplished. We often find ourselves "worlds-apart" in our thinking. The problem finds root in our disparate and conflicting worldviews.

Our worldviews essentially create a personal and unified picture and interpretation of our environment. The environment, it might be argued, is essentially the same for each of us. But it is obvious that the "views" that we individually experience are very different. Maybe a better way to see this is by envisioning a suspended three-dimensional object. The view from every angle is of the same object, but it looks different, and is described differently, from each point of viewing.

Beliefs are the starting points for the things that we consider worth doing. Of equal importance are those things we believe should be avoided. The ability to live a life that is consistent with one's beliefs is at the heart of the feeling we are at home. We are clearly alienated and relationally distanced from those whose fundamental beliefs are different from our own. This is a function of our evaluation of the relative rightness or wrongness of the alternate belief-sets of others. Additionally, and to the extent that our values are mis-aligned, we lose our interest in forming a relationship with "them." When the presence of *them* exists, the group is not a community. Mind-Heads do not view community in terms of tribes. They view them in terms of outputs. Soul-Heads sense the loss of community and see the impending challenges in the soul of the organization.

"You people . . ." is the beginning of the sentence expressing a contrary set of values and an alternate worldview. We would all like to believe that this is not so, and that we have evolved to a point where values-based conflicts are a throwback issue for the history books. This is especially true in our large institutions which are ostensibly held together and naturally "bonded" by forces of the institution's makings. It is the unfortunate case that the larger the mass, the greater the exertion of the forces of beliefs-based entropy. And this is the reason that large and successful organizations are the home to beliefs-based disconnects that incrementally tear away at their institutional souls. It is only a matter of degree.

DISCONNECTED BELIEF SYSTEMS

"We have a million customers, who cares if we make one really mad?" is one belief-set speaking. "It just kills me when any one of our customers gets treated that badly." is another. I have heard those comments come out of different individuals during the same meeting. Is one lost sheep worthy of the effort to retrieve? Maybe, or maybe not, depending on one's worldview. When the next decision needs to be made about what to do with a failed customer experience, what will be the result? It will be a struggle between these opposing views, and the person with the most relative political power will win. Energy will be drained from the organization, alienation will occur and the soul of the organization will be carved away.

In many of my working capacities, I have spent nearly all my time resolving for belief-centered conflict issues. Most of that time was spent reconciling the internal value systems, and only a small part was directed at the problem itself. The actual problems were relatively easy to figure out. The belief system discontinuities were the hard part. None of us enjoys fighting and negotiating compromises with the people that are supposed to be on our side of the table. This is classic "rot-from-within."

"Can you give us an example of some of the beliefs and values you are talking about?" came from the audience. So I reflected for a moment and then proceeded to give them a story from my day earlier conversation with our Legal Department. I was managing an organization that had history of fairly reckless financial advice to customers, or let's at least say, "very high-risk investing." That definitely needed to change. I went on to talk about a client that had filed a suit claiming that we had caused him great financial harm. He had been a train engineer his whole life and had accumulated about $300,000 dollars to support himself and his family during his retirement. My question to the group was, "How much money do you think the guy had left when we were done with him?" Silence ensued. "About thirty thousand dollars" was what I said next. They all looked at me with a single question on their faces: "How do we keep this situation from happening going forward?" This was not a matter of right or wrong, but rather a coming to grips with a conflict in approaches to the organization's values. The investor might have ended up a big winner using our methods. The question was not one of risk-taking, but of the belief systems, values and related outcomes. And while this example is quite stark, the differences of opinion as to how an institution should conduct itself run rampant in most large organizations.

Post-Sufficient organizations are the home of *conflicting* values messaging to their members. These organizations have come to believe that values exist in a vacuum and that they can "have it both ways." To believe that values do not involve highly critical and oft times painful trade-offs is to live in a world of one's own making. The situation where "all the price tags have been shifted around" is not fatal, but it is very organizationally disconcerting. Organizations simply cannot "will" the real-world trade-offs away.

THE VALUES DELUSION

Every once and awhile, the sun comes out, the clouds and fog go away, and the world around us becomes more clear. I was on my way to no place of any importance one day when I noticed that the car ahead of me had an interesting license plate "frame." The message of the frame said, "Let's make our children our highest priority." It was at that moment of my life that the sun came out and the fog of the "values delusion" became clear.

The expressed Core Values of many large organizations had always appeared to me as addressing things of *value*, although seldom did they seem to say anything about *values*. Since the advent and subsequent collective mandate for the corporate "Statements of Core Values," this had always bothered me. But I had never spent any time thinking about the reasons why. The license plate frame provided the answer to my dilemma.

I went home and created an inventory of the Core Values from the websites of a half-dozen large organizations. The long list of values included some of the following: Building Strong Relationships, Giving Back, Excellent Customer Service, Creating Shareholder Value, Entrepreneurial Spirit, Taking Care of Our People, Doing the Right Thing, Leadership, Excellence, Integrity, Diversity, Respect, Teamwork, Professionalism, Collaboration, Accountability, Passion, Diversity, Quality, Market Focus, "Work Smart," Act like Owners, "Be the Brand," and Execution. As I looked at a few additional sites, the themes began repeating themselves, so it seemed I had largely covered the "Statement of Core Values" waterfront. But what do all of these words and phrases have to do with making our children our highest priority?

The best guess I had as to the political and emotional message of the driver of the car ahead of me was that this was just another San Francisco liberal who wanted more taxes to create even more school funding. While I couldn't agree any more vociferously with the underlying message, *my* suggested solution would have been a very different one. While we agreed on the object, we likely did not agree on the associated right actions. For purposes of this example, however, it makes little difference as to whose opinion was the most valid. The point is that most things in life are subject to some level of evaluation and that in almost all cases the evaluation as to the absolute goodness of the object is universal. And we can almost all agree that children are an important priority and of very high value.

The difference between things of value and values *themselves*, however, is when we take the next step and talk about the relative priorities attached to the choices we have amongst the various "goods" and "rights." Said differently, not until we compare and create preferences for one object (or party) over the others are we talking about values.

Values always, and by definition, make statements about relative preferences. Values are permanently linked to "who gets what, and who pays for what?" Alternatively, Vladimir Lenin thought in terms of "Who is doing what to whom?" It is a difference without a distinction. So while my license-frame friend was expressing a sentiment, it does not turn into a value until we talk about "who gets what and who pays," or we determine "who is doing what to whom." Successful human institutions often do the same thing. They substitute an adjective for a noun. In so doing, the purposes of the values-based words and phrases are decimated.

In an attempt to create statements of unique collective values, they simply create lists of things that *have* value. And in so doing, they cause more harm via confusion and misinterpretation than they create good. Of much greater consequence, however, is that they come to *think* they have addressed the issue of beliefs and values and have not, in reality, come anywhere close to actually doing it. When organizations come to believe that the existence of a Statements of Core Values is sufficient to solve for the "values issue," they are in real trouble. Values defy objectification. Mindishness sees the completion of the Statement of Core Values as a victory and a point of progress. Soul-Heads recognize the dangers that are present. Some organizations "get the 'values thing,'" and others do not.

We can use a few of the Core Values sited above to examine the differences between things of value and values themselves. My favorite example is that of "doing the right thing." This is an absolutely classic example of what logicians call a *rhetoric tautology*. All the words "rhetoric tautology" mean is that the response to the question (or the example) uses different words to say the same thing that was implicit in the question. Additionally, the words used in response to the question fail to provide additional clarity in their repetition. It is obvious that the question of values is by definition a claim about "doing the right thing."

The real *values* are based on what the answer to the question: "What is the right thing?" really is. Did they create this logic error intentionally? It can be seen that many of the words and phrases listed above fall into the same category. And it can just as easily be seen that the alleged value of the statement is of no value to anyone actually attempting to rightly express the value in their actions. The right thing to me and the right thing to you might be very different. The sentiment expressed in "doing the right thing" is outstanding. It just lacks meaning without further priority-rich context.

The other values delusions are seen in the form of statements that 1) just recapture the role of the institution, 2) are simply statements of strategic intent or, 3) represent blinding glimpses of the obvious. To "create value for shareholders" is what capitalist organizations, as agents for those owners, are supposed to do. A real value statement would be found in talking about the trade-offs that are made to facilitate the end of creating the shareholder value. An example of this is whether the organization prefers short-term profits at the potential cost of long-term profits, or the other way around. "Taking care of our people" is a similar values-less comment. Spewing notions like "working smart" and "operating with integrity" are equally inane from a pure values communications standpoint.

Who is going to disagree with these statements? Real values, by definition, always contain topics for which rightfully differing views exist. Something is dreadfully wrong with an organization that feels the need to state that integrity or "operating intelligently" should be stated as values-based goals. To determine that an important message within a human institution is the need to turn people's brains back on is to conclude that the picture is troubling. We are never conflicted over issues with which we all agree.

Values are guiding in those situations where as individuals we do not know the organizationally correct path to take, but for adequate values-based guidance from the institution. Organizational attempts to negate the impact of disparate values through rank simplification are doomed.

Lastly, the class of indicated values that contains sentiments like execution, quality, and building strong relationship are just strategic focal points, and have nothing to do with values at all, albeit that they are all relatively virtuous things. Values come into play as we get to the inevitable forks in the road, and need to figure out which of the paths is the one most consistent with the prevailing preferences. No formula can guide us at those points, only embedded values. When organizations espouse the value of "building strong customer relationships" and then cut the "customer visit" travel budget by ten percent, what does it mean? It means something; it is just hard to tell what that something is. It is a contradiction, and it clearly does not inspire confidence.

Post-Sufficient organizations say one thing and then proceed to approach things very differently. They think they can have it both ways. They believe in their own rationalizations, as if the members of the organization think the way they do. But what they create is an organization stripped of its soul. Communities do not tolerate this type of abject hypocrisy. They know that they cannot afford to.

VALUES IN CONTEXT

Beliefs and values, to gain any traction within an organization must be placed in context, or they become the object of cynicism. Context comes in the form of identified reference points. The reference points indicate real choices based on principles, as opposed to situational choices based on the "flavor of the day." Statements of beliefs and values are powerful in their immutability. That is also whats makes them "Handle with Care" items. Values must be carefully guarded within any organizational setting. And they are likely not conflated into a single word or expression. Some examples as to statements that actually contain beliefs and values are as follows:

"As questions arise as to the equitable and fair resolution of issues we have with our customers, we error on the side of customers as our first priority. We attempt not to be abused or taken advantage of by our customers, or to create the unequal treatment of customers. But, we universally try to give them the advantage in any and all situations when trade-offs are being made." This says that the customer is the *recipient* in the "who gets what" question, and that the organization is the one that generally pays. The exception is in those unusual situations where the customer is being intentionally abusive. This type of statement is hugely self-identifying.

"As questions arise as to who gets paid the most within our organization, we reward those who have shown their loyalty to the organization and to its long-term growth." This statement says that the organization values commitment and long-term thinking over get-rich-quick schemes that someone might concoct. If this is in-fact what the organization actually values, the impact on its actions will be both noteworthy and profoundly obvious to the members. This type of statement will radically shape the organization's outcomes.

"As economic times get tough, we error on the side of taking care of the economic and financial interests of our member associates, rather than the investment-return interests of our shareholders." I am waiting to hear this one come out of some CEO at an annual shareholder meeting. Some organizations actually have this value set and some do not. The "right" answer is that there is no right answer, and that is what makes it a belief system. It represents a choice. This type of statement addresses the real issue of how important its associates are. It is a tremendously loud statement.

"If one of our associates has done something wrong, we make a conscious decision on the side of remediation, as opposed to punishment." Some organizations want to hold up the severed heads of offenders as examples, while some choose a slightly more personally dignified path. The difference in the messages is not difficult for the members to discern. Remember, the mighty Roman Empire was built against a backdrop of severed heads. Your belief systems dictate whether this is thought to be a good thing or not.

The list of these values and preferences goes on indefinitely. And that is the reason that organizations want to create a Statement of Core Values. It is a form of short-hand for a language for which the short-hand communicates little of the substance. It is just another "sub-formula" that makes up part of the "grand success formula" of the organization. And like most formulas, it falls short of the mark, as they fail to incorporate the humanity in the situation.

The incorporation of beliefs and values into an organization is not a project, leading to a values-list, or to a fancy banner resting atop the corporate newsletter. Values define the nature of the interaction and the rules-of-engagement between the seriously self-interested parties in the melodrama. They cannot be simplified or formulated away. And it is critically important to understand that once a "people group" has been wronged from a values standpoint, they never, ever forget the violation. The wrongs are passed down through the years.

Values speak to the soul. They can, as such, only be addressed in the language of the soul. And they are only addressed by Soul-Heads. The format is never words or short phrases, as those are not the linguistic form of the Soul-Head. The format is always most effective in the stories that are baked into the history of the organization. Those stories stand as memorials and future reference points as to the effective choices, sacrifices, and trade-offs made in the past.

When five people are working together that share a common set of values, their energies are multiplicative or even exponential. When five thousand or fifty thousand people are working together, the energies are multiplied and then a factor is subtracted based on the level of beliefs-based discontinuities. The presence of these discontinuities within human institutions causes a dramatic reduction in output of all kinds given first, the energy absorbed in the internal fights and second, the lack of any meaningful imagination that can emerge during exhibitions of divergent values and worldviews. Varying opinions are great starters for the collective imagination. Varying values and worldviews are just the opposite. Diversity of thought leading to creativity is essential to advancement. Diversity of people groups representing fundamentally different worldviews, however defined, is completely antithetical to success and durability.

It is the foremost objective of all human institutions to spend whatever time and resource is necessary to maintain the group version of a home and a community. To be given the opportunity to understand what is important, to emotionally and logically agree with the rationale of the priorities, and to feel protected within the context of the organization is to promote the institutional version of a home.

If you were to ask most company's senior executives whether these things have been accomplished, my sense is that they would say yes. "We have our mission and vision statements and our statements of values, and they are communicated regularly." My observations have been to the contrary. These corporate statements basically tell us that the institution's mission is to be a "World-class company that will work together as a team, utilizing a customer-focused approach, to outperform the competition and to fulfill the interests of our associates, our shareholders and our communities." Has it occurred to the world that if everyone has the same statements of intention that they might actually be completely meaningless? What this says is that the world is one big community, which it clearly is not.

Mission-Vision-Values statements are on the checklist of every large entity and they are basically substitutes for substance. They are substitutes for real sharing and substitutes for the establishment of a real community. It is easy to believe most of them are actually well-intended. But this is positive intent as understood by the Mind-Head. The attempts at establishing consistent value systems are just not of an "industrial strength" and fall woefully short of what is actually necessary to maintain community. Within Post-Sufficiency they become laughable, given the naïve notion that they are actually impacting anyone or anything. They seem to provide the organization something to talk about and little else. They have become the institutional equivalent of talking about the weather in our personal relationships. They are interesting, but without the substance necessary to actually change anything. They do not provide any guidance. The lack of substance in these statements is not so much the problem. The problem is that organizations talk about them as if they actually did.

VALUE AND WORLDVIEW NEEDS

So what is it that we need as individuals within our institutions in regard to establishment of the foundations of consistent values and worldviews? We need two very basic things. The first is to exist within an organization that lives with a set of values that are both essential and demonstrable. The second is to be educated in the values at a level consistent with their creation of personal direction and mobilization. All well-functioning communities are essentially fueled by a set of broadly understood and mobilizing values. The further we are removed from values, the closer we are to disintegration and chaos.

It is impossible to understate the importance of addressing the "why" questions existing within our institutional settings. We need to have the organization "open our eyes" as to the value systems, such that we can understand the real nature of the environment in which we operate. And we need to understand the importance of that unity of opinion in accomplishing our objectives. Call this the development of the sense of "sameness." It is the sense that we are all on the same side, not just in a competitive sense, but also in a community sense. To face a common enemy is to be part of a team. To face an identifiable common enemy with a common set of values is to create a winning team. To exist within an institution that is mobilized by a set of common values that are mobilizing without the presence of an identified enemy is to create real community. Only true community endures.

The keys to developing a valuable and productive worldview consistency, requires a series of presuppositions and mindsets that must exist. The first of these essentials is the simple acceptance that worldview disparities systematically destroy the intentions of an institution. More specifically, it must be understood that a *strategy* is not a force operating opposite the values discontinuities. That these differences, either by acts of ignorance or passive-aggressive behavior, are the creators of significant under-performance is a notion that is very difficult for many organizational leaders to accept. This is mostly a function of their relative over-confidence in the efficacy of their strategies and the communications of their strategic values.

Precedent to that, the organization must develop the capabilities to capture and communicate the nature and content of their values and worldviews. The ability to stand in front of an organization's members and begin an address with "This is how we see the world working and here is *why* we are going to act in accordance with that set of views" is a good start. To discuss the essential goodness of the group's undertaking and to speak to the values that are personally inspirational represents a great second step. Speaking to the "rightness in approach" as to the nature of the relationships that are encountered within the organization is to essentially complete the picture. This is an alternative to "Here is what we have concluded we are going to *do* and here is what we expect to *accomplish*." When we don't know the reasons why, we generally just don't care about anything else.

The next thing that organizations must do to establish worldview consistency is to rid themselves of both positivism and paternalism. It is in our institutional natures that we project a positive and protective stance opposite each other as members. But this creates a contorted view of how we really see the world, and everyone within the organization knows it. We must be willing to trust each other with the truth. We must be willing to share the depths of our belief systems without fear that the disclosure will somehow destabilize the organization.

The notion that the truth will set you free is, in this context, absolutely true. Optimism is a virtue. Positivism is a curse. And while being protected from the world's ills represents a nice sentiment, the protectors in this setting are creating more risks for members (in their protective stance) than they are solving for. Human beings can handle a challenging environment that is personally well understood. What we all struggle with is the semblance of stability against a backdrop of uncertainty created by positivism and paternalism.

In the balance of this chapter, we will look at four areas of concentration which may be seen as both critical and fundamental to the establishment of durable foundations for the institutional homes in which people live and are sustained. They represent some practical and values-based supports for a durable community. They are just examples, but they cut across all structural and reporting lines within any organization and have nothing whatsoever to do with any of the operating functions of an entity. They are almost completely devoid of quantification and therefore very challenging for the contemporary analytic manager to "manage." The results of the outputs of the areas of concentration are more *felt* than comprehended by those who are impacted. But they contain the essential ingredients of real values that can become the foundations for long-term durability.

THE SENSITIVITY IMPERATIVE

As I sit in the office in our home, our cat is often sleeping in the chair in the corner of the room. It has always been intriguing to me that in the midst of his sleep, if I whisper his name, whichever of his ears that is closest to me tilts towards me. I suppose this is some kind of protective mechanism, as opposed to a reflection of his relational interest in me. But the metaphor seems instructive. Napoleon is very alert and sensitive to his environment. He has a sense that is so finely developed he can even use it in his sleep.

As a musician, I have had to learn to play my instruments in tune. Most of us have the ability to hear whether something is generally being played in tune or not. Over the years I have developed the additional ability to hear the "vibrations" that are processed through my ears and into my brain from two notes that are not in tune. The slower the vibrations, the closer the notes are to being in tune. Any guitar player can demonstrate how this works and sounds. Some of us, however, are not so musically inclined. We can't hear that one note is different from the other. Pitch eludes our best intentions and attempts. And it is frustrating.

Napoleon was born with his audial sensitivities. No training was required. I have had to work to develop my sense of intonation. The same combination of traits exists within human institutions as it relates to hearing and responding to the interests of customers and other constituencies. Insufficient organizations, whether by instinct or development, are very good at "hearing the whispers" or "feeling the vibrations" of their constituencies. Large and successful organizations are often on a path to losing both senses. The reasons for this are many. But stopping the progression is an organizational imperative.

Included among the reasons that organizations lose their customer orientation and sensitivity is they end up with so few of their members who actually have contact with customers. As a matter of fact, many people who work in large organizations do so as a way of actually *avoiding* contact with real customers. Customers can be scary. As a result, much of the insight into clients that should be gained through direct contact is substituted for by artificially gained "Customer Knowledge Management" or "Competitive Intelligence" which are no substitutes at all. The lack of sufficient and direct customer interface also creates a situation where continuous improvement of the offering, whatever it is, becomes the only method of innovation. When major changes to the offering are needed, which always ultimately happens, the ability and willingness to make the hard decisions is highly compromised. In a situation where so many decision makers are not exposed to customers, the likelihood of "missing the market" goes up significantly as well. Even getting to any level of agreement on core strategy issues becomes nearly impossible as the consistent feedback and customer-based sensitivities are missing.

In Insufficient organizations, nearly everyone has good customer interaction. The effective distance between customers and the average member of many large organizations becomes a very large gap. The further removed we are from the real object of our attentions, the less attuned and sensitive we are to the needs of the object. Customers end up becoming an abstract concept, something for our Mind-Head to figure out. As human beings are always the customers (very few machines ever make buying decisions), the sensitivity imperative is directed at Soul-Heads. The distance from customers is the source of an anesthetic numbing of the sensitivities of an organization.

I once worked in an organization that did a tremendous amount of market and customer research. That research indicated that customers were willing to pay significantly more for the services of the Company than they were currently paying. As the costs to provide services were largely fixed, and as the organization was a scale provider, the profit margin magnification resulting from price increases were extremely large. Interestingly, the entire Board of Directors bought this logic with the exception of one lone Board member. He simply did not believe what all the research was saying. In retrospect, he was the sole Soul-Head on a Board consisting almost entirely of Mind-Heads. And while the jury is still out, it looks like he was the only one on the Board that saw the picture correctly. The price increases likely have destroyed the competitive position once owned by this organization.

Additionally, in large and successful organizations, a level of fascination of "things-internal" takes over and drives much of the organization's energies. To the extent that by some coincidence the internal machinations create end-customer value, this is, in a small way, an acceptable situation. But more often the customer perspective in Post-Sufficiency is just missing. And talking with customers about their needs is only a very early step in actually understanding their current and future needs. Even efficiency initiatives, while appearing internal, should have an external perspective. "This is why the efficiency and infrastructure-building efforts that we are involved with today create improvements that will have an impact on our pricing and competitive positioning. They also are directly related to the ways we can add even more value for our customers as an organization. This is why this initiative is so important to our customers and for our organization and our associates."

If you imagine a triangle that is intersected and sliced horizontally into four segments, it creates an interesting view of an organization with respect to customer sensitivity. In the top of the figure is a group of people with incredible insight and understanding and sensitivities to the needs of customers. The bottom slice is represented by those in the organization with no understanding of customers at any level. The slices in-between represent those with some modest level of understanding and those with what might be called a "good" amount of understanding. I have worked in an organization where only one percent of the members were in that top grade . . . call it Grade A. I would guess that about five percent were in Grade B, with the other ninety four percent in the bottom two grades. I don't know what the right configuration is, but I know that the mix in that organization was way too heavily consigned to Grades C and D. Over the long-run, this is not sustainable. Distance creates a major sensitivity and empathy challenge. We care little over that with which we have neither contact nor understanding.

The Sensitivity Imperative requires an organization to constantly apply pressure in an effort to continually migrate their members towards increasing insight and sensitivities towards customers. The means available to accomplish the desired end of greater customer sensitivity are without end. More significant is the discipline and desire of the organization, as a function of the universally recognized need for customer sensitivity as a value system, to simply engage in the affair. This is a core value that some organizations embrace and some do not. Clearly the needs within organizations are different. At the same time, over periods of years, many organizations slip into Post-Sufficiency as they narrow their exposure to customers to fewer and fewer people within the organization. This is classic utilitarianism in action. It is often easier to limit customer exposure to a few people as possible who are paid to be customer sensitivity "specialists." This is not a strategy for long-term durability.

Some of the pertinent questions related to the Sensitivity Imperative include: 1) What percentage of the members of the organization is engaged with customers at Grades A and B? 2) Why are members of the organization distanced from customers and how can that situation be remedied? 3) What insights about customers are the most critical in understanding how the organization can situate itself towards meeting those current and future customer needs? 4) What would change in the organization's priority and decision-making processes if customer sensitivity levels were significantly higher?

This imperative speaks not to gaining complete exposure of the organization to customers. Rather it speaks to maintaining a certain minimum level of appreciation and "closeness" to customers to keep the enterprise from customer-atrophy. With sensitivity to the needs of customers comes an enthusiasm for meeting those needs. Without sensitivity, the members are subjected to the "Bokanovsky Process" and become "Gamma-Minus Semi-Morons" in the words of Aldous Huxley.

Sensitivities to the needs of others are the food for the soul of the organization. Communities are built to serve. When members cannot meaningfully serve their constituencies, they diagnose their contributions as without value and they act accordingly.

This value system takes a significant amount of organizational time and energy. I was once in a conversation with the new business unit controller for one of the institution's business units and we were talking about what the customer-facing people did in their jobs. Additionally, we talked about the dual roles of financial people in terms of creating the financials on one hand, and on providing data for decision support of the customer-facing people on the other. It was apparent that this individual was pretty clear on her role with respect to maintaining the debits and credits. Her lack of understanding as to how the business of our customers worked, however, made the discussion of any decision-support for the sales and service people a wasted exercise. This was a marvelous human being with a tremendous attitude. But her lack of customer sensitivity and context represented a huge opportunity cost for the organization. The organization should have been willing to invest in this type of person in order to bring them to a better level of understanding—beyond the fact that debits are on the left.

Someone once asked me the question, "What is the most important piece of a jigsaw puzzle?" After allowing me to ponder the question for a few seconds he offered the answer. He smiled and said "the top of the box." The ability to see the whole picture, and to be sensitive to the implications of the whole, is a starting point without equal. We develop sensitivities to our world by being in contact with it. And that is the key to the sensitivity imperative.

Mind-Heads don't even like the word "sensitivity." Soul-Heads actually *see* the world in terms of sensitivity.

THE CREATIVITY IMPERATIVE

Thomas Sowell, the noted social commentator and economist, wrote a book on opportunity costs that exist within closed systems. In the preface to the book, he made an off-handed comment that I could only assume he had concluded all the rest of us already knew. And maybe everyone else already did, but his insight had clearly eluded me to that point. He basically said the history of progress is that of taking things (materials of whatever variety) that had formerly operated in disparate spheres, and assembling them by the use of new ideas in ways that create additional total utility and usefulness. These new things simply had not existed before their integration. So I looked around the room and saw the scenario having played out in everything around me. Whether it was my wrist watch or the latex paint on the walls, it all spoke to Sowell's observation. Undoubtedly, others had come to similar conclusions previously, but the idea seemed very powerful.

As a result of Sowell's observation, I then came to see creativity as a more deductive, versus inductive, process. As a deductive process, the knowledge of (and sensitivity to) the big picture was much more useful. To be able to place "all the pieces" on the table in front of a group of people who have a broad understanding of the uses and meanings of the pieces now was of tremendous creative value. And it was infinitely doable. Instead of looking at creativity as an exercise in sitting back and thinking glorious and innovative thoughts, the notion of creativity was made available to those of us with IQs of less than 160.

In this light, everyone has the ability to be creative. The Marketing or Product Development people in any organization are not (and cannot be) the sole keepers of the creative spark within the organization. Creativity is applicable to everything, everywhere and at all times. We sub-optimize our futures greatly when the organization, in whatever ways it selects, decides to cordon off creativity and force it into the domain of the few. It is also the case that to the extent creativity does come to rest in a small group; they will be very unwilling to share their "creative wealth" for fear of its commoditization. For many organizations the imagination "decision" is one of whether they either are or are not creative. If they deem creativity to be their strategy, then it is made an important value. If they deem themselves to have other attributes of their business on which they are building their futures, then imagination is thought to be something that "the other guys do." But that can only be a short-term mindset.

Some of the organizations I have worked for have considered themselves creative—at least to a degree—and some have not. More often than not, however, creativity is considered at least moderately strategically dangerous, and they decide that they would actually prefer to follow a more well-traveled path. The idea of the "fast follower" becomes the norm in Post-Sufficient organizations with a value system that has morphed into one of risk reduction at almost any cost. Becoming a fast-follower is a fools game, but not because an organization cannot follow closely enough over the long-term. Nor is it a function of the disproportionate rewards that come to those who are early entrants into a market. Rather, the problem with the fast-follower strategy is that it robs the organization of the soulish energy generated by being in the position to drive "industry" growth through innovation. As the old line goes, "If you are not the lead dog, every view is the same."

There is a belief held by some that the only effective brand positioning strategy is that of being the leader. Leadership comes from creativity manifest in some form of customer satisfaction. The question is: "Has the organization completely lost its ability to innovate and imagine?" This would seem to be impossible in a large group of very smart people. But, as we all observe, much more innovation (on a per capita or even absolute basis) comes from Insufficient organizations than from those who are Post-Sufficient and large. It is left to the large to simply do those things that require large amounts of "throw weight." We are then back to the fundamental question of why large organizations are less effective at innovation, with all their seemingly insurmountable advantages, than the small and nimble

One of the reasons organizations fail to innovate is that innovation is quietly thought to be too dangerous. When things are going well, why would you mess it all up by coming up with something new? Systems are good at innovating because individuals are good at innovating. Within the Post-Sufficient organization, innovation causes an imbalance between the known and the unknown where there is more perceived downside risk to innovation than there is perceived upside opportunity. The situation is reversed amongst the Insufficient. And that is why creativity is a value as opposed to a process or approach.

The second reason for the creativity deficit is that many organizations just do not embrace the significance of creativity and imagination. They value the science of execution and essentially minimize the import of the art form that is creativity. In order for imagination to flourish, the organization has to say that it actually values creativity and then act in like manner. And in this connection, the notion of imagination is not limited to the creation of "the next big thing," but includes imagination in even the most basic functions of an institution. And it includes the imaginative opportunities of literally every member of the organization. This is not a utopian thought. Imagination can and must come in all sizes and shapes.

Additionally, a history of innovation can lull an organization to sleep. It is in innovation, broadly defined, that organizations are propelled forward. They initially become successful as the result of innovation. Then they become apathetic and rely on past innovation to author their continued success. An organization's relative level of innovation, at any point in time, may be sufficient for the time. It is infinitely simple to rely on the past as the author of future success. The belief system that is the Creativity Imperative says that that is not true. It also says that all the collected innovation of the past is the foundation on which future innovation can be built.

As Edmund Burke indicated, societies (communities) are partnerships with our ancestors, the living and the yet unborn. Without that values-based sense of our connectedness with people and time, the accurate understanding of who we are is lost and our organizational souls are diminished. Innovation is always built on that which has come before. I have seen dozens of situations where my organizational affiliations have found themselves effectively behind the competition. The reason was that they would periodically take creativity breaks and coast for a time. And then, they would be five or eight years behind, and the challenges of catching up became immense.

Some of the questions to address with respect to the Creativity Imperative are: 1) How does the organization define creativity and where is creativity needed? 2) What sources of creativity currently exist in the organization and how do those sources match with the organization's needs? 3) Is the organization's "creativity culture" sufficient to advance the overall needs of the entity? 4) Does the creativity of the organization inspire and further incent the group's members? 5) Has the organization taken into account the "new" level of complexity that exists in the current environment?

"Then one day you find, ten years have got behind you. No one told you when to run. You missed the starting gun." *Pink Floyd* makes a very interesting point. Some events in our lives have starting guns and others do not. If the race is already going on and we are found to be waiting for the gun, the race will be lost. Creativity is one of those things where there is no gun. It therefore has to be a value and a part of the organization's worldview.

Mind-Heads logically appreciate the importance of creativity and imagination, but can be intimidated by its implications. They are also concerned with the lack of quantifiability of the impact of investments in imagination and cultures that actively embrace creativity. Soul-Heads see creativity as an avenue to a brighter and more relationally positive future. They recognize the broad implications of creativity as a deeply-held value system, particularly as it impacts the souls of all the members of the organization. Nothing is as motivating as coming up with something new and positive.

THE MOBILIZATION IMPERATIVE

Whether represented by the Gettysburg Address or the "I Have a Dream" speech, the combination of outstanding character, a passion for a better future for the whole, and the ability to put deep meaning into words changes the future. Deep meaning always comes from an equally deep set of personal beliefs and values. The change occurs because the words pierce their way right through to where we live. These speeches speak to our souls. And a soul, once spoken to, will never forget. Souls actually cannot forget. They can ignore, at least for awhile, but they can never forget.

Our minds, alternatively, are just the opposite. They hear what they want to hear. Mindishness creates a desire for things we want. Minds create push-strategies. Souls are focused on betterment. Souls create pull-strategies. This difference between betterment and "things we want" is seminal. Only when a soul is attached to betterment is it fundamentally mobilized. Mobilized is a combination of both *prepared* and *willing*. A group that is effectively mobilized is both emotionally and mentally capable of almost anything it decides it wants to do.

Betterment as the source of mobilization looks outside of the self and, in so doing, frees people of the challenges associated with tiring and relentless self-interest, which is ultimately and universally enslaving. When a soul is inspired by something that is both worthy of attention and beyond the self, it is the most powerful force in the universe. To capture just a part of the potential soulishness of the individuals in an organization is both a major accomplishment and a major source of organizational durability.

Dave Drury, as President of the Principal Financial Group, was neither Abraham Lincoln nor Martin Luther King. Actually, as an orator, he was far from it. He usually read his addresses to the organization. Dave was not an aggressive man, nor was he a gifted speaker. His background was as an actuary; the ultimate bean-counter. But when Dave spoke, people listened. And it was always my impression that nearly everyone in the organization would Storm the Bastille if that is what Dave thought should be done.

The reason for the organization's loyalty to Dave has become more apparent to me over time. He was a person of outstanding character that was totally committed to the outcomes of the organization and the people who worked there. Everyone knew Dave was doing everything in his power to move the organization ahead in a manner consistent with the historically instilled values of the Company. And his words, though usually few, were always very impactful. Dave might say three words in a meeting. But it was important you heard each one of them. Dave rightfully claimed moral authority (and it was readily granted to him by his followers) and the result was the very effective mobilization of his army. The voice of character and values was always heard above the cacophony of the crowd.

Self-interest creates much of the underlying driving incentive for people to act as individuals. We all know this and we see it every day. Mobilization, alternatively, is driven by group interest. Mobilization is infinitely more powerful as a long-term solution to the issue of institutional durability. There are organizations that use personally focused self-interest as their chief motivator, but those organizations are playing with fire. Goldman Sachs may be an example of a company that can get away with using personal incentives in this way. But Goldman would be an exceptional case, and not any sort of prototype for the rest of us to follow. Greed as a value system actually seems to work at Goldman, an organization that has made an art form out of the movie line "Greed, for lack of a better word, is good."

Personal incentives, as a mobilizing force, represent a very shallow view of humanity. That the rewards system in an organization is limited to self-interest bespeaks a view of humanity that is an insult to the human spirit. If there is nothing being done in the organization that represents a broader interest in the betterment of the world, such that it cannot become a mobilizing force, then we are talking about a sad situation. The identification and heartfelt communication of the opportunity for the organization to advance the whole is critical to avoid Post-Sufficiency.

In some ways it is right to say that the reason that capitalist organizations exist is to make money. It may be concluded, at least by some, that it is the only reason that these institutions exist. No one, however, is personally and directly motivated by their organization's ability to make money. They are personally motivated by the connection between the company's ability to make money and their personal ability to make money. And they are motivated by the security which comes to their lives by working in an entity that appears to provide them an opportunity to make money into the future. They may be motivated by the notion that their organization is making money, as a means of keeping score and an indication that their team is winning. But the simple fact that an organization is making money is of little use to most of us. Yet, much of the discussion in large and successful organizations is around "returns", and not that which is truly mobilizing. Personal security and predictability and mobilization around a greater good are the real and enduring sources of energy.

As a general rule, if the statement involves a number, or set of numbers, don't expect it to do anything other than inform. While I personally like the numbers (most of my colleagues think of me as a numbers guy), numbers do not represent the language of the soul. Numbers tell a cryptic tale that creates a level of disinterest in their sheer abstraction. Numbers are usually not well-enough understood to resonate, and actually tend to confuse or look like intentional misinformation.

Stories are the language of the soul. The soul speaks in the terms of relationships. Not just inter-personal relationships, but all types of relationships. And it speaks in the language of hope. In the case of the Abe Lincoln or Martin Luther King, the relationships being spoken of were of very large groups of people who were divided by vast differences in worldviews. This is the same situation existing in large organizations. Imparting the story as to why we are "put into right relationship with one another" is the ultimate mobilizing theme. It speaks to the "better angels" of our nature, as President Lincoln indicated.

These better angels are a critical ally in fighting Post-Sufficiency, as large and successful organizations create more than enough opportunities to house the organizational "gremlins" that always take up residence. Gremlins are birthed in break-rooms and become nasty little life forms that emanate from insecurity. At issue is the ability to effectively summon the better angels with enough authority and clarity as to draw them out. Without the voice, or voices, within an organization that can accomplish this, the gremlins just take over. The message is of the Gremlin's choosing. The nature of the dialog then changes within the organization and all sense of mobilization is lost.

Angels and gremlins both speak the language of values. They both talk to the issue of relationships and justice. Angels talk about group justice and gremlins talk about personal injustice. Angels think and act in the future tense. Gremlins want to focus on what is wrong today and to the whole history of wrongs. Angels drive the conversation towards answers, while gremlins would like the conversation to trend towards expansion of the problems heretofore identified. It takes a strong and credible voice within a large entity to drown out the message of the gremlins with a message that collectively resonates and mobilizes a large group of people. The ability to speak meaningful truth into the life of a human institution is invaluable. It is also very doable. But it takes the right voice or set of voices. Preparing and positioning those voices is an imperative second-to-none.

I was attending a dinner with about fifty of my colleagues and was sitting next to the President of the organization. At one point in the meeting, he leaned over to me and asked if he should stand up and say a few words. The obvious answer was "Yes." After he addressed the group, he sat down again and said to me, "That just wasn't as good as (his predecessor) would have done it." He was forlorn. He was trying to mobilize and inspire the group and he had failed. His problem was that he was a classic Mind-Head guy. His predecessor was a very smart Soul-Head. He was perplexed why his Mind-Head continued to fail him. The point was that it hadn't. Mind-Heads aren't any good at mobilizing large groups of people. It is not their job. This was also a very smart guy, but with only one head, and it hurt the organization. Leaders must be able to speak life into the soul of the organization as a means of mobilizing the members to a higher level of commitment than exists in a world of abstract and numerically denominated notions of advancement.

Some of the questions to address with the Mobilization Imperative are: 1) Who has the character, passion, and ability to express mobilizing values? 2) Who in the organization has the ability to speak with mobilizing authority? 3) How many people in the institution can provide this type and level of mobilization? 4) Who is effectively being trained or mentored to carry all these torches? 5) Who has enough transparency within the organization to allow the organization's members to see their character, passion and values?

And yes, the need for resources, time and money are readily apparent here as well. There is a need for a set of competencies in this imperative that are very unique. Who taught Mr.'s Lincoln and King their skill sets? How did they grow into the trenchant leaders they became? How much of this was a part of their DNA at birth? What life events caused them to emerge with the authority to move millions? Why did people listen? Machines do not talk, and they clearly do not communicate. Nor does the system talk or inspire. Numbers are mute as well. The mobilizing role is left, and always will be left, to high-character, passionate, and group-serving individuals with the competencies and credibility to mobilize the masses. While most organizations will not find themselves in the company of the political and religious leaders mentioned here, the issues are again only those of degrees of separation.

Mind-Heads are inclined to see the mobilization of their teams in terms of things that are logically motivating. They see numbers and theories as those sources of mobilization, because those are the things that motivate them. And they tend to look at the motivation of the group as the motivation of individuals within the group. Soul-Heads are inclined to see mobilization as a group exercise, with rhetoric and stories the device, and humanity the object. The goal of the Soul-Head is never to impress. The goal is to do whatever is necessary to speak with moving clarity to the audience.

The imperatives of Sensitivity, Creativity, and Mobilization all address the need that human institutions have to create appropriate relational linkages between themselves and the world around them. They do not conform to physical laws and are difficult to put into tightly-wound theories or formulas. It is true they are very easy to understand at a high-level, and at the same time very difficult to discuss. They are deeply personal topics and subjectively evaluative, and in that we tend to shy away. And they are in many ways lost-arts in a SMUTy world, with its shriveling Soul-Heads and "financial engineering" approach to organizational development.

At the core, humans are a collection of two things. We each represent a set of beliefs and values and a store of potential energy. Beliefs are uniquely human. Creativity is a uniquely spiritual exercise. Sensitivity and empathy are the things of mystery. And to be mobilized is to have our souls engaged in something significant. Our ability to care about anything other than ourselves is an unexplainable human phenomenon largely beyond our ability to logically understand. And in our vile humanity there exist a number of very important questions that are in continual need of answers.

In aligning the real and critical institutional values, and in developing and mobilizing the organization's members, is to release the potential energy embedded deep within our humanity. In this continued "releasing" is the force behind the advancement and durability of all human institutions. It is in this freedom of release that we are able to operate as a community. And in so doing, we find ourselves at home.

The establishment of a common base of beliefs and values discussed in this chapter is the baseline component in the building of essentially durable foundations for human institutions. The organization can then move towards building onto that foundation. The next foundational building blocks are found in the establishment of "meaning." Our values and belief systems provide the context for our actions. Meaning then goes on to provide the set of deeply held and personal human *incentives* for action.

9

Organizational Teleology

Large and successful organizations are challenged to maintain any sense of organizational meaning, other than simply existing. Meaning is the importance the organization attaches to their contribution to the whole of the community, and serves as the mobilizing force in their advancement. Mind-Heads are ill-equipped to deal with issues of meaning, as they are not of an analytical nature. Accordingly, the Soul-Head must speak to issues of teleology and consistently deliver the message of organizational significance.

WE HAD JUST COMPLETED the release of our new and "first-ever" variable annuity product in one of my affiliations, and I was giving an address to an audience in the Company's auditorium (the purpose of the address I have long since forgotten). I was attempting to be at least somewhat profound. So I asked the group "Why do people buy variable annuities?" I was fishing for a wrong (but anticipated) answer that would come in the form of a description of some kind of death-benefit rider or our cleverly crafted "M&E" charge schedule, just to make a point. When no one said anything, (as I had also anticipated), I offered that the reason people buy annuities had nothing to do with the value of the annuity product itself. Rather, they were buying a product in the hopes of one day funding the purchase of a vacation home in the Carolinas. The group seemed to accept my philosophizing, so I went on. I said that the hope of the ownership of property in Beaufort, South Carolina was in-fact *not* really the reason either, and that another more fundamental reason actually existed.

As I went on, it came out that the core rationale for doing almost anything was always relational, and that a Low Country home in

Beaufort was essentially useless unless you could enjoy the residence with people you know and love. That might include the grandkids, a lifelong friend or some old college buddies. What I was trying to say was that we were not in the annuity business; we were engaged in a much more significant enterprise. At the same time, I was attempting to direct the group's attention to the next essential in attaining organizational durability in the form of the development of soulish and solid foundations.

The point of my discussion was to make our efforts in building and distributing the product part of something much bigger than just putting another fancy financial services product on the street. Rather than thinking about exchanging a customer's money for a piece of paper on which a number of promises were written, I was hoping to impart a more purposive message. For most of us to think about the outputs of the "factory" is not very interesting. And it is pretty clearly not very motivating. On the other hand, to think about the goods and related *good* that the outputs of the factory create moves us from the point of thinking in terms of "what we do" to thinking about "how we are contributing." And the latter is a very different thing from the former, especially over the long grind which can be the organization's existence.

We all want to be a part of doing something that is significant. We all want to be proud of the work we do and the associated and positive public images of our institutions. The old story that talks about the mason who comments that his work is "laying bricks" versus the one that concludes "I am building the world's greatest Cathedral" speaks directly to this point. Building great Cathedrals is inspiring and brings out the best in each of us. Building great Cathedrals invokes in us a fiery passion that is only in operation when the object of our attention is truly worthy of that level of personal intensity. We hold that level of passion within us, and release it into the world when the situation, as a function of our values and objects, is merited.

In the life of nearly all organizations, there exists a period of time when that fiery passion is released by the organization's members. It is an emotional rush, and it propels an organization in its formative period for months or years or even decades. The impetus for the display of passion (and energy and creativity and hopefulness) is a belief that the organization is "building a Cathedral." There is almost no stopping an organization in this phase, as the accomplishments that are experienced towards meeting the goal, which are always bigger than life itself, continue to add fuel to an already raging fire. The commitment levels of the members are directed by a notion that is bigger than the group itself. The group is being swept along by a purpose and destiny that is both meaningful and "worth the price" that is to be paid in its accomplishment.

At one point in my career I was presenting the strategy of my business unit to the Supervisory Board of ING. They were mostly Europeans and were in America reviewing some of their recent acquisitions. I was doing my part to educate them. I was the fifteenth out of sixteen presentations. My presentation was the first one after lunch on the second day. How fortuitous was that? By the time we got to my presentation, even I was fighting to stay awake. The preceding fourteen presentations all went like this: "Here is the list of financial products we produce, here is how we distribute these products, and here are the financial projections. Are there any questions?" So at lunch I decided, against my better instincts, to try something different. I was going to tell a bunch of European executives a little story and then see how they would respond.

The fairly lengthy tale I told was of a family situation where a financial advisor had essentially become "a part of the family" as a result of being of tremendous value. This was during a difficult period resulting from the loss of one of the elderly spouses. It was a story of a relationship forged between a financial advisor and an elderly woman who was devastated by the loss of her husband of nearly fifty years. I concluded the story with "and while Joan still misses Floyd in ways many of us will never understand, she is forever grateful for her financial advisor, who spent the time and relational energy to make sure that at least her financial affairs were taken care of." I went on to indicate that this was the story of my in-laws, and that I too was grateful to Mark, the financial advisor.

I was the person who had introduced Mark to my in-laws twenty years earlier. The rest of presentation was then linked to "And that is what we do in our business unit. We support the Mark's of this world." And I concluded with "We expect this level of financial result if we are successful in providing a high-quality of support." As I walked off the platform, the Company's US President handed me a note that said, "Great job, you almost brought me to tears." He had heard the meaning.

Over the years I have always been aware of the need for any organization to have that "edge" that is created by the passion to accomplish something that was really important. I once heard the former Chairman of Principal Financial Group, Dave Hurd, comment to a large group of people that "If we can just be just a little better (and he would hold up his thumb and pointer finger) than the competition year after year, we will find ourselves much better than the rest of the competition before not too many years will pass." And while I agreed with the mathematical accuracy of the comment, I was left uncertain what the *thing* was that was supposed to actually drive us to be "just a little better." The competition was likely all saying the very same thing.

What I was looking for was the identification of the *spark* that was supposed to ignite our collective will towards incremental betterness. All I heard was that betterness is betterness. And with that comment we would all agree. Mr. Hurd was not in a philosophical discussion, and I appreciated his remarks greatly, as he was a very sincere and well-intended man. At the same time, I remember walking away from that encounter thinking about why it would be that any organization would have the desire and will to be "just a little better" over the long-term, and what their response to that interest would then be.

The summary conclusion that I have reached is that organizations with a unified sense of purpose and meaning are always willing to pay a price to be "just a little better." In some cases it is to be truly a whole lot better. They are also more successful in their endeavors than those whose motivations come from alternative sources of reward. The "spark" that lights the fiery institutional passion is a knowledge that the object of attention is going to make a difference that will be noteworthy in the lives of both the members of the community, and those outside. We don't want to live our three score and ten and then vanish without leaving a legacy and a memorial to our lives. The building of "monuments" is the best way to leave a legacy, and our monuments come in all shapes and sizes.

Monuments are built with passion. They are nominally and poorly sustained, however, as a result of apathy. Post-Sufficiency nearly always chronologically follows the completion of a monument, irrespective of how long it took to complete. Even the completion date is sometimes difficult to define, but the members know when the work has been done, and the legacy established. And as surely as day leads to night, apathy follows passion. Since the beginning of time, the search has always been for the "next act." Failure to define the next act is usually fatal. Playing the same scene over and over may be comfortable, but it is never inspiring.

SPUDS

I have come to call these "sparks" that ignite our communitarian passions SPUDs. SPUD is an acronym for "significant, plausible, understandable and desirable" outcomes. The combination of significant, plausible, understandable and desirable, is highly combustible, and creates in us the sense of purpose and the sense of destiny that pushes us in ways that no other sources of motivation can. SPUDs are mobilizing as they speak to issues of personal dignity, the worth of relationships, the creation of just and equitable outcomes, and of a contribution to the whole of mankind. I once asked a stranger that I met on an airplane about what he did for a living and he told me that their company "built something that allowed one machine to talk to another machine." That struck me as the least valuable thing of which anyone could to be a part.

"I work with Down Syndrome adults to help provide them with the dignity of vocational employment" is felt much more deeply than "I help rich people get richer by selling them whiz-bang financial products." The point is not that helping Down Syndrome adults is innately better than peddling whiz-bang financial products. The point is that we can be more effectively mobilized when the cause is both defined and worthy of our attention, based on relational concepts.

SPUDs address things like comfort and beauty, truth and liberty, health and hopefulness, and peace and faith. SPUDs don't address operating efficiencies, output levels, process improvements, business models, or performance metrics. SPUDs don't care about industry leadership, branding, margins, or scale. And they are immune to quantification. Actually, as you attempt to quantify a SPUD, you simultaneously obliterate it.

I was sitting in a fast food restaurant during one of my business trips to Portland. I think it was a KFC. In walked a thirty-something year old women with a *very* old man. I assumed that the thirty-something was maybe the man's granddaughter. It became clear though, as they came and sat down at a table just a few feet away from me, that these were not members of a family. The woman had a name tag on her blouse with a title under her name. I don't remember her name, but I do remember her title. Apparently, she worked for a nursing home or skilled-care facility. She was the "Director of Vitality." SPUDs create vitality.

Essentially all that a SPUD represents is a narrative that demonstrates and allows the member to visualize where it is that the organization is going in terms that are either relational or otherwise humanly attractive. It includes the rationale as to the destination, "why we are going there," and why everyone should be proud of the anticipated accomplishment. It is essentially a well-articulated picture of the world "that could be" if our community is successful in its endeavors. And it captivates the attention and emotions of all the members. It becomes something worth doing, as opposed to just something to do.

The mailroom supervisor of a mutual fund distribution company that I once managed did an exceptionally efficient job. She had been with the company for a number of years. She never made any mistakes. One day she said to me, "Brian, my husband and I have never really had any money. So I don't understand a lot of what it is we actually do. At the same time, my husband and I have always been very happy, and our kids are now grown and doing well; so life is very good. But I have a question for you. Could you spend a few minutes and explain to me *what a mutual fund is?*"

She had very lovingly just dropped a load of bricks directly on my head. All she wanted was to understand what it was that we were providing and how she fit into the bigger scheme. She wanted the sense of worth that came along with something she sensed was a good thing, but really didn't understand. I was so happy she asked. It forever impacted how I thought about the individuals that make up the team. She wanted to know that what she was doing was part of creating a grander good. What a simply marvelous thing to want to know. And from that day, not only did she do a great job, but her very essence came alive. She inspired everyone she came in contact with as a result of her new and infectious attitude. She was now part of building a cathedral.

CREATING SPUDS

So how do institutions create and preserve passion-producing SPUDs? In the early days of an institution it is very simple. Survival, as a result of all the hard work and dedication to the animating idea of the institution, is a monument onto itself. After the organization reaches a level of success, and the original monument is being polished daily, the creation of a second or third generation SPUD becomes one of the greatest challenges for leadership.

I once heard the story of the personal commitment of a ten year old boy. As the story goes, it was during a time of war. There was a critically injured soldier who was in need of blood, and as the boy was available and had the right blood-type, he was asked if he would give his blood in support of the life of the soldier. With some trepidation, he agreed and went to the hospital to give of himself. After a few minutes, the boy's eyes began to well-up with tears which then ran down his cheeks. The nurse asked him if he was experiencing any pain. He indicated that he was fine and not in pain. The nurse said, "Well what is wrong then?" The boy paused for a moment and then solemnly asked "How long will it be before I die?" The nurse didn't know what to say. The little guy had falsely assumed that to give blood was to give his life. Ah, the beauty of a child and the power of a human being with an important and sacrificial purpose. This was an expression of "meaning" in its purest form.

"What? You are saying that we need a new animating and stimulating force to keep us going? We have so much momentum that nothing is going to get in our way. We are a finely tuned machine and we don't need another bedtime story at this juncture in our organization's life!" Many leaders in organizations become so accustomed to speaking solely from their Mind-Heads they can no longer hear their soul saying anything at all. They couldn't define a SPUD is they tried. The Mind-Head just does not think that way. They have created (by committee) their otiose "Mission-Vision-Values" statements, and that box has now been checked off as completed. Post-Sufficiency issues are a function of the denial of the need for more human depth.

SPUDs are value systems that look and act like faith systems. Having the faith that your community can accomplish something monumental creates a completely different environment than Woody Allen's notion that "Eighty percent of success is just showing up." I actually agree with that comment. But the other twenty percent is tied to the passion that the members bring to the jobsite everyday. It is the passion driven by meaning that is the key ingredient in making the real difference in terms of long-term organizational success.

I am always intrigued when I hear the word "transparency" in the context of an organization. You wonder about what is happening when the transparency antecedent is *not* being used. Communities always just assume transparency, and it does not need to be identified as such. When you hear the word transparency, be very afraid.

SPUDs, alternatively, are the ultimate voice of real transparency and they clearly don't need to be labeled, as they are felt, not calculated. They are abstract yet sincere; visual and not characteristic. They are conceptual, not linear. They defy objectification and quantification, and they really don't like it when people try to characterize them in that way. How do you quantify a Cathedral? By counting the number of bricks? Counting bricks might be transparent, but it is completely devoid of any real and humanly descriptive quality of the monument and its purposive meaning.

As large and successful organizations begin loosing their sense of purpose and meaning, as naturally happens, they often don't identify the problem as such, and they go in search of other solutions to the "obvious lack of passion" problem. They are looking for the spark, but have not identified their need. In the political era in which we all live, leaders who succumb to Post-Sufficiency generally search for answers in terms of governance and how the organization is lead. "How can we better orchestrate and direct the voices of our members towards a more civil and engaged public square?" "We need to get people more excited about participating around here, and here's how we are going to do it!" All the while, the organization's members are looking for something very different. Building a Habitat for Humanity house is a great idea, but it has little bearing on the impact of meaning within the institution sponsoring the work or the workers.

I have watched organizations follow several courses in their quest for a spark of institutional passion. The first course of action seems to be "leaders as cheerleaders." I have observed many a senior leader in front of their charges talking about "how personally excited I am about the completion of our XYZ acquisition." The new acquisition looks like just more work to most of the people in attendance and they have no idea as to whether the acquisition is a good thing or just another opportunity for someone else to take their job. The leader actually looks foolish in front of the group because the enthusiasm differential between themselves and the audience is so great as to be laughable. The same can be said of any number of product launches, new employee benefit programs, big investments in technology or whatever else comes along.

I particularly remember sitting in a meeting when the senior people were doing cartwheels (and had donned their party hats) in the announcement of a big acquisition. This, after the group had just had their bonuses radically reduced. "Oh, now we know where our bonus money went!" was the response of the group. No one else picked up a whistle . . . and no one ate the cupcakes. The leaders were actively destroying the soul of the organization with their financial data points, industry leadership statistics, and "brand enhancing momentum" that was spewed *ad nauseam*. And they did not have a clue as to why the organization's members just sat and stared.

The next course of action undertaken to address the "passion problem" are the attempts at "Distributed Governance." The thought is that the troops are not engaged because they are not involved. The notion that "People will not support that which they are not engaged in developing" takes over the search for the spark. So they set out to have the troops get engaged in many aspects of the organization's existence only to find out that what people are looking for is not so much involvement but *understanding* and the associated *meaning*. Most of us would rather understand why we are "here" than to simply engage with others in an environment where no one else has any better ideas than we do. Distributed governance contains a very positive set of values. Defining the spark of an organization's meaning and destiny is not one of them.

A big part of Distributed Governance is found in the creation of very broad-based measurement systems that are allegedly designed to create the spark of passionate expression. "If you can't measure it, you can't manage it!" It might be better suggested that if you can measure it, it is not very directly correlated to the long-term durability of the organization. In the context of organizational durability, the relentless quest to quantify and objectify has been driven to an extreme where measurement has taken over for thinking. The evolved thought would seem to be taken as far as "If you can create enough measurements, you don't need a strategy." Or, even more extreme is that measurement can actually become another institutional foundation. It is thought that in measurement is found the internal definition of success. But measurement is no substitute for purpose and meaning.

The most troubling course taken by organizations as they seek to find their spark in governance is when all else fails, revert to autocracy. When SPUD-based unity is absent, the natural response of leaders is often simply to attempt to centrally control the unifying forces within the organization, as the ubiquitous control of the SPUD is now sensed to be no longer functioning. The forced unity attached to autocracy is the path of least resistance. All that is required for autocracy to prevail is just the power to claim the position. And this vacuum is always quickly filled.

It is very obvious that the seizing of *power* is much easier than the creation of legitimate *authority* to which we all wish to be subject. Power is the drug that is reached for in the event of authority-dysfunction. Power is impotent in the face of the challenges of SPUD creation and distribution. Power and SPUDs just do not go together. Authority and SPUDs do. As individuals we push back against power, while we readily embrace legitimate and desired authority. The question becomes that of the appropriate form of authority. SPUDs actually create authority.

SPUDs have two important elements in their effective use within human institutions. The first element is that SPUDs are communicated in the form of coherent stories that speak to our souls. Numbers and theories are not the raw materials of meaning. Meaning is a much more primitive concept than can be communicated in a form beyond the simplicity of a story. Mind-Heads cannot tell stories with a moral, as they think in facts and equations. Soul-Heads see the child in each of us, and the desire we all continue to have in seeking to better understand the world we call home. Meaning lives in stories and cannot be stored in other media. Soul-Heads begin most communications with "Let me tell you a story." This first element is just that simple.

The second element in the development of an effective SPUD is that the stories must directly speak to our human relationships, and not to "the way things are working." The story must tell the tale of the community and to the value created by the community. Every human institution impacts the relationships within the community and with other human beings by definition. The nature and magnitude of that impact is tremendously important to each of us. Those organizations that retain their initial, agreed-to and positive relational focus remain soulish. And they retain the spark that allows them the edge that separates the durable from the remnants of the historical. The second element is just about as simple as the first. The focus must be on the relational, and not on the "inputs and outputs." That is all.

The unity created by a SPUD can eliminate the need for a large amount of "means-planning" as the "ends' are so much better instilled in both the hearts and minds of the members. When meaning is established by those who speak from a position of authority as opposed to power, the results are infinitely different. SPUDs clearly grow the best when planted in the rich soil of shared context and shared values. Meaning emerges out of shared values and the associated context that is created by those values. But it only can emerge when the messenger is considered a legitimate authority. And the message must be considered significant, plausible, understandable and desirable, from a relational standpoint to impact the soul of any human institution.

* * * * *

When an organization can in unison say, "This is what we stand for, this is what we are pursuing, and this is the reason why" it has developed two of the four foundational elements that we are discussing in the establishment of a durable human institution. As common beliefs and values create the baseline for organizational durability, we see the addition of "meaning" as the second level of the foundation. At this point, however, the organization has not yet done anything . . . it has just begun establishing who it is.

The natural foundational extension of meaning is into growth. Meaning creates an interest in growth. Without meaning, no one would care if anything changed or progressed at all. We would just exist. And we would all be "happy" with our state of nothingness. As values create the opportunity for meaning, meaning creates the opportunity for advancement and growth. Accordingly, we will now turn to the topic of growth as the next layer in the establishment of durable foundations.

10

Growth Defines Life

Large and successful organizations redefine the humanly important notions of growth by confusing organizational and personal growth. This occurs as personal growth is devalued, and organizational growth is defined in terms that speak only to size and not to contribution. Mind-Heads see growth in numbers. Soul-Heads look for growth in the non-quantifiable and personal.

Chico Marx, in one of the Marx Brothers skits, asked the question, "Who are you going to believe, me or you own two eyes?" Unfortunately, there is sometimes a difference between what other people tell us and that which we actually see and believe. The Marx Brothers use of a "reverse rhetorical" question is remarkably illuminating as to the nature of one of the major challenges that we face in our lives. Discerning fact from fiction is one of the critical links in our ability to grow as individuals. We grow as individuals and organizations through truth and truth-telling and not through distortions. And we can only grow within our communities when we can trust our fellow members.

As growth is innately linked to life, we all desire to grow as individuals and community members, and to experience the alive-ness that we humans are prone to desire. We desire to personally grow for reasons both internal and external to our communities. To grow within the community is to experience the joys of contributory association. To grow externally is to learn to adapt to the eventuality of life outside the walls of our current communities. I have found very few people across the course of my life that do not have a deep desire to grow. And this is growth in all areas of life: physically, spiritually, emotionally, mentally and materially. At the same time, I have found a very large percentage of those same people who have just given up, for any number of reasons. It remains a truism that most organizational growth comes as the result of the growth of individuals within the community, which in turn drives the growth of the community itself. The converse simply breeds frailty.

Growth is the evidence of life itself. While it may seem more intuitive to view our surroundings as either organic or inorganic, that is not where most of us draw the line. Instead of looking at "all living things" in the same light, we more rightly discern a finer gradation amongst the living. That finer line is between the alive and growing, and the alive and "stable" or declining. The lack of growth is seen as the precursor to decay, and the impact on the souls of our communities is marked. Said simply, when we experience a lack of growth, either as individuals or as institutions, we begin to fear for our longevity. The fears associated with stagnation are real and very challenging.

I once had a friendly conversation with one of my neighbors. She was an eighty year old woman at the time. She told me about her recent "gym membership" and how excited she was about her new workout routine. This was a vibrant woman who continued to experience growth as an octogenarian. My respect for her was immense. But more importantly, the respect that she had for herself was determinatively positive. As we age, we come to a decision point: grow or stagnate. The same is true in our institutions and communities.

I was told early in my career that it was very critical for me to "build my library." By that, the individual who shared the thought intended for me to understand it as my collected capabilities, sensitivities, understandings, and maturity. He went on to say, "Corporate organizations can take away your employment and your livelihood. But they can never steal your library." We all want a library, but most of us need help in its assemblage and its management. Libraries represent the sum total of our acquired capabilities. They are immense sources of both capability and self-worth. What we ask of our organizational affiliations is then part monetary "compensation" and part personal "library."

Empty shelves in our libraries leave us feeling unprotected from the randomness of life. And this shelf-filling process becomes essential to an organization characterized as having networks of healthy individuals and improving relationships. People without expanding libraries become defensive and non-cooperative. They become naturally defensive as a result of lack of confidence in themselves. Vulnerabilities and individually experienced susceptibilities are always frightening. But our vulnerabilities to viral colds are different from our vulnerabilities to unemployment and disassociation in general. Colds are annoying. Unemployment, and other episodes of being "expelled from the family," can destroy one's whole life.

Empty organizational shelves are the same. When we perceive our institutions to be failing to grow, we become concerned over that relative level of stagnation. Growth can be experienced in any form, but the evidence of some advancement must be felt by the members. The growth might be seen in the "sales" results or in the improvement in the organization's abilities to create imaginative solutions. Growth is naturally and positively a very broad topic. But there is no such thing as a "healthy steady state." While an institutional steady state may exist in theory, the way we process the perceived lack of growth through our souls indicates to each of us that something that is not growing is quickly becoming inorganic. And inorganic is innately immobilizing.

STOCKING THE LIBRARY

We all generally know that much of our personal development is dependent completely on ourselves. At the same time, we come to view our organizational affiliations as sources of both the content associated with personal development as well as the discipline. "As hard as I am expected to work around here, I really don't have a lot of time for self-development, so I really *need* the organization to help me with that." In some institutions, the reason for the affiliation of members is purely focused on that institution's ability to assist in personal growth.

In an earlier era where most of us lived on farms, enjoyed personally controllable sources of our food supplies, and no mortgage payments (and no college funding or retirement planning to attend to), the world was a very different place. We were not nearly as vulnerable to the unpredictable actions of political and corporate entities which are now, unfortunately, looming fixtures in most of our lives. The absolute need to grow in that earlier (and more physical as opposed to mental) environment was much less pronounced than in the intellectually-charged and creativity driven environment of today.

There are basically two types of development that are available to us in our institutional affiliations. The first is the technical knowledge to do the unique things that are required for one's job. The second is the relational knowledge that is necessary to effectively interact with other people. Both are necessary ingredients in the accomplishment of one's job. The problem is that as Mindishness takes over an organization, the development of individuals skews rapidly towards the technical.

I began taking music lessons when I was in the first grade. The piano was my first instrument and a solid starting point for my musical interests. As I got older, I began to realize that playing an instrument was a very different experience depending on the venue. When I was "backstage," or in a practice room at school, the exercise was easy. When I was "onstage," with an audience, the exercise was very different. It was also much harder. When it was just me and the instrument, everyone was comfortable. As the number of people expanded, so did the number of errors. Nothing changed except the fact that I was now "onstage." The performance was now relational, not just technical.

The technical element, the playing of scales and preludes and etudes, is a critical part of becoming an accomplished musician. The relational element of playing those same exercises in the presence of others is also part of becoming a musician. For most of us, it is the more challenging part. Five decades after first beginning to learn the technical components of music, I am still working very hard on fulfilling the relational component. And as life mimics art, the same is true in our organizational lives. We get pretty good at the technical parts, and then spend a lifetime working on that which touches others.

Most organizations, especially as they grow, take the idea of growing their associates pretty seriously. They come to see that the knowledge-gaps created by the growing complexity of the enterprise are important to solve for on a current basis. These are the knowledge-gaps that represent the space between the issues faced by the organization and its abilities to solve for those issues. But what they usually create as a means of coping with the advancing complexity is a group of fairly technically accomplished twelve-year olds. They don't do this because they like children. They do it because they are thinking only with their Mind-Head.

So they offer as part of the development curriculum classes on word processing and spreadsheet tools. They do training on the effective usage of the associate performance management system and the company's mission-vision-values statements. The curriculum will likely have some guest speakers who will address the organization's products and distribution channels, and might throw in an offsite training class provided by an industry source. Then comes the time-management training, and then some reference materials are provided on how to develop a "personal goals statement." In the advanced classes, the organization's finances may even be discussed. These efforts all resemble the creation of software, but not of humans. They are all designed to make people more technically proficient. They are all "backstage" learning.

Yet, with all that, most people are both unsatisfied and under-developed. They need onstage training, and they know it.

Onstage training is scary. Onstage training is about who we are as individuals, and not about whether we can press the right keys on a timely basis. Onstage training addresses one's emotional state and social presence. Onstage training looks at leadership and communications abilities. Some people are really good at those things and others are not. And that difference in abilities is always frightening. Onstage training asks "Are you confident enough in yourself that you can deliver 'this' message with enough presence of mind to do it convincingly?" Or, can you "just say the words." Onstage training always brings in a "heckler" just to see how you react. Onstage training is personal with a capital "P." This is obviously because onstage training is all in the realm of the relational. And most Post-Sufficient organizations don't want to touch any part of it.

DEVELOPMENT AND GROWTH AGENDAS

If you ask a Soul-Head what the training and growth agenda might look like, they would start with theatre, move on to rhetoric and persuasive skills, proceed to "interesting life topics, and finish with "peace negotiations." They might tack on a summer course on "fullness of life." This would actually be a curriculum that would not resemble the implementation and mastery of a new "accounts receivable" system. The problem is, sometimes Doctor Frankenstein creates a monster. More often than not, however, he creates an adult. And it is an adult with the combination of technical and relational skills to effectively contribute. It is a fully formed adult with two heads.

The problem with Post-Sufficient organizations is not that they don't have development programs available. They are just misdirected towards the technical side. Insufficient organizations are cross-developmental by their nature as they recognize that they have gaps to fill in order for them to effectively compete. They recognize those gaps as personal development gaps of both the technical and relational variety. Post-Sufficient organizations, on the other hand, do not see themselves as particularly needy of anything, and that includes the expanded investment in usable intellectual capital and "emotional intelligence," as Dan Goleman has described it.

I was once asked to put together an inventory of training needs for a group of people within our organization. I put the list together and it contained about fifty items. Most of them were of the relational and soulish variety. I then submitted it to the requester, my boss, and asked "what is going to happen next." I got good feedback on the list and it was determined to be ready-for-implementation. So, the next logical question was, "And how is this training going to be administered?" The answer was, "Oh, you are going to do it." My thought was that I had just been the recipient of another unfunded corporate mandate, of which I was in little position to respond. This was a classic example of the organization understanding the need for the development of the troops, without a value system that would actually provide the resources to make a meaningful dent in the "needs-bank." I basically threw the inventory in the trash and went about doing the rest of my job.

There are some things in life that are infinitely easy to talk about and rarely implemented with any level of effectiveness. Development, along with the associated personal growth, is one of those things.

THE DEVELOPMENT AGENDA

At what pace does development just *happen* if no attention is paid to it? What if no one cared about development and growth of the members at all? The answer is that it likely advances at a pace that may be sufficient to meet the needs of the organization over the short-term. People learn a lot from life. The problem is that the amount learned likely fails to meet two other important hurdles: the personal needs of the members and the long-term needs of the organization. This is especially true as measured opposite the growing field of threats to an organization's continued existence. So this topic represents just another in a long line of short-term versus long-term trade-offs that create human suffering in large and successful organizations, each singly focused on attempting to maintain and grow their profit margins.

If the real cost of the "development gap" was somehow quantified and placed on the balance sheet of the organization, it would create quite a conversation amongst the stakeholders. If the real magnitude of the development gap could be identified, it would likely refocus much of the attention of the leadership of the institution. It is very feasible to believe that at some point, the opportunity cost represented simply as a function of the personal development gap approaches the sum of all future earnings. Said differently, the liability attached to solving for the development gap reaches a point where it is as large as the value of all future earnings. That point may be described as the point where the organization reaches "Intellectual and Emotional Capital Bankruptcy."

Without intentional technical and relational development, the troops are fearful of their futures. Without development, the looming challenge of the increased complexity of the future becomes even more pervasive. Organizations become more complex by virtue of building onto what it is they already do. Without adding the myriad complexities created by the marketplace, the "complexity-weight" of organizations grows from within at a rapid rate. Without development, the insightful and imaginative solutions to solve for both the internal and marketplace challenges and opportunities lay dormant under a blanket of blissful somnolence. It is one of those really important things that cannot be measured and for which the short-term implications are small. The short-term implications of the expansion of the gap may actually appear positive. And this is true in every organization. Not just those characterized by rapid change. Without adequate personal development, the people perish, and their organizations with them.

The simple question for organizations to address is "Do we have a development gap that will impact our future—either technically or relationally?" Does the organization have a concern that the skills and abilities of the organization's members are defective in any way opposite the demands that the organization will face in the years to come. If the answer is in the affirmative, the next question is "In what areas must we concentrate?"

On the other hand, are the deficiencies weighted on the side of the members? Do the members perceive a set of gaps that are personal to themselves? The development gaps run in both directions. How do our members perceive their abilities in terms of creating a level of security for themselves and their families?

Mind-Heads look at the economic and operating statistics and determine whether the machine appears to be running at peak efficiency. Soul-Heads look at the machine and inquire as to whether any of the parts might be loosing their resiliency or effectiveness. Mind-Heads look at the machine and *wonder* how fast it might go if more fuel is delivered by stepping harder on the gas pedal. Soul-Heads understand the needs of the machine parts and the increasing needs of those parts as more fuel is applied. And they *know,* or at least have an informed idea, as to how it will do under increased stress. Mind-Heads are surprised when the machine fails to perform at levels seen in the past. Soul-Heads are only surprised when things proceed exactly as planned.

Mind-Heads worry about over-investing in the development of their people. They would rather just assume that all is proceeding according to schedule and wait for something bad to start happening. The more likely case is that something bad will not happen, but rather that everything good will quit happening. Soul-Heads think about the future and look for ways to provide their members with the tools to cope and thrive. They recognize that hope, and hopeful optimism, only resides in those with the tools to adequately address the challenges and fears that life presents. Hope, like acceptance, is mobilizing and freeing.

A group without the requisite tools to meet the perceived challenges is a group without hope. And it is our collection of hopes that propels us forward, in the face of sometimes challenging odds. The alternative to mobilization through hope is mobilization that comes from fear. That theory works exceptionally well for a short period of time. That theory also begs a whole raft of interesting ethical issues. And it always fails in the long-term. Communities rightfully care about the long-term.

Consistent with the development of an understanding of trust in an organization, the notion of the development of a "Development Gap Map" is applicable here as well. To simply talk about the broad-based development needs of the organization is a step in the right direction. To talk in terms of the leadership and relational and maturity needs of the organization is to take the conversation to the next level. And to move beyond the "succession plan" of a few roles within the organization to seeing the development of the entire organization as a staple of future existence is to re-arrive back at the point where most successful organizations began. When the topic of the development of the overall skill set of the team members (whether there are one hundred people or one hundred thousand people) is expanded beyond the ability of the organization to assess its meeting of sales quotas, or the successful launch of the next new product, the conversation becomes meaningful to future success.

Most Post-Sufficient organizations don't take the time to think beyond the human resource needs of the next year, suffice to say the next ten years. And they think little of the relationship building needs. Apparently the assumption is that if they run short on talent and ability, they will go out and buy it. And yet, most organizations know that this type of thinking simply creates a new and expanded set of problems down the road. It is impossible to just go-out-and-find-the-necessary-talent, if for no other reason than at least half the people brought in from outside will be chewed up and spit out by the organization's existing culture. And half of the rest will fail from incompetence. Those are not very good odds. But that is the game that is often being played.

The seminal question is whether an organization believes it can build a successful organization, or whether it believes it must build a group of contributing organizational members that will in turn build a successful organization. The differences in the thought process and associated actions are radical. The associated question is whether the organization is willing to put themselves at the risk of falling into a steady state, one without the perception of growth, and think that the situation is survivable.

I often ask the question, "How many people in this organization could do their organizational superior's job if something happened to the boss?" Alternatively, "What percentage of the people in this organization is positioned to be advanced without further intentional development?" If you believe in 'just-in-time' manufacturing, you might conclude that the answer should be nil for both questions. That would be consistent with a SMUTy mindset. From a current output and productivity standpoint, that would also be the right answer. Why invest in anyone if that investment might never be needed? Why pay someone for a higher level of performance-driven growth than is needed for the next twenty minutes? If, however, something akin to the present value of all future outputs of the organization where selected as the denominator, the nil answer is obviously a very bad answer. And yet, with such extensive and current discussion as to the importance of intellectual capital as the lifeblood of organizations, massive sub-optimization occurs in Post-Sufficient organizations.

The assumption implicit in this thought process is that personal growth is the leading indicator of community growth. While community growth bears within itself the opportunity for personal growth, the correlation is much less strong and certainly not fixed. People can be growing their libraries as organizations stagnate, but the perceived growth of individuals is sustaining. When organizations get to the point where neither the organization nor its people are perceived to be growing, Post-Sufficiency manifests itself in all manner of negative outcomes.

* * * * *

Does the organization have a belief system that instills a set of values that are directional in the lives of the members of the organization? Does that belief system inculcate the requisite depth and breadth necessary to address the real life-issues that members confront in their organizational and personal lives on a day-to-day basis? Have the value-systems been placed in a mobilizing context that provides the members with a sense of purpose and meaning that transcends the mundane? Is their something happening within the community that the members would determine is "good?" Does the community see that the results of their directed and principles-based efforts are making the world a better place for themselves and their constituencies? Do the members of the community experience within the affiliation a sense of growth and advancement in their personal libraries?

As the answers to these questions continue to be "yes," organizations continue to support the foundations on which future performance and durability are built. The combination of "yes" answers then positions the organization for the successful fulfillment of the last of the foundational elements. When beliefs and values come together to form meaning, and meaning is converted into an interest in growth, a large percentage of the foundation has been created. The remaining need is for an environment of trust.

11

Free-Agency and Trust

> Large and successful organizations are constrained by their lack of willingness to allow their members to think and act. In the absence of trust, an institution's energies are directed towards personal protection and not on the advancement of the community. Mind-Heads cannot "see" trust and thus proceed to minimize its importance. Soul-Heads understand that all human progress is a function of trust.

"Your mission, Mr. Phelps, if you chose to accept it . . ." was the classic opening line of the 1960's and 1970's television show *Mission Impossible*. Phelps was the ultimate free agent. He was in control of everything. He was not just a cog in the big wheel. He was able to use all his faculties in solving the problems that had been identified. He knew who the bad guys were, and he was always conscious of their plot. And it was his job, along with his team, to thwart their mischief. The team had values-systems and a worldview that were well understood, and were operating with a common mind. This was a seriously seasoned team with highly-developed members. And they all deeply sensed the importance and meaning in all that was to be accomplished.

It was Phelps that crafted and created both the means and the master plan. The imagination and foresight of both Phelps and the team created all the intrigue and all of the spell-binding outcomes. And the intensity of the musical and rhythmic backdrop was equally captivating. Most of us who are old enough can still hear the musical theme in our heads yet today. As the team would walk away quietly into the night after the completion of the mission, the rewards were evident. They were accomplishments of the heart. They were rewards of the soul.

We each felt those same sensations as we came to the completion of each mission, and each episode.

Phelps was the perfect two-headed specimen. His mind-head formed the plan, and his soul-head dealt with all the unforeseen issues that were driven by the idiosyncrasies of human behavior. His team respected his Mind-Head. They loved his Soul-Head. The result was always magical. Phelps was the consummate free-agent. He is the stuff of legend. We all long to either be a Phelps, or work side-by-side with one.

When this concept of free-agency becomes inverted, and liberty in thought and action is denied, the soul begins to die. Phelps' competency and free-agency provided the basis for the hope of a successful set of outcomes. Willie Nelson sings a song that indicates that "Our heroes have always been cowboys." Cowboys are heroes because we think of them as free-agents as well. In the movie *The Matrix*, as with so much of science fiction, we humans are taken over by an alien and sinister force, and we have had our free wills completely usurped. In *The Truman Show*, Truman lives in a bubble of someone else's making. Without his knowledge, everyone is watching his completely staged life. What was worse, the stage was actually a venue for grubby capitalist advertising. This list of musical and theatrical works that are based on our relative ability to exercise our individual free will goes on indefinitely. The list is possibly as long as those featuring the concept of coming home. And they all speak intimately to the issue of trust. Trust is not a relevant issue in the absence of will and choice.

In order for us to trust one another, a number of systems of alignment must be in place. The first of these alignments is in connection with our values. Different values create different sources of personal motivation which in turn create sources of mistrust. The second of the "alignments" is connected to how the members of the community are organized and directed. Again, motivations are altered within organizational structures, and the impact on trust is significant. Lastly, there must be alignment at the soulish level. To the extent that we place our confidence and faith in differing sources of our future success, we are on inherently different tracks. And failure to trust is the inevitable result.

VALUES ALIGNMENT

As individuals, we will only trust others who we deem to be 1) decent and 2) competent. Decency is the proxy for agreement as to fundamental worldviews and values such that others can be trusted to do what they say they are going to do. Competency goes one step further and asks the question, "Ok, I believe that what you say is true, by our joint definition of 'true.' But, can I trust that you will actually do what you indicate you are capable of doing?" If we deem people to have integrity and ability, we have moved a step towards trusting them. If the "others" definitions of decency and competence are altered as a result of differing values, resulting in differing definitions of right, true, and good, then trust is the victim.

When I was in high school I worked for a small commercial homebuilder and real estate manager. I drove an old beat-up red Dodge van and did whatever odd-jobs needed to be done. Some days I cleaned up construction site debris, other days I might have been mowing grass at an apartment complex. The next day I would be painting a rental house. I was well-paid and I worked very hard. One day I asked the President of the Company about a concern that I had that I might not be doing the job as well as I should. I just wanted to make sure that he was happy with my work. His response changed my worldview.

He said, "Brian, are you doing what you think is a good and responsible job?" I answered that I was doing my best. He said, "Then that is all I can ask. I trust you and believe that you would tell me if something isn't working the way it should. I also ask that you just use your own good judgment in making the decisions you need to make, and I am certain everyone will be happy with the outcomes." What he was saying to me was that he and I shared a set of values, and that he trusted me as a result.

That statement freed me and turned me into a productivity-crazed free-agent. I came to recognize later that the range of the potential screw-ups I might have created was probably small, but the sentiment of the response was the same. At different times in my career I have heard that same message. At other times the impression was just the opposite. With trust comes liberty and all that accompanies it. But trust is never granted when we believe that the basis on which another person thinks about how the world works is different than our own. Insufficient

organizations share a common view of the world, its priorities, and the importance of those priorities within their organization. Post-Sufficient organizations are deemed "political" as a result of differing values and worldviews. This would be true: they are political. And to trust anyone else in a political environment is to act in the role of the Village Idiot. The organization's personal energies are then diverted to "idiot avoidance" as opposed to advancement of the community.

When trust is compromised as a function of the lack of decency, competency and common values, the results are predictable. Organizations without trust are "managed to death." The alternative is to invest in the members to the degree that they need nearly no management. Only self-management will prevent the individual "brain-drain" that occurs in Post-Sufficiency. When people are not trusted, they quit thinking, as it pays no demonstrable dividends. Conversely, they become free-agents, and can accomplish nearly anything.

COMMUNITY ALIGNMENT

As organizations grow, they generally grow in both size and complexity. Size or "scale growth" entails doing the same thing, but doing it many more times. Complexity growth entails integrating more "moving parts" into the overall operating equation. Scale growth is not the usual source of trust problems within organizations. Complexity growth, however, is a very different issue.

Complexity cannot be left unmanaged within human institutions. We all recognize that at some point, the sheer complexity of the environment begins working against us. In order to deal with complexity, all large organizations make decisions that effectively create two different operating models to deal with the complexity. Some organizations tend toward the Monolithic, and some towards the Modular. The former of the two models attempts to continue to use complexity to its advantage. The latter of the models attempts to break down the complexity into small enough pieces such as to make the complexity manageable.

Purely Monolithic organizations are those that are completely integrated from beginning to end. Every part of their overall delivery of value to the customer is dependent on all the rest. These types of operations can be stunningly efficient as the component pieces of the organization have been painstakingly placed in the system in a way that maximizes their overall and integrative utility. Think of these companies as having one of every part, and all the parts are inextricably linked. These are organizations that have "heads of functions" and not "heads of business segments."

The challenge with this type of configuration is that at some point, the absolute number of points of inter-connectedness gets to be so large, that keeping the whole machine running without one faulty part negatively impacting the whole becomes very challenging. When one part breaks, the whole machine stops. Monolithic is then a higher-risk, but higher reward strategy.

Purely Modular organizations, while representing an integrated whole, do not rely on the efficacy of the entire system to meet their ends. They have rather decided to deal with the issues of complexity by creating "modules" that are pieced together in a way that creates utility with "modular simplicity." Organizations in this mode break the operation of their institution into an assortment of pieces, all with their own management and unique objectives. They make an assumption that the orchestration of all the pieces is easier, or less risky, than attempting to manage the institution as a single object. The good news with this type of entity is that the failures of the modules do not represent the complete failure of the whole. On the other hand, the give-up is that the totality of the system does not operate at the kinds of levels of peak efficiency as do their Monolithic friends.

From a trust standpoint, the use of the Monolithic model is infinitely better. The reason is easy to see in that everyone working within the system is effectively responsible for the whole system. Everyone has the same incentives and everyone feels the same pains. The reverse is true within Modular organizations. The modules can be described in any number of ways, but the problem is always the same. When someone else is working off a different sheet of incentives and down-side risks, we naturally distrust them. And we have good reason to.

I worked for a technology service organization that had historically operated under a Monolithic operating model. As a means of coping with the looming complexity challenges, and to "better align personal incentives" a large number of product and technology groups were "modularized." The thought was that the complexity could be more effectively cordoned off and be better managed. It was also apparently thought that the better alignment of incentives would create more of *something*. And it did create more of something.

The modularization of the organization literally rendered it massively dysfunctional. People who used to literally sit next to one another, now were parts of uniquely identifiable and warring tribes. The dependencies all changed, the wiring schematic was altered, and there were short-circuit outages everywhere. The goals and incentives were different, and so were the pressures. And it was trust that suffered. The creation of client value was reduced to a fraction of its former self. The tribal disconnects emerged rapidly, were vary palpable, and the result was internecine warfare.

When people groups within an organization are allowed to "go tribal," they are forced to act in accordance with the rules of their tribe. Tribes are formed when the nature of the rewards and the nature of the security measures are different from the other tribes. Give a group of people a different and unique set of goals and resources (even if a subset of the overall organizational goals and resources), and a tribe is born. Now you have a trust problem.

As a response to the challenges of modularization, organizations attempt any number of compensating measures. The preferred method of reconciling the tribes is to bring them together into "large group meetings" and talk about the overall goal of the enterprise. The thought, it could be presumed, is that the better angels of our natures will prevail, and that we will all act in concert as a result of our newfound knowledge. And lo, this always fails after but one day.

The second method of reconciliation is a set of mutual incentives, which negates much of what was hoped to be gained in the first place. Next, an appeal to "universal morality" and the "brotherhood of man" is made to the leaders of the tribes. Apparently, the thought is that the disparate incentives and security issues can be overcome with discussion and moral suasion. And then the organization usually just gives up and decides to leave the tribes alone. The result is that they have forced themselves to deal with the carnage created in their newfound inability to provide value.

If an organization's foundations are not solid, the resort is often to "just throwing money at the problem." Compensation is the mobilizer of last resort as an organization has entered Post-Sufficiency. When incentives-based tribalism, and the resultant lack of trust is in full swing, the thought is that compensation can solve for the "organizational alignment" problems. It is an action that is both desperate and wrong-minded. When the organization likely needs to be working better together, to forge better integrated solutions to the issues faced by their clients, they are actually being pushed even further apart.

When Ronald Reagan used the phrase, "Trust, but verify." he was heard and understood very broadly by the world's political observers. The thought that remains to this day has seemingly become contorted to infer that all relationships are somehow naturally subject to verification and that it is, accordingly, rationally and relationally justified. Reagan was speaking of an international relationship, however, with a government that was not part of *our* United States community. Within communities, on the other hand, the idea that verification is an acceptable goal is contrary to the fundamental notion of community. In a community, people do what they say they are going to do, and they do not do what they say they are not going to do. Communities create internal trust and do not need to spend the massive amounts of energy needed to verify the actions of all the members. When tribes form, the ability to verify is compromised, and the verifying act is viewed with creativity-absorbing suspicion.

When trust is compromised as a result of the tribalism associated with a misalignment of both goals and risks, the impact is always very predictable. Organizations of the modular variety spend nearly all their time attempting to determine if the "other tribe" is operating in the overall best interests of the community, or if they are self-serving. What begins as a well-intended attempt to control and manage complexity, ends in a nightmarish political game where the enemy is everyone and anyone.

SOULISH ALIGNMENT

If the decency, competency and values hurdles have been successfully navigated, and the organization is aligned such that the tribal factions are not an impediment, then one series of questions regarding trust remains. That list of questions is "How is it that I can believe that you will not change your mind? What is the basis on which your belief systems are operational? How deep does your credibility go?" This is the point where we begin to see and exhibit trust as a matter of faith.

To array the various levels of trust and faith along a continuum is to see the power of faith in indirect correlation with its empirical tangibility. Said more simply, as elements of faith are added to the trust equation, it deepens the absolute levels of trust. When people have faith in those things that are less tangible, and "less easy to see," the human inference is that these objects of faith are more substantive in the minds of the faithful. People who jointly believe in the unseen are more likely to trust one another than those who are not part of the faithful.

It may be posited that there are four "stops" along this continuum, ranging from the wildly spiritual or faithful on one end, to the blandly knowable, but completely uninspiring on the other. Levels of trust are seen to increase as people experience greater levels of consistent faith in any particular object. There is little relational commonality gained by a common belief in the forces of gravity. There is, alternatively, significant relational cohesion when the object of faith is an ideal, or that exists in the transcendental.

To start at the first stop along the continuum is at the far right and can be described as Ideological Fanaticism. This represents the stop for cults of all kinds. And in this context, a cult may be a very good thing, or a very bad thing. The only difference is the object of worship. Ideological fanaticism always claims an overall and over-arching understanding of the "truth" and uses the inculcation of values as the means of fueling the fanaticism. Ideological Fanaticism is characterized by an impressive level of zeal. Some of the world's great accomplishments come from Ideological Fanaticism, as have nearly all of the great human tragedies. And it is in the latter connection that it, Ideological Fanaticism, has acquired such a bad reputation. It is also the fuel that has powered most of what is good in the world today. Amongst fellow ideologues, there is never a fear of betrayal. The faith system just runs to deep. Trust is naturally taken for granted.

The second stop on the continuum is Faith-Infused Idealism. Faith-Infused Idealism creates an object of attention and it takes the time to create a set of cohesive values that are the direct outcroppings of the object. It also takes the time and energy needed to develop a well-defined and very specific object of worship. The idealism is fueled by the desire of the members to pursue the perfecting of the values-system as a means to happiness, fulfillment, or whatever the system describes as the end-state of the complete incorporation of the system. Unlike Ideological

Fanaticism, Faith-Infused Idealism has a generally long half-life, as it a personal *choice* as opposed to a personal *reaction*. It is then more "rational" or objectively defined, but still requiring a certain level of faith in that which may not be positively proven. Like ideologues, the "faithful" are always true to one another. And they are more comfortable to deal with, given the perceived "rational" foundations of the faith.

The third stop along the continuum is Cultural Behavioralism. Without going into any detail, this next stop is characterized by a set of actions that are predicated on the existing values of the group: whatever they may be. There are no fixed points of focus, nor are there any unique sets of values, other than that which emerges spontaneously and over time from within the group. This point, or stop along the continuum, is that which is often thought utopian, as it is not based on a fixed notion of the good. Cultural Behavioralism is not in any way mobilizing of its adherents, but rather is an accommodation to the security needs of its adherents. "We really don't stand for anything, but if you don't do anything completely principled or hateful, you can be a part of our community. Just don't cause any trouble and all will be fine."

It is not that there are no values or beliefs within the Cultural Behavioralism camp; it is rather that the values are, by definition, purposefully attached to the benign. Everyone gets along, but nothing is advanced and no cause is identified other than simple co-existence. Cultural Behavioralism is not a prescription for a community or for advancement. It is, by design, a prescription for peace, and not for progress. That would be unless your definition of progress is just peace.

The only faith required within Cultural Behavioralism is that people can actually, if given the right conditions, get along with each other. It is a faith in "us." It is hard to be trusting of people who are purely situational in their orientation to the world. As a result, organizations that fit this characterization are thought "political" (read immature), and are not likely to inspire any level of real trust.

The last stop on the continuum, Blind Empiricism, is simply that of logic and observation serving as the basis for the notion "the right." Blind empiricism completely denies the notion of any ideal or anything transcendental, and seeks to gain authority by virtue of its objective truth-claims. Trust, here, is not a function of any idea or ideals, but is rather a function of the group's carefully selected "incontrovertible data." If trust emerges from shared values, then Blind Empiricism does not engender trust, as it simply has no mechanism consistent with that end. Blind Empiricism can only say w*hat,* and it doesn't care as to *why.* And with no why, there is no personal and relational level of trust. I call this continuum the *Noetic-Fideistic* Continuum for like reason. Noetic is from the notion of knowledge and *Fide* from the notion of faith.

But what does this Continuum have to do with the whole idea of trust? Trust involves not just confidence in the causes and associated effects that emerge from our actions. It also involves the perceived nature and efficacy of the objects of our trust. If we are left to simply trust whether the chairs we are sitting on will keep us from crashing to the floor and injuring ourselves, we are left with an incomplete picture of trust. The ability of organizations to prove durable over time actually mandates the incorporation of all the stops along the *Noetic-Fideistic* Continuum.

The Noetic end of the continuum is characterized by facts and analysis. The Fideistic end is characterized by symbols. It is important to trust in the potency of facts and analysis. But it is readily observable that the Noetic type of trust is one that is both shallow and without any emotional substance. It is a dead trust. The "living trust" comes from the other end of the continuum. And it is to the living trust that symbols speak. By symbols, my reference is to any person, place or thing (including language) that holds within it a set of values that link an organization's members to the thing itself. Our Mind-Heads work on the facts, our Soul-Heads focus on the symbols.

Symbols are the constant reminders of the personal connection we have with our institution and our fellow members. They can take almost any form, including everything from common stories, to bronze statues, to memorialized engineering feats, or to the carved-in-stone values of the organization. Symbols are the surrogates that fill in and remind us of that which we truly believe and rely on. They are the anchoring points to which we attach our value-systems. And they have the ability to create a sense of security from their symbolically emotional coherence.

Communities are seekers after objects of common worship, as Fyodor Dostoevsky reminds us, and our symbols represent those objects. For true trust to be gained within an organization and for that organization to endure the trials of their existence, they are forbidden from living their lives at the left end of the continuum. They must have roots that sink deep into the Fideistic end of the continuum. Common belief systems are critical to community. Communities are rooted in beliefs.

Living at the left end of the continuum is the natural outcome of a Mind-Head-guided human institution. The right end is the result of an organization that recognizes the trust and belief needs of the Soul-Head. Said simply, human institutions must exist across the continuum's entirety for their durability and for their organizational soulish health. Trust is not built on a foundation of numbers and data points. Trust is built on a foundation of faith in something whose essence transcends the anodyne and formulaic. Post-Sufficient organizations are told that they must stay away from the "right," even though that is where their ancestors undoubtedly lived. The Mind-Head does not believe, as it is not in their nature. The job of believing is left to the Soul-Head. Mind-Heads have a hard time with understanding the whole concept of beliefs. Soul-Heads are only challenged in regard to the selection of beliefs. But they are constantly in search of the truth and beauty found in the natively unknowable. Hope can only exist in the presence of the unknown. Belief is that which connects that unknown future to our souls. Our Soul-Heads have the role of relieving the stress of the unknown with the hope found in belief.

The decline of religion in America over time has lead to a situation where fewer and fewer organizational leaders are at all comfortable talking about anything that is beyond "concretism." The language of faith has been lost and the emotionally bonding and trust-building implications of faith along with it. As we observe leaders who substitute facts for beliefs and ideals, we see Post-Sufficiency blossom. These leaders look to us as those with no heart, no passion, and no inspiration. We prize and respect their command of the relevant subject matter, as they speak with the skill of a nuclear physicist. Yet we quietly wish they could speak with the compassion and prescience of a prophet. Can the leader express anything that actually inspires the group's members at the level of the Soul-Head?

Trust is a Soul-Head function, and is accordingly, impossible to measure. But what is known is that once trust is lost, it takes a very long time to regain. When organizations create lay-offs, the amount of trust lost in the organization is large and the effect is the creation of an emotionally implacable mob. Lay-offs are perceived as just another form of "cheating." When organizations go out of their way to sustain an environment of trust, the rewards are, on the other hand, significant loyalty. When an organization's members wonder who is being taken to the ovens today, as opposed to reveling in the trust that is provided the member in the accomplishment of their duties, the differences are absurdly dramatic.

At one point in my career I received quarterly updates to the Company's Severance Policy. This was "Lay-Offs" as a way of life. This was a company that made billions of dollars a year. It was also an organization that demanded its members to be completely committed to the organization's strategies and schemes. And yet I received the updates to the severance policy because layoffs were part of that organization's informal contract with its members. It is impossible to personally commit to a strategy when the severance policy might reasonably be thought to apply to *me* in the next round of rolling layoffs. The situation reminds me of the radio spots that I heard as a kid. "This is a test of the Emergency Broadcast System. In the event of an actual emergency you would be instructed . . ." It is almost as if my company feels like it needs to "stay fit" by testing the lay-off and associated severance systems regularly to make sure that it is maintained in prime operating condition. In the end, one can only commit to, and actively engage with, an object that is worthy of trust.

A friend of mine once spent nine months in a state penitentiary for "borrowing" a few hundred thousand dollars from his financial planning clients. And this was without the clients' knowledge of the actual "lending relationship." It was a sad story, but one that ended well. The truth that emerged from the whole ordeal was the idea that "forgiveness is granted, while trust is earned." His other friends basically told him that we were willing to let his past actions remain a part of history, but that he would have to prove himself once again trustworthy over time. We told him that the trust building would take years. We were willing to let go of the past, but we were unwilling to blindly trust him again until he showed himself worthy.

Organizations build and lose trust the same way. They lose it quickly and they build it slowly. Violations of trust, especially those that represent important value systems, are greeted with the very sad knowledge that the path to renewed trust is a long and winding road. The abuse of trust within organizations is akin to being abused by one's parent. The scars never go away. I spent years working with one of my organizations rebuilding trust after a very nasty episode where people's employment lives had been threatened. I honestly could not believe how arduous that journey actually was and how much energy was absorbed in the process.

Trust cannot be just "created." The preconditions of trust must be painstakingly built and then, and only then, can trust enter the arena. I once heard a consultant tell a bunch of financial advisors that they should schedule "relationship reviews" with their clients. This was supposed to help in the development or creation of the "trusted advisor role" of which they were all seeking. Only in that role could they maximize their impact on the client and their personal incomes, at least in the mind of the consultant. That seemed like very odd advice to me. Wouldn't the better advice have been to actually *create* trusted relationships with their clients as opposed to having "reviews?" Trust is about objects, and values and symbols. There are no short-cuts. Defining and living the preconditions of trust is the only path to its actual establishment.

BUILDING TRUST

Trust within most human institutions starts with a well-documented and oft-celebrated heroic and trust-building event somewhere in the annals of the organization's past. At one point, the organization stood up and said very definitively, "We care about the levels of trust that people have in us. We are demonstrating our trustworthiness in the actions we are taking today. Let this episode serve as a beacon for all that will come by this way in the future." Subsequent actions are measured against a fixed standard that is instilled in the member's souls. Every action an organization makes is subject to the evaluation of its members as either certifying its trustworthiness or chipping away at it.

It is usually the case that it is in our short-term interests to cheat, or to chip away at the block of trust that has been built. The benefits of cheating are always an allure for us as individuals, and we measure the costs in terms of the likelihood of being caught and the associated severity of the short-term implications. Organizations are the same. It is hard to draw a line against the short-term benefits of activities and decisions that defy trust. Trust is built with the celebration of big events and life-enhancing symbols and is usually destroyed by a blood-letting from a thousand little cuts.

TRUST AND FEEDBACK

The feedback mechanisms that exist in most large organizations are little equipped to handle the magnitude of the trust issue. The reasons are obvious. As trust is waning within an enterprise, the ability to effectively inquire inside the institution whether trust levels are good is all but lost. No one is willing to say to someone that they do not trust, "I don't really trust you." That is until the moment right before the door swings shut behind them. So the organizations that don't need to ask the question are those that don't have to, and organizations that do need to ask get bad or completely inaccurate feedback. It is just another paradoxical aspect of organizational life. And it is another reason that organizational success is determined ontologically and not as the result of a management process. Organizations are trusted to the degree they deserve to be trusted. There is no trick here. Organizations that do not display a sufficient level of internal trust expend most of their available energy fighting the dragons of cynicism, anger, and fear.

We humans are magically mobilized when we are both told, and it is being observed, that we are being trusted. The opposite is equally true. I once spent months interacting with (mostly listening to the painful lament) of a friend that had been fired by Home Depot. He was a long-term employee who ended up with new boss, and is so often the case, the new boss needed to demonstrate that she could "shake things up . . . and get this unit moving." My sense was that Bill was just a "civilian casualty" or collateral damage in a broader war. But the scars of the lack of trust were very deep.

In a completely different situation, a friend of mine told me of that he had spent months assembling a strategy for a particular development effort which had been heavily supported by his boss. At the end of the process, the boss "changed his mind" and effectively used my friend as the fall-guy for his now "ill-conceived and poorly thought-out plan." In both cases, the lack of trust created disastrous results. These were both highly talented and highly committed people that just got accidentally hung up, and crushed, in the gears of the machine. These stories go on forever in the presence of Post-Sufficiency. We never have to wonder how trust is lost. When personal self-aggrandizement or self-protection becomes the *modus operandi* of the machine, the battle for trust is lost.

On the other side of the ledger, to continue with examples, is another friend who told me "My boss really tries to let me steer my own ship. It actually makes me nervous." This friend was a sales guy who was good at the sales game, but was lacking in complete knowledge of the new organization he was representing. He went on to tell me that his boss would tell him that he trusted him, but that a big component part of that trust was in knowing when he needed to ask for help. And in those instances where help was needed and asked for, help was always provided. But his boss wanted him to be both responsible for his actions and to get the much-earned and appropriate credit for the results. It was a classic win-win-win situation.

To analyze and understand the complex essence of trust within any human institution is to go a long way towards understanding its future performance and durability. My sense is that most large and successful organizations pay little attention to the "relationship and trust" needs of the individuals within their organizations. While distribution and product development strategies abound, little thought is given to the significance of trusting relationships, even though most leaders would see trust as an element critical to their future success. But they see the issue as one external to the organization. They comprehend the importance of trust with respect to their customer relationships, and then proceed to either assume that trust operates well within their organization, or that it is just too quotidian an issue to require any effort on their personal part.

Organizations would do well to create "Trust-Maps" based on decency, competence, organizational dependency, and belief systems, defined both vertically and horizontally. If every area of the organization were to assess every other with these metrics, the results would be illuminating. And the correlations between progress, durability, performance, and trust would become immediately apparent.

* * * * *

The building of the essential foundations necessary for the durability of human institutions is the role of the Soul-Head. Only the Soul-Head has the ability to speak the language of mobilizing and cohesion-building values. Only the Soul-Head can attach the meaning that is necessary to create the universal incentives for an organization to advance their cause. Only the Soul-Head can understand the needs of the organization to experience real personal and collective growth. And only the Soul-Head can manage the organizational belief systems in a way that engenders facilitative trust.

The challenges attached to Post-Sufficiency are deeply engrained in any organization which is its victim. When changes need to be made as to the organization's processes, the actions are generally both discernable and implementable. When changes need to made to the core nature of the entity, the magnitude of the challenge is multiplied a hundred fold. We rarely see the innate problem in any situation as "ourselves." And yet that is exactly what is needed, this "self-identification as cause" in Post-Sufficiency. The entire notion of creating a new self-identity with a group of thousands of people is almost unthinkable.

Human institutions die when they forget who they are. Human institutions die when they come to believe that they have everything figured out. Human institutions die when they try to control for everything, except for the need of their members to continue to use principles-based thought processes to drive their actions, their relationships and their creativity. Free-agents bound together with a common definition of community find their way through the maze that is the present, and into a more hopeful future. They are always able to find their way home.

The Mind-Head is the master builder of all that is seen. The Soul-Head is the master supporter of all that is unseen. Great and enduring communities are built when the mind and soul work in concert. And to find ourselves at home in our relentlessly changing universe is the happiest of all happy endings.

Conclusion

On a drizzly winter Saturday morning in San Rafael I was emerging from my breakfast at McDonalds when I came across a good-looking blonde kid of about twenty. He was obviously living the life of a homeless person, and was looking for a handout to feed himself and his little dog. I passed him by and was then somehow convicted to go back and talk with him. The conversation was short. I addressed the handsome, but pretty dirty-looking young guy, with only a backpack and bowl for his dog: "I would be happy to buy you breakfast if you would just answer one question for me." He eyed me with a quizzical look, but was not in much of a position to decline my offer. So I asked, "Why are you doing this?" He understood that I was asking about his homeless situation. Without hesitation, and indicating a deep sense of the basis of his answer, he said, "I don't have anyone." I handed him a five and said, "I truly hope you can find someone." And I walked away. He was just a man without a home.

If we could each find ourselves at home within our institutional affiliations, we would not solve for world peace, but we would find ourselves in a world where everyone would feel much more personally secure and much more personally fulfilled. And that would be a good thing for each and every one of us. "Just home."

Definitions to Commonly Used Words

Abdicate: To give up or renounce

Abject: Utterly hopeless

Adumbrate: To provide a rough sketch

Anodyne: Not likely to offend

Antebellum: Before the Civil War

Attenuated: To weaken or reduce

Autarkic: A policy of self-sufficiency

Automaton: Behaves mechanically

Banal: Completely common

Beneficent: Causing good

Begonias: Type of flower

Bulwark: A protective structure

Callow: Immature

Canard: An unfounded story

Conflagration: A consuming fire

Comity: A friendly atmosphere

Dank: Damp and cold

Denizen: An inhabitant

Detritus: Disintegrated matter

Dialectic: A logical argument

Disaffection: The absence of goodwill

Effete: Barren and without vitality

Egalitarian: Belief in equality

Emollients: To assuage

Enervate: To reduce the moral vigor

Epistemology: The study of knowledge

Ethereal: Highly refined

Euphemistic: A vague expression

Exsiccated: To dry up

Extant: Still existing

Febrile: Feverish

Feckless: Without purpose

Hackneyed: Repeated too often

Hokum: sincere but untrue

Immolation: To destroy

Incipient: An initial stage

Inculcated: To impress forcefully

Indefatigable: Incapable of tiring

Ineluctably: Not to be changed

Inexorable: Unyielding

Inscrutable: Not easily understood

Jettison: To throw away

Labyrinth: Torturous maze

Lionize: To treat as celebrity

Litany: Tedious account

Milieu: Setting

Meliorate: To make better

Moribund: In a dying state

Nascent: Emerging

Nefarious: Wicked in the extreme

Neoteric: Modern or new

Nettlesome: Tending to vex

Obdurate: Hardened and intractable

Obfuscate: To confuse of dim

Obviate: To prevent of eliminate

Officious: Meddlesome

Ontology: Regarding nature of existence

Opaque: Not transparent

Ossification: To harden into bone

Ostensibly: Outwardly appearing

Otiose: Having a lazy nature

Otolaryngology: Ear, Nose and Throat

Palliatives: To relieve without a cure

Palpable: Plainly sensed

Perforce: Of necessity

Pernicious: Causing insidious harm

Plenary: Complete or full

Plenitude: Abundance

Polyglot: A mixture of languages

Precocious: Premature development

Progenitors: An originator

Prophylactic: To prevent of defend

Quotidian: Commonplace

Rabble: A disorderly mob

Recondite: Difficult to understand

Regalia: Emblems of royalty

Rubric: A class or category

Sacrosanct: Extremely sacred

Sagacity: Keenly farsighted

Salvific: With redemptive power

Sine Qua Non: Most foundational

Skein: A loosely wound thread

Spurious: Lacking authority

Tacit: Unvoiced

Tendentious: Biased

Ubiquitous: Being everywhere

www.ingramcontent.com/pod-product-compliance
Lightning Source LLC
Chambersburg PA
CBHW070248230426
43664CB00014B/2441